W9-CZU-555

MODERN
AMERICAN
HISTORY ★ A
Garland
Series

Edited by
ROBERT E. BURKE
and
FRANK FREIDEL

NIXON AND THE POLITICS OF PUBLIC TELEVISION

David M. Stone

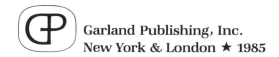
Garland Publishing, Inc.
New York & London ★ 1985

© 1985 David M. Stone

Library of Congress Cataloging-in-Publication Data

Stone, David M., 1958–
  Nixon and the politics of public television.

  (Modern American history)
  Bibliography: p.
  Includes index.
  1. Nixon, Richard M. (Richard Milhous), 1913– —Views
on public television. 2. Public television—Govern-
ment policy—United States. I. Title. II. Series.
  HE8700.8.S87 1985   384.54'4'0973   85-15918
  ISBN 0-8240-5674-4

All volumes in this series are printed on acid-free,
250-year-life paper.

Printed in the United States of America

NIXON AND THE POLITICS OF PUBLIC TELEVISION

David M. Stone

ACKNOWLEDGEMENTS

This book has taken a long path from college thesis to publication. Along the way I have benefited from the help of many generous people. I would like to thank all of those who agreed to be interviewed and those who gave me wide access to their files and photocopy machines for this work. Among these individuals and organizations are Clay T. Whitehead, Fred Friendly, Blair Clark, Bill Moyers, James Killian, James Day, John Macy, Frank W. Lloyd, Henry Loomis, Brian Lamb, Henry Goldberg, Jack Valenti, Tom Moore, Allan Lewis, the Corporation for Public Broadcasting, and the Public Broadcasting Service. Special thanks go to Robert MacNeil, Jim Lehrer and Richard D. Heffner for all their aid and encouragement.

My deepest debt of gratitude is owed to Professor Nancy J. Weiss of Princeton University. As my thesis adviser she guided this work from its inception and has remained a valued teacher and friend long after her official responsibility for me ended.

Thanks, too, to Susan Finta, for making sure that my words looked good on paper.

And finally, my love and thanks to my wife Wendy Horwitz whose useful criticism and loving support helped bring the manuscript to completion. I dedicate this book to my mother and the memory of my father.

D.M.S.
Philadelphia, PA
February 1985

CONTENTS

LIST OF ILLUSTRATIONS

Following page

INTRODUCTION

There have been relatively few times in its
brief history when public television was not struggling
through some crisis; either fiscal, or political, or
both. Throughout its existence public television has
been criticized by some for reflecting a left-wing, or at
least a consistently liberal political bias. Others have
charged that public television, sensitive to pressure
from its government and corporate underwriters, is overly
safe and conservative in its programming choices.
Ideology aside, there is a growing perception that new
telecommunications technologies which allow a virtually
unlimited number of viewing options make the very idea of
a government-supported alternative to the commercial
television networks an anachronism. Since scarcity is no
longer a problem, this argument goes, competing private
entities can effectively supply diverse and high quality
programming to the market public television was intended
to serve. Moreover, this new abundance of voices makes
it unnecessary for the government to be involved in the
business of enforcing fairness on the airwaves. After
all, such financial and editorial involvement by
politicians cannot easily be reconciled with our notions
of freedom of expression under the First Amendment.

This book examines public television's struggle
during its first years of existence in the early 1970's
to maintain its independence from the federal government.
They were controversial years, marked, above all, by the
hostile and destructive relationship between the many
public broadcasting organizations striving to define
their respective roles, and the President of the United
States, Richard Nixon. President Nixon and his aides did

not like the idea of a publicly-supported television system, and they were usually angered by its actual performance. Yet, the responsibility for developing crucial legislation for the long-term federal funding of the non-commercial media was thrust upon them. Creating "Public Broadcasting" out of a collection of educational television stations had been a Johnson administration project, a much-heralded extension of the "Great Society" to the nation's airwaves. But Lyndon Johnson never answered the critical question of how to pay for the system he had mandated. It could hardly have been given to a less willing benefactor than the Nixon White House.

In 1973 and 1974, public television appeared to have won a long and difficult battle with the Nixon White House. But as recent developments suggest, Nixon's personal fall from grace might not have given public television much more than a few months in the spotlight and a few years of breathing space. Today, the technologies and structures that created the need for a non-commercial alternative in American television are undergoing drastic changes. Of necessity, the federal government is seeking to redefine its responsibilities in the entire communications field. Public television could prove to be a casualty of this process of change. A decade ago, however, it was unquestionably the victim of the partisan antipathy of the Nixon White House. This is the story of how public broadcasters attempted to cope with that antipathy and prove their indispensability to viewers and patrons both in and outside of government.

In this country and elsewhere, one question about broadcasting is inescapable: What is the proper relationship between broadcasters, politicians and the "public interest" they both claim to serve? A democratic society must decide how to balance the need for some government regulation of the electronic media with a tradition of free speech and thought. The decision is never an easy one and the resulting balance is often unstable. "The autonomy of a broadcasting institution," wrote Anthony Smith, "is a delicate flower, nervously planted, tenderly nurtured and easily plucked up by the roots."[1] Certainly this was true of the fledgling public television system at the outset of the Nixon years. But this proved, to some extent, true of the commercial networks, as well.

Broadcasters everywhere owe their continued existence -- their right to make use of the public airwaves -- to the government. Radio and television organizations can be run by the state; funded by the state; or, merely licensed by the state. Somewhere along the line, the politicians inevitably play a role. In the United States we have tried to make that role as small as possible. We encouraged the development of the most competitive, commercial television system in the world in preference to the kind of government-supported systems employed by other western democracies. Where other countries -- following in one way or another the basic example of the British Broadcasting Corporation -- created some form of social control of broadcasting, we placed our trust in the free marketplace of goods and services as the best available mechanism for guaranteeing a free flow of ideas over the airwaves. The creation of a national non-commercial television organization in this country during the 1960's was based on the realization that the commercial marketplace -- the advertiser supported networks and local stations -- had failed to provide the American people with the kind of quality and diversity of goods they had come to expect from private enterprise. But irrigating the wasteland of television with the taxpayer's money brought politics and the politicians a giant step closer to the delicate creative process. Noncommercial broadcasting became accountable not merely to its audience and public trustees, but to the Congress and the President, as well.

Our communications law vests the ultimate responsibility for what goes out over the airwaves in the local station -- the licensee -- as long as it serves the "public interest, convenience and necessity." But just how broadcasters are to serve the "public interest" has always been subject to controversy. Though a host of new technologies might alter old assumptions about the need for statutory enforcement of "fairness" and "equal time" in programs that deal with current public issues, we have come to expect journalism on television to adhere to these broad guidelines. There are many voices in society, but only a few sets of microphones, cameras and channels. We expect fairness from those few who decide what so many people will see and hear.

Our government grants broadcast licenses and it can refuse to renew them, though it rarely does so. Advertisers can simply refuse to underwrite programs that cause controversy, and often do. The real test of freedom for public and commercial television alike is how well they cover issues that involve the hands that feed them, or give them license. Journalism on television consequently has faced tough battles against broadcasters who view it as more trouble than it is worth, too dangerous to the survival of the rest of the organization. Commercial network news faced harsh criticism and outright intimidation from the Nixon White House, but public television's journalists faced more direct threats. In a newborn system that depended not just on government licensing, but on government money to operate, there were many who believed that it was worth removing current affairs programming rather than risk the survival of their whole enterprise. Non-commercial

broadcasters had wanted federal dollars in the system
because they saw it as the only way to fulfill their
potential. But, as many warned when "educational"
television went "public" in 1967, the government's
involvement could prove a mighty threat to the creative
spirit of their endeavor. Public television was created
to be free of the pressures of conformity that had so
dominated commercial broadcasting. The Nixon experience
quickly showed that with tax dollars came even more
compelling pressures, particularly with an administration
that demonstrated its own warnings about the dangers of
government interference. The success of public
television had been predicated on the passage of
financing legislation that would insulate it from the
political pressures of annual congressional
appropriations and presidential appointment of directors.
Without such funding -- as it was until the mid-1970's --
public television was uncomfortably bound by the
underlying assumption of its critics that "he who pays
the piper calls the tune." Like commercial advertisers
concerned about the image of their products, few elected
officials like to hear the dissonant chords of
controversy on the air. For public television, the
politics of funding became divisive and destructive in
the face of Nixon administration opposition to the
creation of a "fourth network" with government money.
This White House believed it had quite enough battles to
fight with the three networks there already were. Its
hostility to public television was, in part, just one
aspect of its antipathy toward all of the news media for
giving attention to those who opposed it, for providing a
forum for dissent.

The broadcasting institution, as Smith wrote,
"sits at a precarious point in society, assailed by
critics for encouraging violence or radicalism or

escapism, berated for bias or for being anodyne, for overheating its audience and simultaneously for trivializing them; it picks a path through the cultural battlefields of history."[3] The 1960's and early 1970's were the setting for some of the fiercest cultural and political battles in our recent history. It was a discordant, contentious and often violent era, distinguished by mass movements for civil rights and against the war in Vietnam, by political assassination of our most charismatic leaders, by a counterculture that expressed its disdain for older tastes and values in all things, and by the pivotal role played by the mass media as both a chronicler and an agent of change. In 1968 the nation seemed, in one author's words, to be "coming apart,"[4] polarized into opposing camps: Black and white, young and old, hawk and dove. It was a particularly precarious time for all our broadcasting institutions as they tried to choose a path through the fighting. During the late 1960's, the extraordinary power of television to shape the public discourse itself became a major issue of concern and debate. The commercial television networks, relatively free from the interference or control of the elected, were sharply criticized by those all along the ideological spectrum because they were controlled by an un-elected elite. Throughout the decade, as an increasing majority of Americans said they received most of their information about public issues via television news, the network news broadcasts became the focus of much analysis and disparagement. Conservatives labeled television news as "left-leaning," enamored of the anti-war, anti-establishment groups and their leaders. Radicals of the left criticized television's dependence on established, official sources and its reinforcement of the social and political status quo. And more moderate commentators lamented, as they still do, television news' superficiality, its tendency to oversimplify and finally trivialize the complex issues and events it tries to report. Broadcasters, both commercial and public, seeking refuge from the storm, claimed to maintain the values of balance and fairness in the presentation of the nation's bitter controversies. The events of 1968 and 1969 proved, however, that there was no such safety to be found, even for broadcast news that claimed neutrality as its ideal.

In 1968 Lyndon Johnson decided against running for re-election to a second full term as President because of the rising opposition to United States involvement in Vietnam. With that winter's bloody Tet offensive, he and his commanders in the field believed that American and South Vietnamese troops had dealt a crushing blow to the military capability of the Vietcong and North Vietnamese, but that the news media's coverage of the fighting made it seem as though we had lost the decisive battle.[5] Near the conclusion of a year that also witnessed the murder of Martin Luther King and Robert Kennedy, violence in the streets among blacks, students, anti-war protesters and the police, Americans elected to the presidency a man with a bitter history of antipathy toward the news media and a strong belief that the country had seen quite enough of the dissent that had been filling the evening news.

Richard Nixon came into office convinced that the media -- dominated by those with an "eastern, liberal" view of the world -- were biased against him personally and against the conservative political and social values he espoused. From very early in his tenure, President Nixon and others in his administration sought to control what they viewed as the unwarranted and sometimes subversive power of the press, and television news, in particular. His battle with the news media and

with the "eastern liberal establishment" became one of
the running themes of his presidency, as it had been
throughout his political career. For the brand new
public television system which was both part of the media
and the ward of such eastern establishment institutions
and the Ford and Carnegie Foundations, the Nixon years
would provide a most inhospitable environment.

As White House speechwriter Patrick Buchanan
later explained, by the autumn of his first year in
office President Nixon felt that the news media had
focused far too much attention on the activities of left-
wing, anti-war groups, particularly during the October
1969 Moratorium against the war. Nixon viewed this
emphasis, Buchanan said, as an attempt by "an unelected
and arrogant elite" to challenge his constitutional
authority to make the nation's foreign policy.
Therefore, the President felt, "the time had come to take
the question of who would make American foreign policy
over the heads of his critics" in the media, directly to
the American people.[6] On November 3, Nixon went on
national television and appealed to "the silent majority
of the nation" to support him as he pursued his plan to
bring all American troops home from Vietnam on an
orderly, but secret timetable. "Let us be united in
peace," he said. "Let us also be united against defeat.
Because let us understand: North Vietnam cannot defeat
or humiliate the United States. Only Americans can do
that."[7]

The "Silent Majority" speech received what the
White House considered blatantly unfair "instant
analysis" by the network correspondents and guest
commentators. In the President's view, the journalists
had "openly sided with the men and the movement" seeking
to force him into new concessions on the war. Ten days
later, as Pat Buchanan triumphantly declared, Vice

President Spiro Agnew arrived in Des Moines, Iowa to "settle the account." November 13, 1969 marked the first infamous salvo of the Nixon White House's attack on the power and prestige of the news media. The speech was broadcast live by all three television networks who preempted their regularly scheduled newscasts for the occasion.

"The purpose of my remarks tonight," Agnew said, "is to focus your attention on this little group of men who not only enjoy the right of instant rebuttal to every Presidential address, but, more importantly, wield a free hand in selecting, presenting and interpreting the great issues of our nation. . . . The American people would rightly not tolerate this concentration of power in government. Is it not fair and relevant to question its concentration in the hands of a tiny, enclosed fraternity of privileged men elected by no one and enjoying a monopoly sanctioned and licensed by government?"[8] Said Buchanan, "The purpose of the Vice President's address -- 'the greatest sustained polemic in the English language in the twentieth century' in the estimation of one media analyst -- was not simply the settling of an account. It was the opening of a national debate on the power, the responsibility, and the fairness of the network news."[9]

But many of Buchanan's colleagues in the White House proved less interested in debating in the ensuing four years than in harassing and intimidating their "enemies" in the press. The "them versus us," "press versus government" siege mentality was rampant throughout the Nixon White House, communications director Herb Klein later wrote. "The President himself spent a disproportionate amount of time complaining about the press."[10] Many on the White House staff spent a disproportionate amount of their time trying to punish those in the news media who criticized the President.

From 1969 until the summer of 1973, when the multiplying revelations of Watergate finally blunted the administration's offensive against all its enemies --both real and imagined -- they conducted a public campaign challenging the integrity of the news media, and a covert effort to undermine their freedom. Wiretaps of newsmen, lawsuits calling for prior restraint of publication, subpoenas of television documentary out-takes and reporters' notebooks, and explicit threats to broadcast licenses were all employed by the government to mute the questioning voices of the press. The White House strived to create an atmosphere in both broadcast and print journalism perhaps best described by the title of the 1973 book on the "First Amendment crisis," <u>Fear in the Air</u>.[11]

Among the many issues raised by the administration's battle with the media, the situation of public broadcasting was exceptional. Certainly the smallest fish in the "Big Media" network pond in 1969 was the newly-chartered Public Broadcasting Service and its quasi-governmental benefactor, the year-old Corporation for Public Broadcasting. Although non-commercial television had been in existence for some fifteen years as educational television, the structure of public broadcasting as we know it today was created in 1967 with the passage of the Public Broadcasting Act. The Act established the Corporation for Public Broadcasting as an independent, non-profit entity responsible for developing and leading a national system of non-commercial television and radio stations.[12] The commission and the congressional sponsors of the Public Broadcasting Act hoped that, in the autonomous corporation, they had devised a structure that could provide politically insulated funding for the public media. They considered such insulation vital since one of public television's

most important mandates was to produce programs that
dealt with contemporary political and social issues.
Essayist E. B. White wrote at its creation that public
television should at once be "our Lyceum, our
Chatautauqua, our Minsky's, and our Camelot." It should
strive to "restate and clarify the social dilemma and the
political pickle."[13]

Yet the relationship between broadcast
journalism and the government was ambivalent enough
without the injection of direct federal financial
support. The experience of the Nixon years proved that
an institutional heat shield alone was not enough to
guaranty creative freedom from determined White House
pressure. The problem, as former aide to Lyndon Johnson
Douglass Cater put it, was that the political predicament
of public television in the early 1970's was inextricably
tied up with its economic plight. Public television,
Cater wrote, was a journalistic enterprise "singularly
vulnerable to governmental pressures."[14] The threat to
public television from the Nixon White House was more
serious -- though often less noticed by the general
public -- than the threat to CBS News of The Washington
Post not only because the federal government helped
underwrite its expenses, but because the President
himself appointed the membership of the Corporation for
Public Broadcasting's board of directors. In the words
of political columnist and onetime panelist on public
television's Washington Week in Review program, Peter
Lisagor, public television "lost its virginity" when
government money was put into it. "After that," he said,
"every two-bit politician felt compelled or obliged or
somehow able to say, 'I'm not going to vote money for the
kind of garbage that fellow is speaking on public
television.'"[15] The real problems occurred when such a
politician was the President of the United States.

The Nixon administration and public television began at virtually the same turbulent moment in our history. Their relationship proved mutually disadvantageous at almost every turn. Richard Nixon was not good for public television. His administration very nearly succeeded in strangling it at birth. And public television, ironically, was not good for Richard Nixon, either. Its highly acclaimed coverage of the Senate Watergate hearings during the summer of 1973 allowed an entire nation to watch the dramatic unraveling of his presidency. The broadcasts undoubtedly helped bring about his downfall.

The battle between the Nixon administration and the public broadcasters was marked by inconsistency and confusion on all sides. Conflict over methods and goals within the administration made the broadcasters deeply mistrustful of White House intentions, and rightly so. All at once the administration was pressuring public television to decentralize its program production and decisionmaking, while also pressuring the board of the Corporation for Public Broadcasting to take central control in order to remove all political programs from the national schedule. The administration emphasized the importance of "localism" in the system, but refused to support the kind of congressional appropriations that might make localism attainable. The inherent contradictions of the administration's actions and pronouncements were quickly perceived and, perhaps, magnified by a press and a public television system that were prepared to believe the worst. Sadly, their concerns about White House influence proved entirely justified. Nixon and his closest aides wanted to take control of public television -- or get rid of it altogether. They failed to do so. The White House's Office of Telecommunications Policy wanted to alter the

structure of the public television system by
decentralizing it. They met with only slightly more
success after four politically destructive years. Often
OTP's policy formulations, under the leadership of
director Clay T. Whitehead, seemed little more than
elegant smoke screens for the partisan objectives of the
White House itself. Indeed, it became impossible to
distinguish between the two.

Public television was itself regularly engulfed
in divisive intramural battles. The system was straining
to organize itself and the lack of sufficient funding was
both a cause and a result of its internal bickering. The
issues went to the heart of the dilemma faced by any
broadcasting institution supported by government money,
with a mission to provide both national and local
service. They were, and remain, difficult to resolve:
Who is to have final responsibility for programming?
What kind of standards should inform the decisions made?
Who sets the standards? How, in short, do you balance
creative freedom with fiscal accountability to
government?

Public television, once noted for granting its
producers and broadcast journalists greater editorial
freedom than that accorded their commercial counterparts,
began applying a more restrictive definition to the terms
"balance," "fairness," and "objectivity" during the Nixon
years. The infusion of federal funding made it
impossible to have done otherwise. Public television
wanted credibility in its journalistic offerings, the
same credibility and independence as commercial
television news. But with a President and an
administration that believed in neither the credibility
nor independence of the commercial network news,
journalism on public television -- even if it was
scrupulously balanced and fair -- was in for serious

trouble. Each successive program controversy boiled down
to the same old question: Who should define the "public
interest" in this publicly-supported institution, the
local station, the national program agency, the producer,
the politically appointed trustees or the government
itself? For journalism on public television, this
question of sovereignty is always a divisive one. It was
made far more divisive by the presence of an
administration hostile to it. Public television had
plenty of problems on its own. The Nixonian threat
succeeded only on exacerbating tensions and conflicts
that were inherent in the system's unwieldy structure and
unusual status.

The full documentary evidence of the Nixon
administration's "war" on public television became
available for the first time publicly in February of
1979. At the request of the second Carnegie Commission
on the Future of Public Broadcasting under the Freedom of
Information Act, all White House documents dealing with
public broadcasting were released. These materials
constitute the single most important documentary source
for this work. The other most vital source is personal
interviews by the author with a number of those who
directed the Nixon administration's Office of
Telecommunications Policy and with many of public
television's managerial and journalistic leaders of the
period. Also many thousands of pages of documents from
the Public Broadcasting Service, the Corporation for
Public Broadcasting were made available to me. Of
course, the battle over the future of public television
was no secret at the time it was occurring. The New York
Times, The Washington Post, and Variety covered the story
and a number of critical events received nationwide
attention in the press. In fact, in the spring of 1973
CBS News' Sixty Minutes did a segment on the politics of

public television. But there are wide gaps between what was reported while the struggle over public television was raging and what is known today. This work seeks to fill in some of those gaps and thereby shed some light on issues that are still very much with us. Many outside the broadcasting industry do not recall Nixon's war on public television. But it is, if nothing else, a good story, with an extraordinarily dramatic plot. Its final chapters are tinged with more than a little irony. It is the story of a fledgling and divided institution whose unification, momentarily at least, was brought about by virtue of the administration's attacks against it and whose popular success was made very much at the expense of those in the White House who tried to control it.

CHAPTER ONE

A PECULIAR INSTITUTION

"Public television is a series of meetings occasionally interrupted by a TV show."

—someone in public television

Non-commercial television is a peculiar institution in the United States. It is peculiar because it contradicts our belief in a strict separation between the government and the free press. It is peculiar because it does not fit comfortably into the competitive economic framework that underlies America's basic social institutions. Its difficulties during the Nixon era -- and since -- stem from our difficulty in rationalizing these peculiarities and in adequately resolving the conflicts they present. When Richard Nixon took office in January of 1969, public broadcasting, as educational television had only recently been renamed, was in a state of disarray. As one veteran of the industry observed at the time: "Public television is crackling with static -- an uncertainty about objectives, a dissonance of conflicting interests, a plethora of double-images."[1] The tensions within the public broadcasting community which the Nixon administration would soon exacerbate were an organic and consistent feature of the relatively brief history of the institution. It is not the purpose of this book to recount the entire history of non-commercial television in the United States; it has been well documented elsewhere.[2] Nonetheless, some understanding of the internecine institutional, political, and philosophical struggles taking place when Richard Nixon entered the White House seems a necessary prerequisite to appreciating the threat posed by his administration's efforts to further divide and intimidate the industry. Nixon and his advisers hardly created the divisions that racked public television between 1969 and 1974, but they certainly recognized them and sought to capitalize on them in order to achieve their own objectives. And the intrinsically fractionalized, and factionalized, structure of public television made it an easy target for such governmental pressure. It was partly because of just such a danger that the United States had been the last of the western democracies to develop a government supported broadcasting system, and it finally did so only with great hesitation.

With the beginning of large scale radio broadcasting in the industrially advanced nations during the early 1920's, governments had to decide how to structure their country's broadcast systems. Radio was recognized as a revolutionary communications tool with far greater power over the masses than print; and such decisionmaking was informed by the belief that because of its unique power, broadcasting could be either a danger to free society or an important vehicle for social and intellectual improvement. The great question was how to direct this potential. In Great Britain and the many European countries that followed its example, it was decided that the public airwaves were far too important to be left in private hands. The British Broadcasting Corporation served as a popular prototype of a government-chartered public broadcasting institution that remained well insulated -- if not completely aloof -- from political pressures. But the BBC was a monopoly in Britain and it remained so for many years after its creation. Its executives were entrusted with extraordinary power over the listening habits of an entire country. In the United States, distrust of such centralized control fostered a fundamentally different answer to the question of how to make broadcasting a positive reflection of the common values -- but diverse viewpoints -- of the nation. Here the commercial marketplace was allowed to serve as the controlling force over broadcasting's development. After all, in the 1920's, America's business was supposed to be business. So it was to be with radio. Here freedom of speech over the airwaves would be guaranteed not by public servants, but by a free competition of voices financed by the desire to sell products. In Britain, where radio was funded by a tax on everyone who owned a receiver, cultural diversity was mandated by government. In the United States, it was to be bought and paid for by advertisers.[3]

In the local station was placed the ultimate responsibility for what went on the air. The Communications Act of 1934 established the Federal Communications Commission to oversee the regulation of broadcasting. The Commission's primary task -- until 1927 undertaken by the Secretary of Commerce and then by the FCC's immediate precursor, the Federal Radio Commission -- was the licensing of these local stations. In doing so, it was responsible for allocating a public resource, the airwave, to private interests, provided they acted in the "public interest, convenience and necessity."[4] To most broadcasters, however, those were little more than rhetorical flourishes on their fundamental objective: making money in the new and rapidly expanding industry. But they were not alone in wanting to develop the potential of the broadcast medium. Many of the first radio broadcasters in the early 1920's

were educators interested in using radio for more
instructive purposes. Many colleges and universities
founded their own stations for teaching extension and
credit courses over the air. Unfortunately, compared to
the growing number of commercial stations filling the
spectrum, most of these operations were woefully
underfinanced and suffered from their confinement to low-
powered, part-time channel assignments from an unsympa-
thetic Federal Radio Commission. "Many educators," Erik
Barnouw wrote, "saw radio as an extraordinary educational
resource that in a few years had been handed over to
business control, with active help of the Federal Radio
Commission."[5] The non-profit broadcasters and others
who were alarmed at the rapid commercialization of radio
organized a campaign to force the government in its 1934
Communications Act to reserve a significant portion of
the broadcast spectrum for non-profit, educational
stations. Supporters of the campaign, including some in
Congress, charged that advertiser supported "pollution of
the air" threatened to undermine the national culture.[6]

But proponents of educational, non-profit radio
lost their fight to become a major force in American
broadcasting. The Communications Act of 1934 contained
no provision reserving a section of the broadcast
spectrum for educational stations, although many of the
college stations did continue to operate in the ensuing
years. When the widespread development of television
began after the Second World War, the veterans of the
non-commercial broadcasting movement were somewhat better
prepared and more successful in guaranteeing for
themselves a role in the new medium. Between 1948 and
1952 the Federal Communications Commission put a hold on
the granting of all television licenses. No new
applications for channels in the Very High Frequency --
channels 2 to 13 -- were granted and the development of

the seventy possible channels in the Ultra-High Frequency
was delayed.[7] In 1951 the Ford Foundation created the
Fund for Adult Education to "assist experimental
activities and to support promising programs in voluntary
education after formal schooling."[8] The fund made
sizable grants to the National Association of Educational
Broadcasters and the Joint Committee on Educational
Television to support their efforts to have both UHF and
VHF channels allocated by the FCC for non-commercial,
educational use. The NAEB used its grant from the
Foundations' Fund for Adult Education to undertake a
series of "monitoring studies" of the current program
offerings on commercial television. New York viewers,
the studies found, could witness 2,970 "acts or threats"
of violence in a single week, more than seventeen "acts
or threats" of violence during children's viewing
periods.[9] Such figures were used to powerful effect by
the supporters of channel reservation for educational
purposes. In 1952 the FCC's Sixth Reporter and Order set
aside 242 channels for educational television -- a number
which was later increased. The Fund for Adult Education
then provided a half million dollars to finance the
creation of another organization, the National Citizens
Committee for Educational Television, to assist the NAEB
and the Joint Committee on Educational Television in
their efforts to help stations acquire broadcast licenses
and in generating public support for the new ventures.

The Ford Foundation's unique level of support
and encouragement of educational -- and then public --
television's alphabet soup of organizations continued
into the late 1970's. Its cumulative investment totaled
nearly $300 million. During the Nixon years the
Foundation's special role in the medium became a major
political issue both to those within the White House and
to many within the industry itself, but educational

television might never have gotten off the ground and on
the air had Ford not committed itself to being what Jack
Gould of The New York Times called its "financial
kingpin."[10] From 1953 until 1969 money from the
Foundation underwrote everything from the construction of
new local stations to the production of experimental
programming for national distribution. At first, the
emphasis of all programming tended toward the purely
instructional: video classes and lectures by college
professors. Educational television programming did not
aspire to greatness in production values. It simply
could not afford to.

Despite serious financial and technological
constraints, educational television grew tremendously
during the 1960's. In 1961 there were only 56 non-
commercial television stations in the United States. By
1966 that number had more than doubled (to 177). The
nationwide viewing audience also doubled, numbering by
1966 14 million evening viewers and another 6.3 million
who watched daytime instructional programs.[11] In 1962
Congress passed the Educational Television Facilities Act
to finance, through the Department of Health, Education
and Welfare, the construction of new stations throughout
the country. The largest source of funds for many of the
stations, however, was state and local government, since
many of the educational broadcast licenses were held by
state universities and local school boards. Funding also
came from individual viewers, private corporations who
underwrote specific programs in exchange for on-air
credit, and the Ford Foundation.

The largest single source of programming was
also a Ford creation, National Educational Television
("NET") in New York. Until 1969 NET was the preeminent
force in educational television. It was founded in
October 1952 in Ann Arbor, Michigan with money from the

Fund for Adult Education, and its original role was to
acquire programs from diverse sources -- particularly
from the non-commercial stations themselves -- and to
supply these programs to cooperating stations by mail.[12]
The program distribution service began operation in 1954.
Five years later, in an effort to upgrade the technical
and artistic quality of its nationally distributed
productions, NET moved its headquarters to New York City
and discontinued its activities in radio and
instructional television.

     The center provided only five hours of national
programming each week and the cumbersome mailing process
put serious limitations on the growth of a truly national
audience. There were only a few regional electronic
interconnections between stations, most notably the
Eastern Educational Network which linked stations in
eight northeastern states.* Most educational stations
received their package of NET programs only through the
"bicycling" system. In bicycling, NET duplicated its
programs on a number of videotapes for distribution by
mail. Through a complicated system of mailing and re-
mailing, most programs could be seen within a two-week
period, but at different times and on different days
within each community served by an educational station.
By 1966 educational television was thus capable of
reaching two-thirds of American households. But despite
the impressive increase in viewership, only 12.5 percent
of the American viewing public actually tuned in during
the average week.[13]

---

*   An electronic interconnection is the system by which
    stations are simultaneously linked together. This can
    be done with telephone land lines or via satellite.
    Such an interconnection can be used to broadcast
    programs on many stations at the same time, as the
    commercial networks most often do; or simply to
    distribute material instantaneously for recording and
    later broadcast by individual stations.

By the mid-1960's educational television seemed to have reached an impasse. Without some significant change its potential for greater impact on American society was limited. Commercial television achieved an extraordinary prevalence -- as radio had -- through the networks. The networks simultaneously linked together their affiliate stations around the country and thus had the ability to reach many times more viewers than their non-commercial counterparts at NET. The only way for educational broadcasters to tap the full potential of their medium was to build a true national system. But building such a system would take money, a great deal more than educational television could expect from its current supporters. The possibilities for increased funding had ceased to expand. In December 1964, the National Association of Educational Broadcasters convened a national conference of educational station representatives in Washington to examine the problem of long-range financing.

There was a nearly unanimous sense at the conference that some kind of presidential commission should be established to undertake a comprehensive study of the current state and future needs of the educational television system. During the following year the Carnegie Corporation agreed to underwrite the formation of a panel of distinguished citizens to perform the task. In January 1967 the Carnegie Commission on Educational Television presented its report, <u>Public Television: A Program for Action</u>.

The Commission's central conclusion was that a well-financed and well-directed educational television system, substantially larger than the existing one and far more pervasive and effective, must be brought into existence if the full needs of the American public were to be served. As an indication of the broadened scope and potential it envisioned for the non-commercial medium, the Commission suggested that educational television in the future should be known as "Public Television." The Carnegie report argued that if the non-commercial stations that had been struggling for years in comparative obscurity were to be pulled together to produce programs on a technical and artistic level comparable to that of commercial television, then a truly national system had to be created, with a new source of guaranteed annual income. This new source, the report said, should be the federal government.[14]

The Commission called on Congress to establish a federally-chartered, non-profit, independent corporation to serve as the channel through which both public and private funds would flow to the public television system. The Commission said that it considered the creation of the corporation "fundamental to its proposals and [that it] would be most reluctant to recommend the other parts of its plan unless the corporate entity is brought into being."[15] Though the financial lifeblood of the new agency would be the federal government, the Commission also insisted that the public funding NOT be subject to the yearly appropriations process in Congress. The authors of the Carnegie report recognized that the infusion of federal money inevitably created the danger of partisan political control. Commission Chairman James R. Killian said, "If the future means of financing the [system] were to remain tied to annual appropriations, it would in our view seriously compromise [its] independence, and should be rejected."[16] President Johnson echoed the concern about government control. "Non-commercial television and radio," he said, "even though supported by federal funds, must be absolutely free from any federal government interference over programming." The Commission suggested that the best available method for providing such politically insulated financing was through an excise tax of between two and five percent on television set manufacturers. The revenues from the tax would go into a trust fund to be used at the discretion of the federally-chartered corporation in its support of the public television system.

Another theme fundamental to the Carnegie report was that of "grass-roots" localism in the new system. The Commission believed that the "bedrock" of the medium should be its local stations, the "heart" of the system, the community. Local public television stations would not be simply affiliates of a fourth network funded by the government. Initiative, the Carnegie report said, should flow up from the bottom instead of down from the top, as it did in commercial broadcasting. But the only way of achieving this ideal of pluralistic broadcasting service would be through a major new financial commitment. In 1966 the entire educational television system operated on an annual budget of only $34 million, with a cumulative capital outlay of $108 million. But the Commission estimated that the minimum annual operating cost for a viable national non-commercial television system was $270 million. The minimum capital investment required for such a system was impossible without a massive infusion of money at all levels of the operation. More money would be the key to assuring both higher quality and increased diversity of viewpoint on the public airwaves.

In February 1967 President Johnson, as part of his comprehensive "Message on Education and Health," recommended that Congress enact the Public Television Act of 1967. "Non-commercial television can bring its audience the excitement of excellence in every field," he said, but it "is reaching only a fraction of its audience

-- and achieving only a fraction of its potential
worth. . . . I am convinced that a vital and self-
sufficient non-commercial television system will not only
instruct, but inspire and uplift our people."[18]

The Johnson administration's legislative
proposal was based almost entirely on the recommendations
of the Carnegie Commission. Almost, but not quite. The
draft bill called for the creation of a Corporation for
Public Television, as well as for an increase in HEW
funding for television and radio facility construction.
Sensing, however, that Congress might not accept the idea
of permanently insulated financing, the White House
sought only a single year, $4 million appropriation for
fiscal 1968 as seed money for the new agency, instead of
asking for the excise tax and trust fund as Carnegie
implored. "Next year," Johnson said in his message to
Congress, "after careful review, I will make further
proposals for the Corporation's long-term financing."[19]

The idea of educational broadcasting was a
popular one in Congress, but there were many on Capitol
Hill who had serious questions about the unprecedented
concept that the corporation proposal represented.
Republican House members in particular voiced concern
about the government funding an independent communications organization. Minority members of the House
Interstate and Foreign Commerce Committee had qualms
about the large amount of federal funding that the
Carnegie report had envisioned; about the political
composition of the proposed Corporation's board of
presidentially appointed directors; and about support of
partisan editorializing with taxpayers' money. Though
all asserted that they wanted to devise a public
broadcast system free from government interference, many
were hesitant about creating a publicly underwritten
system whose fiscal and editorial policies were beyond

the reach of Congressional scrutiny. In a separate
opinion attached to the House report, Congressman
Hastings Keith warned that the proposed legislation would
make of educational television "an entity unlike anything
we know now. The potential good from educational TV is
limitless and much to be desired, but the potential
dangers are not to be ignored; we should not consider the
Corporation, which we are creating, so independent an
entity that at some later date the Commerce Committee may
not review and reshape its form and function."[20] Congress
decided to hedge its bet on public broadcasting by
opting, for the time being, for single year
appropriations to finance the Corporation. The Carnegie
Commission's plea for politically insulated funding would
have to wait until public broadcasting had proved its
value to the public and its responsibility to the
Congress.

On the floor of the House Congressman William
Springer defended the public broadcasting bill and the
decision to make the federal contribution to the
development of the system through appropriated funds.
"It will be a man-sized job," he said, "to maintain the
principle of independence of action for the Corporation
while holding the life and death purse string. That will
be the next chapter in the drama of public television and
will be played on this station next season. . . . For the
present we can create the machinery and see how it
functions."[21]

The Public Broadcasting Act of 1967 was passed
by Congress and signed by President Johnson in November.
The act expanded the functions of the new agency to
include radio as well as television and thus established
the Corporation for Public Broadcasting ("CPB") as an
independent, non-profit corporation authorized to:

> . . . facilitate the full development of
> educational broadcasting in which
> programs of high quality, obtained from
> diverse sources, will be made available
> to non-commercial educational television
> or radio broadcasting stations, with
> strict adherence to objectivity and
> balance in all programs . . . of
> controversial nature. . . .

> . . . assist in the establishment of one
> or more systems of interconnection to be
> used for the distribution . . . of
> programs . . . .

> . . . engage in its activities in ways
> that will most effectively assure the
> maximum freedom of the non-commercial
> television or radio broadcasting systems
> and local stations from interference
> with or control of program content or
> other activities.[22]

The Corporation would be governed by a board of fifteen,
whose members were presidentially appointed, but no more
than eight of whom could belong to the same political
party.

The first chairman of CPB's board of directors
was Frank Pace, Jr., who had served as director of the
Bureau of the Budget and Secretary of the Army under
President Truman. After leaving government in 1953 he
became chairman and chief executive officer of the major
defense contractor, General Dynamics Corporation. Since
1964 Pace had been president of the International
Executive Service Corps, which provided the management
and technical skills of American executives to business
enterprises in developing countries. Presidents
Eisenhower, Kennedy, and Johnson had all asked Pace, a
prominent Democrat, to serve on a variety of quasi-
governmental groups, among them the American Council on
NATO, the President's Commission on National Goals, the
Foreign Intelligence Advisory Board, and the Committee on

the Political Activity of Government Personnel.[23] He was someone who knew his way around Washington and the workings of presidentially appointed boards.

Pace's choice as the first president of the Corporation was an old colleague from the Truman administration, John Macy. Although Macy had had no professional experience as a broadcaster prior to his appointment to the CPB post, he had held a variety of governmental positions in the field of personnel administration. He and Pace had served together in the Air Force during the Second World War. From 1947 to 1951 he was director of Organization and Personnel for the Atomic Energy Commission's research facility in Los Alamos, New Mexico. Macy then became Pace's assistant Secretary of the Army. Under Eisenhower he served as executive director of the United States Civil Service Commission and under Kennedy and Johnson was its chairman. Macy worked as LBJ's principal "headhunter" for positions in the highest levels of the federal bureaucracy. Macy himself thought, in retrospect, that his appointment to head CPB was probably a mistake. Because of his extensive experience in the federal government it may have seemed, he said, that public broadcasting as an institution would be too closely tied to the government. Also, he was closely identified with President Johnson and might not be acceptable to a subsequent administration.[24]

Since Congress had rejected the Carnegie idea of an excise tax-supported trust fund, the crucial issue of permanent funding for CPB remained unresolved. President Johnson had assured public broadcasters that the White House would soon propose a long-term funding plan, but when he left office in January of 1969 one had yet to be drafted. The Corporation received no appropriation from Congress in fiscal year 1968 instead

of the $4 million promised by the administration. Until
a method of long-range financing could be devised, the
Corporation for Public Broadcasting would remain
dependent on annual appropriations. Thus, CPB was a
federally chartered agency, funded by the Congress on a
yearly basis, directed by presidential appointees and
headed by a lifelong government bureaucrat. From its
inception, public broadcasting was not nearly as
"independent" as its architects had envisioned it would
be.

  "I think that the 1968 statute was seriously
deficient," Macy said. "It was deficient primarily
because it failed to come to grips with the financial
issue; but it was also flawed in the structure of
governance it gave the Corporation."[25] Although the
Carnegie report had assumed that CPB itself would manage
the nationwide public television interconnection (the
satellite or land line system by which programs could be
distributed to the local stations) Congress had
prohibited the Corporation from owning or operating any
broadcast facilities. The potential of a government-run
national television system -- a domestic propaganda
agency, perhaps -- seemed too great. So CPB was
authorized to finance productions, but not to actually
produce or broadcast them. Macy and the Corporation's
lawyers interpreted this provision to mean that there had
to be another vehicle responsible for the technical
aspects of networking public television's national
programs. Local station leaders also felt strongly that
no single entity should have complete control over the
funding, production and distribution of programming.
Their suspicion of centralized domination resulted from
their recent experiences with the old combined national
production and interconnection organization, National
Educational Television. NET, many station leaders

complained, had been able to act as both judge and jury over its productions and therefore over all of educational television's national programming. The Carnegie report's recommendation that there be two national production centers and its emphasis on the "bedrock of localism" seemed an excellent prescription for those stations which were jealous about the amount of funding NET received from the Ford Foundation and the near absolute power NET producers had in developing the national schedule. The Carnegie Commission, the Congress, and the stations themselves were in harmony on the importance of decentralizing power in the new public television system.

By the beginning of 1969 CPB had replaced NET as the dominant force in public television, although NET's leaders were still hopeful that their organization would be chosen by the Corporation to manage the interconnection. But criticisms like those voiced by Thomas Petry, president of public station WCNY in Syracuse, New York, illustrated the political necessity of creating a totally new, station-oriented entity to run the system. In early January of 1969, Petry publicly expressed his dismay over the fact that all of the major forces in public television -- NET, CPB, the Ford Foundation and its latest creation, the Public Broadcast Laboratory (PBL) -- were located in New York City. His comments reflected the uneasiness many local stations felt about the concentration of decision-making authority over programming. They questioned "whether the structure, with its extensive cross-fertilization of personnel, was not inherently parochial rather than genuinely national in its composition and attitudes."[26] Robert Pepper explains it:

Station opposition to NET arose
basically from two issues. One was
station dissatisfaction with NET
programming. NET's public affairs
programs were considered too liberal,
anti-establishment, and often
unbalanced; other programs raised
questions of profanity, obscenity, and
matters of taste. The second issue was
a feeling of powerlessness on the part
of the stations in dealing with NET.
The two issues were inexorably
interrelated, as the lack of NET
response to programming objections led
to the impression of an arrogant and
unresponsive NET.[27]

Local station objections to the kind of
programs that were sent "down the line" from New York's
NET and PBL were one factor that led public television's
leaders in 1969 and 1970 to propose some fundamental
institutional changes. The new dependence on public
money through yearly congressional appropriation also
created pressure on public television to minimize
controversy and appeal to a wider spectrum than it had
previously. Stations themselves received criticism from
their boards of directors -- which often reflected the
more conservative elements of the community -- because of
programs with questionable language or anti-establishment
political viewpoints.

In the spring of 1969, James Day left his
position as manager of San Francisco's public station
KQED to assume the leadership of NET. Under Day, KQED
had gained a reputation as one of the most innovative and
successful stations in educational television. As NET
president he lobbied forcefully to have the Corporation
appoint NET as the new interconnection agency. His
position was that while there should certainly be both
greater diversity of stations involved in the NET program
decision-making process and a decentralization of

production sources, there still had to be a single source of responsibility. Someone, Day argued, had to be willing to put his head on the line to guarantee the freedom of creative risk-taking in public television. It was almost impossible, he complained, to do contemporary drama or documentaries without offending someone at stations in the South or Midwest. Day audaciously questioned whether a local station manager's assessment of a program's suitability was correct simply by virtue of the fact that it was made locally. "Of course NET wasn't responsive," he said, "as a national programmer it was concerned not about the stations or their boards of directors, but about the viewing public." He argued that true diversity had to be planned, that it would never happen through programming by committee or as a natural by-product of a decentralized structure.[28]

Day believed that journalists working in public television should have virtually the same freedom they might enjoy as print reporters. As their editor he believed in exercising a light touch. He granted documentary producers a great deal more freedom than they were usually given at the commercial networks. After all, public television was free from pressure by advertisers to avoid risk and controversy. That, to Day and others, was the whole point of non-commercial television. So while commercial television news strove for objectivity in presenting issues and events, NET's public affairs programs often had a noticeable point of view. "Balance," in the strictest sense, was not necessary in good journalism, only "fairness." But this approach ran counter to the dominant traditions of broadcast journalism. Newspapers and magazines do not need licenses from the government, do not have quite the same power to reach millions of people in their homes instantaneously. Journalism on television always runs

into controversy when it strays from the ideal of equal
time. The networks did occasionally produce strong-
minded documentaries that were highly controversial, but
they did not receive their funds from Congress and their
directors were not appointed by the President. Public
television was obliged to be somewhat more careful than
the private sector. As a local educational station
manager in San Francisco, Day had succeeded by giving his
producers complete creative freedom. Applying the same
laissez-faire approach to running the one production
center for the national public television system at a
time when the entire country was violently polarized over
politics and social mores resulted in conflict within the
system and controversy on the air.

From his perch atop the organization charged
with bringing harmony to what was intended to be a
pluralistic system, John Macy saw NET's continued
predominance as a major stumbling block to bringing
together the disparate factions of the public television
community. "I felt there were more competitive elements
than were good for the system," he said. "The station
managers were a group unto themselves, but not with a
common approach . . . there were the regional groups that
had formed certain identities of their own and that
wanted to have independence, but also wanted to have
funding. You had a small cabal of producing stations
that had the capability to produce, up to a point; and
yet the cry was that all stations should be equipped to
produce. It seemed to me that, throughout, there was an
absence of any real appreciation of what the financial
picture needed to be."[29] The passage of the Public
Broadcasting Act, with its various limitations on the
role of the Corporation and without the financial support
necessary to carry out its mandate had, if anything,
intensified the competition among public television's

organizations for the power and resources that were available.

In March 1969 the eight largest stations in the system asked CPB and the Ford Foundation to terminate what they called "the most costly and controversial experiment in educational television," the Sunday evening Public Broadcast Laboratory series. PBL had been the Foundation's boldest venture in educational television programming and was the personal project of Fred W. Friendly. Friendly had become media advisor to Foundation president McGeorge Bundy in 1966 after resigning the presidency of CBS News in the last of a number of disputes with the network management. He had worked with the "father of broadcast journalism," Edward R. Murrow, on the influential See It Now program of the 1950's. At a time when the broadcast industry --indeed, the entire country -- had been cowed into blacklisting workers labeled subversive by Senator Joseph McCarthy and his fellow anti-communists, Murrow used "See It Now" to sharply criticize the feared junior senator from Wisconsin. Friendly tried to continue the combative tradition but came to believe that CBS had no desire to place the value of journalism above that of revenue. He left the network in 1965 when he was refused permission to replace the regular program schedule with coverage of the Senate Foreign Relations Committee hearings on American involvement in Vietnam.[30]

Friendly's intense personal style matched his strong professional views. It was difficult to be ambivalent about Fred Friendly. He inspired colleagues to both deep personal loyalty and extreme animosity. He expressed convictions loudly and often and thus collected a large coterie of detractors. Friendly believed above all that serious journalism had an important place on television. But there were many who felt he turned to

educational television as his vehicle when he was unable
to maintain his ideals at CBS.

Shortly after their arrival at Ford, Friendly
and Bundy proposed a novel plan for underwriting a
national non-commercial television system: The
Broadcasters Non-Profit Satellite Service. The service
would use the latest in communications technology to give
educational television a national interconnection at a
fraction of the cost of conventional telephone cable,
then in use by all the networks. More importantly,
excess satellite capacity could be leased to the
commercial networks with the income going to finance
programming on educational television. The Ford proposal
estimated that the satellite would yield $30 million a
year for the non-commercial system -- with no government
strings attached. Though Friendly and Bundy maintained
that their plan was complimentary to, rather than
competitive with, the Carnegie Commission's excise tax-
supported corporation proposal, many believed that the
two represented very different notions about the nature
of non-commercial television. Carnegie's emphasis was on
the local station, Ford's on the national service.

With $10 million in Ford Foundation money,
Friendly then set out to create the Public Broadcast
Laboratory ("PBL") as a way of demonstrating that public
television could, with adequate production funds and a
nationwide interconnection, have a profound impact on the
American viewing public. On Sunday evenings at seven
o'clock PBL presented its experiments in serious public
affairs and cultural programming. Though the PBL project
was grand in design, many felt that it often fell short
in execution. The program won the 1968 DuPont-Columbia
University award for outstanding broadcast journalism for
its documentary, "Defense and Domestic Need: The Contest
for Tomorrow." But stations complained that PBL's public

affairs efforts often caused too much controversy and
that its cultural offerings were elitist and unappealing.
Most importantly, local stations felt that PBL had been
forced on them by an overbearing Friendly and a
meddlesome Ford Foundation.[31]

The stations wanted greater control over the
programs they broadcast. They proposed the "eight
station plan," which called for replacing PBL with a
program that "would place stronger emphasis on cultural
presentations and reduce the proportion of time accorded
to news and public affairs."[32] A month later, Macy and
Friendly announced a major shake-up in the structure and
programming of public broadcasting. Within three months,
CPB would create a new organization to take over
management of the interconnection from NET; in addition,
they made public their intention to begin a new public
affairs production center in Washington. Together, the
new organizations would replace NET as network and
principal production center for national news and public
affairs programs.[33]

After Jim Day was elected NET president in June
1969, he immediately asked the Corporation to delay its
action so that he could consider the plan for a new
organization and, possibly, submit a counterproposal. He
argued that NET should maintain responsibility for the
national interconnection. But since much of public
broadcasting saw NET as the problem, it was unlikely that
it would be considered the solution. In his October 1969
working paper, "The Management and Operation of a
National Interconnection," CPB executive vice president
Ward B. Chamberlin said that the Corporation had
"considered the NET plan at great length. While it has
great advantages, the Corporation does not agree with its
basic concept which vests the system's management and
operation within the present NET structure and does not

believe that it is wise to have the major national
program producer also run the interconnection system.
Having read the NET plan carefully, the Corporation
continues to believe that a new and independent
organization -- one in which the major controlling force
is the stations -- should be formed for this purpose."[34]

The concept advanced by CPB in the summer and
fall of 1969 to achieve greater diversity of production
sources called for the establishment of six to eight
national production centers at stations in different
regions. CPB would fund these stations with large,
unrestricted "block" programming grants -- that is, money
not tied to any specific program proposals but that could
be used only for the production of national programs.
Originally at least, the production centers themselves
were primarily responsible for all such program
decisionmaking and development. In this system, the new
interconnection agency would merely assign each center a
given number of hours to be filled in each broadcast
season. Its pre-broadcast participation would be limited
to minimizing overlap and duplication, and to reviewing
for clear cases of illegality in programs.[35]

The Public Broadcasting Service ("PBS") was
formally incorporated on November 4, 1969. It was to be
a station membership organization. Of its nine
directors, five would represent the stations themselves,
with one representative of non-station production centers
(at the time only NET), one from CPB, and two chosen by
the others to represent the public at large.[36] In
February 1970 Hartford Gunn, general manager of Boston's
WGBH since 1955, was named to head the new service.

The formation of PBS was a clear attempt to
balance public television's presentation by giving local
stations and regional networks a greater voice over
programming. It also marked the end of NET as public

television's network and primary national programmer.[37]
CPB itself was to have no pre-broadcast control or review
over programs PBS distributed. The Corporation would
merely provide the funding for stations and production
groups, while PBS would handle the technical job of
interconnection and determine the schedule of programs
for national distribution.

At the time of PBS's creation, Fred Friendly
had announced that with the inauguration of the new
national system the Ford Foundation would revert to the
role of a "junior partner" in public broadcasting.
Criticisms of the Foundation's intimate involvement in
the institution had increased during the late 1960's.
Local operators felt that Foundation money was
responsible for NET's insensitive domination of the
system and that Friendly had forced the PBL program on
them. Although Ford had undisputably been the "fairy
godmother" in getting the whole enterprise started, they
tended, Macy said, "to have sticky fingers."

They would identify favorites -- favorites in
terms of programming and favorites in terms of
stations."[38] Those who were not "favorites" felt that
those who were cared more about what the Ford Foundation
wanted in programming than what the rest of public TV
wanted. The Ford Foundation had for many come to
symbolize the "New York liberal" predominance in public
broadcasting. Friendly himself was obliged to explain to
Congress and the public that despite the Foundation's
activities in the development and support of a host of
public television entities, neither he nor anyone else at
Ford had ever involved themselves in program content.[39]

The beginning of 1969 until the autumn of 1971
was a period when public television leaders like Gunn and
Macy sought to legitimize the idea of a truly national
public medium while also allowing the local stations to

feel that their power had been enhanced within the system. PBS seemed to be the institutional fulfillment of the "grass-roots" spirit of the Carnegie Report, but according to some critics, the overriding purpose behind the changes taking place was merely a drive for wider popular acceptance and greater financial support from the federal government and the community.[40] The shift away from alleged radicalism of NET was marked by tension between those who saw in the move towards moderation and respectability an attempt to appease those who had power over the purse strings, and those who believed that such a shift was necessary to the future survival of public television.

During the first three years of PBS operation each successive production season saw an increased role for both the Service and the Corporation in the area of program planning. As the two organizations strove to define their respective leadership responsibilities, those on the creative end felt their once unfettered freedom eroding. This gradual assault on what had been conceived by CPB itself as the complete independence of production centers came on two interrelated fronts: fiscal and editorial. The "tax dollar" argument dictated that there be greater accountability both for the money that was spent and for the material that was broadcast. But the partisans of the NET, producer-freedom position believed that public television was choosing a path that would certainly lead to blandness and might possibly lead to government control and exploitation.

In April 1969, Bill Moyers, former Press Secretary to President Johnson, warned the Friends of Channel 13 in New York that the infusion of federal money might not mean the liberation that non-commercial television was seeking, but instead could create a "domestic U.S.I.A." -- a government-sponsored propaganda agency. "Congress," he said, "has a natural instinct to attach strings to its generosity."[41] One week later, forty producers from NET and PBL formed a group dedicated to insulating the public TV from political influence. They also opposed federal government involvement through Congressional grants to CPB.[42] Variety's Bill Greeley soon took to calling CPB the "corporation for PATSY broadcasting" because of what he perceived to be its increased coverage of events that might please the Nixon Administration -- the July 4th "honor America" programs, the President's hunger conference, the State of the Union address.[43] The headlines of his stories neatly described his attitude: "CPB Making Like Government Web," and later, "CPB More Than Ever Like Government Web."[44]

NET president Jim Day pointed out in March of 1970 that since many local stations were accustomed to yearly appropriations from state legislatures, they did not have the same healthy suspicion towards Congress as did those at NET. Faced with what The New York Times called a "steady flow of complaints about controversial NET programs," Day criticized PBS for acting as a censor on behalf of the unprogressive stations. "Most public television stations," he charged, "want programs that won't rock the boat." "Committee control" as exercised by PBS, Day felt, led only "to bland decisions blandly arrived at."[45]

Indeed, less than a month earlier five local stations had refused to air an NET Journal program dealing with United States intervention in the Third World, entitled "Who Invited Us?." The hour-long program, produced by PBL's DuPont award winner Alan M. Levin, was a highly critical examination of the economic and political factors behind American military interventions "from Vladivostok to Vietnam." The emphasis was, for the most part, on Latin America and its

potential for "future Vietnams." Among those interviewed
on the program were Chilean poet and communist
presidential candidate Pablo Neruda, veteran diplomat
Averell Harriman, Democratic Senator Frank Church, and
Republican Senator Karl Mundt. The show included
segments on dissident G.I.'s at Fort Bragg, North
Carolina, preparing an article on the Green Berets for
their underground newspaper. In stark contrast was a
demonstration at the same base of American military
prowess for Latin American military leaders -- hosted by
General William Westmoreland. "Who Invited Us?" also
investigated the role of CIA agents, whose clandestine
efforts, as in the case of Vietnam, were shown to be the
first step towards direct military involvement.[46]

The program, and particularly the decision by
Washington, D.C.'s station WETA not to broadcast it,
caused a storm of protest in both Washington and New
York. "Who Invited Us?" was the first of what were a
very few, but highly publicized NET endeavors over the
next eighteen months that would cause intense reaction in
government and the public broadcasting industry. James
Lehrer, then host of Dallas station KERA's Newsroom
program and later PBS public affairs coordinator, said,
"We're only talking about two or three programs, but
those two or three gave ammunition to those within the
system who were out to get NET for a whole set of
different reasons."[47] NET, even in its diminished role
as national production center, had been isolated from the
public television community. Its fate as an independent
entity was sealed when the Ford Foundation withdrew its
support and denied a $24 million at the very time when
PBS began operations. Such a "one-two punch," Variety
reported, was a "deathblow" to public television's "most
notorious seedbed of controversial programming" since it
was "an open secret that NET programmers [had] been

giving off sparks for years over contrasting notions of
what should be aired on the public web."[48]

By the end of 1970, to the relief of many in
the industry, Hartford Gunn's notions had taken
precedence. He questioned whether "traditional
documentary [was] the way public television should go."[49]
And there were fewer and fewer news and public affairs
programs on the national schedule. It became
increasingly clear to those at NET that at CPB, PBS, and
down the public television line, their New York
production organization was being equated with Vice
President Spiro Agnew's arch villain, the "eastern
liberal media establishment." As Variety's Greeley put
it, their once defiant attitude of "If you can't take the
heat, get out of the kitchen" had been altered by PBS to
"If you can't take the cool, get off the line."[50] A
September 1970 study of PBS clearance patterns -- that
is, the percentages of member stations that carry the
programs sent out over the interconnection -- showed that
"like their commercial counterparts, public television
stations show a marked preference for sports over
programs of controversy or public affairs."[51]

Despite the Public Broadcasting Service's and
the local station's heightened sensitivity to potentially
controversial programs, NET and Boston's WGBH did
occasionally produce programs which PBS "flagged"; that
is, advised member stations about questionable taste or
political content. One such program was "Banks and the
Poor," which aired in November 1970. The show was
controversial not only because it sought to expose the
discriminatory practices of important banking
institutions, but because of the dramatic methods it
employed in doing so. Part of NET's Realities series,
"Banks and the Poor" served its indictment by juxtaposing
the slick, commercial pitches banks and savings and loan

companies made to potential customers with stark
depictions of the poverty living conditions endured by
some less "attractive" would-be borrowers from the black
ghetto of Washington, D.C. It cut back and forth between
separate interviews with Chase Manhattan chairman David
Rockefeller and banking industry critic Representative
Wright Patman of Texas, chairman of the House Banking and
Currency Committee, simulating a debate that did not
actually occur. Most notably, the program closed with a
list of 133 senators and congressmen with banking
holdings or serving as directors of banks -- while the
Battle Hymn of the Republic played in the background.
Before the list appeared, the narrator asked the chairman
of the New York City Bar Association, Louis M. Loeb,
whether he believed legislators should be directors or
shareholders of banks. Loeb said, "I certainly
think . . . that the congressman is not as free to cast
an independent judgment on the merits of the legislation
as he would be if he didn't have a financial interest as
an officer or director in a banking institution." The
program then cited a recent Bar Association report which
had recommended that all congressmen and senators with
financial holdings in banks, serving as directors of
banks or members of law firms with bank clients, sever
such connections. The closing segment of "Banks and the
Poor" clearly implied that conflict of interest on
banking legislation was widespread in the U.S.
Congress.[52]

As it turned out, two of the congressmen whose
names appeared were not at the time connected to any
banks. One senator whose name appeared correctly was
John Pastore of Rhode Island. Pastore, as chairman of
the Communications Subcommittee of the Senate Commerce
Committee, was probably public broadcasting's strongest
supporter on Capitol Hill. He was also a close friend of

CPB board member Michael Gammino, who was president of the same Rhode Island bank for which Pastore served as a director. The program also hit a number of local stations right in _their_ boards of directors and nearly a quarter of them refused to carry it. House Banking Committee chairman Patman criticized the stations that bowed to pressure from local banks not to air "Banks and the Poor." He also said: "I wish the show had been stronger in presenting the shortcomings of the big banks, but the mere fact that these issues were raised is highly beneficial to the public interest."[53]

Few in Congress or even within public broadcasting were as pleased with the show as Patman had been. Whether prompted by fears of continued embarrassments to a vulnerable public television system or by the ideal of objectivity in public affairs programming, the PBS board moved quickly to adopt an interim statement on the issue of program standards and practices. Coincidentally, the day after "Banks and the Poor" aired PBS had scheduled a special membership meeting to consider how the Service should deal with controversies involving taste, language, and journalistic bias. As PBS president Hartford Gunn told the meeting, "It's a big, sprawling topic that is hard for us to get a handle on. It's an area where everyone is an expert --if for no other reason than 'we' know what 'our' personal standards are, and we usually feel that if they're good enough for us, they're good enough for everyone else."[54]

Gunn explained that the new and complex public television system was starting up during a period of tremendous social ferment and political polarization in which words were increasingly used as weapons and "the medium was the messenger." The combination of "expectations for bold new programming and a desire for permanent financing" from the federal government created a framework of tension for which, Gunn said, "simple solutions [were] probably not to be found." But he attempted to place PBS safely on the middle ground: "The balance must be struck between the irresponsibility of NO controls -- and the destruction of the system that this would bring -- and the myopic and bland mix which would result from OVER control." The PBS president was determined "not to gamble needlessly or recklessly with this medium."

A week after the PBS gathering the Corporation for Public Broadcasting assembled for its own scheduled meeting. The minutes show that the "tax dollar" argument exerted a powerful influence on many of those charged with the ultimate responsibility for the government's contribution to public broadcasting. Chairman Frank Pace went right to the issue of the problems involved with government financing and program standards and practices. "How," he asked, "could the Corporation best deal with broadcast material which is objectionable or highly controversial?" Referring to the "Banks" program, the chairman conceded that "troublesome situations were bound to arise" and that the Corporation had to be prepared to deal with them. He went on to say that CPB's difficulty in communicating its performance in this delicate area was causing problems in its relationship with Congress. CPB president John Macy reminded the board that the Corporation "was in the unique position of having to provide leadership and funds without controlling details of administration and was under legislative sanction not to inhibit freedom of programming."[55]

Albert Cole, chairman of Reader's Digest and President Nixon's first appointee to the CPB board, replied that "CPB would in no way delegate or escape its responsibility for spending appropriated funds properly."

Pace agreed, saying, "The White House and Congress would invariably look to CPB as the accountable agency."

The issues of fiscal control and programming power could not, however, realistically be separated. Macy explained that production agencies were fearful that the Corporation's financial support would be coupled with a dictation of editorial policy.

Jack Valenti, former aide to President Johnson and now president of the Motion Picture Association of America, vigorously opposed any involvement by the CPB board in the issue of program content. "It was," he said, "a road strewn with potholes and landmines -- an impossible road to journey down." Valenti argued that the questions would always remain, "What is gratuitous? What are 'good taste,' 'fairness,' and 'balance' and who determines their meaning?" Any attempt to remove objectionable material post production, he said, inevitably results in allegations of censorship. He explained that producers felt an obligation to preserve freedom of expression for the creative artists and their sentiments and opinions were usually at complete variance with those of the board.

Another Nixon appointee was Jack Wrather, president of Wrather Communications, which owned a number of television and radio stations in Tulsa and San Diego. He was also part owner of independent station WNEW-TV in New York and of Teleprompter cable television. Wrather countered Valenti by saying that the obligations of the Corporation and the board were "to all the people rather than to a small coterie of the creative." Bank president Michael Gammino reiterated that the number one obligation of the board was "to insure that the programming it supports meets appropriate legal, moral and ethical standards." He concluded that if the board did not reach a consensus on the proposition it might be lending its hand to "a deterioration from within which could ultimately destroy it."

At that point, vice chairman James Killian, former president and chairman of the board of the Massachusetts Institute of Technology and chairman of the Carnegie Commission which originated the idea of CPB, joined the conversation. Killian said that the Corporation might destroy itself faster by taking too strong a position of censorship. What was needed, he said, was leadership rather than an arbitrary, authoritative approach. Cole warned that the Corporation could not survive many bank programs. "It must keep programming within the sanctions of the Public Broadcasting Act," he said, "or Congress will stop its appropriations." Valenti said that the board would have to read every script for compliance and Pace concluded that the board should exercise "constant vigilance" in the area of program standards and practices. He suggested that the subject was so important that it deserved review at every subsequent board meeting. Macy told the board that in the future, CPB would attach to each grant instrument a brief statement of its legislative responsibilities with respect to both freedom and fairness in programming, "defining in positive and practical fashion such terms as balance, fairness, objectivity and taste." Also, arrangements would be made to bring the Corporation into "timely, periodic discussions involving program subjects, content and treatment prior to the production of even the pilot episodes" of new series. CPB and PBS were determined after "Banks and the Poor" to exercise greater control over what went out to the system for which each group felt responsible.[56]

Nineteen-seventy-one, Pace told the mid-January gathering of the CPB board at the University Club in New

York, would be public broadcasting's "make or break year." The Corporation was moving ahead in drafting long-term funding legislation, but for the current season, Pace reported, insufficient funding would continue to be a serious problem for the entire system. The consensus among CPB and PBS leaders was that increasing public awareness of public television's program service -- with hit shows like the Children's Television Workshop's Sesame Street and Julia Child's The French Chef -- would increase attention to the system's programming standards. With a larger and more attentive audience than in the pre-interconnection, "educational" days, controversy was bound to increase. To help devise a common strategy for dealing with program standards issues the CPB board invited PBS chairman James Loper of KCET in Los Angeles and PBS president Hartford Gunn to its January meeting. There Gunn explained that in all of the media there was a movement towards "reporter power," a desire on the part of producers and reporters to advocate subjective points of view. This trend was particularly strong, he said, in public television which, in order to attract competent talent with limited resources had traditionally offered producers considerable autonomy. Gunn reported, however, that the number of programs raising problems of taste and balance had declined sharply. Whereas 10 percent of all PBS programs were "flagged" in October 1970, only one out of thirty-three was so labeled during the first two weeks of 1971.[57]

Despite the apparently successful efforts by CPB and PBS to control the number of such controversial programs, the few that did reach the air in 1970 and 1971 reinforced the view widely held within the Nixon administration, as well as within some segments of public broadcasting itself, that public television was dominated

by a strongly liberal, anti-administration, anti-war,
anti-establishment point of view. Gunn, Macy, and the
station leaders who were laboring to secure a long-range
funding bill from the White House and Congress did not
appreciate the image, and their efforts at de-politici-
zation did not go unnoticed. The New York Times reported
in June 1971, "some in public TV have been critical of
PBS. They say that since it became the dominant factor
in public television, there has been a falling off in the
number and quality of news and public affairs programs."

In addition to the vexing issue of
controversial journalistic programming, institutional
jealousies continued to afflict public broadcasting. The
Public Broadcasting Service might have served its purpose
in neutralizing NET, but the issue of PBS's proper role
was also a constant source of tension and debate. The
Service, The Times reported, was "plagued by the
rigidities growing out of annual federal funding, the
suspicions of competing program producers and station
managers, the distrust of national, state and local
politicians and the seeming indifference of the larger
viewing public." The network was finding it difficult
"creating a clear picture of itself amid a proliferation
of public television entities."[58]

The architects of the Public Broadcasting
Service had been careful to point out before its creation
that successful operations would depend on formal
agreement defining the relationship between it and CPB.
Because there were many from the Ford Foundation, CPB and
PBS whose professional relationship predated the creation
of the latter two entities, institutional division were
blurred. A confusing informality ruled, and during its
first two seasons PBS maintained a cordial partnership
with CPB. "I didn't feel," Macy said, "that honorable
men needed to have a detailed contract."[59] PBS had

independent responsibility for pre-broadcast control over
programming while CPB held power over grant-making
decisions. The Corporation largely followed PBS's
recommendations in which programs to finance. The system
in 1970 and 1971 remained, however, in a constant state
of flux. As the novel experiment of public television
emerged from the dark, its various elements were
constantly bumping into one another. Within the
heterogeneous public system, whose local member stations
by 1971 numbered over 200, there were some five different
types of stations serving different kinds of
constituencies. They ranged from the local school board
and university-run educational UHF stations, to the large
community stations that were also national production
centers. There were therefore inherent tension among the
diverse groups of stations and organizations. "Those
elements that would make up the system," Macy said,
"really had no desire for a system. What they had was a
desire for support -- without any strings attached."[60]
But because Congress had not yet determined long-term
funding arrangements, battles over scarce resources and
how to use them appropriately continued through the
spring and summer of 1971.

In February 1971, when the Public Broadcasting
Service completed the first draft of guidelines for
public television's journalistic programming, the
production centers began complaining openly about what
they felt was creeping censorship by CPB and PBS. NET's
Jim Day, as a member of the PBS board, remained adamantly
protective of the producer's creative freedom. He
responded to Gunn's invitation to comment on the
journalism guidelines by saying that the document was
"both amateurish in its superficiality and of a low
journalistic quality." Its cry for a higher standard of
journalism in public broadcasting -- accuracy,

objectivity, balance, etc.," he continued, "is fatally
muted by its own journalistic shoddiness." Day
criticized the negative tone and the thinly veiled
hostility towards NET which he felt the draft paper
reflected. "PBS," he said, "must cease regarding the
production centers as refuges for willing falsifiers and
unwitting dupes, and itself as the sanctified guardian of
The Truth and the surrogate father and protector of its
two hundred member stations."[61]

"PBS must come to trust and stand behind those
who produce for it." He concluded:

> As you seek to invoke a code of
> journalism standards, as yourself if you
> can call to mind a single <u>outstanding</u>
> television documentary of the past --
> from Edward R. Murrow's SEE IT NOW on
> Senator McCarthy to the recent CBS
> SELLING OF THE PENTAGON -- that has not
> provoked a debate among "experts" on its
> accuracy, fairness, balance, etc. A
> code of standards could not have
> prevented the debate, but it might have
> prevented the programs.

The national production centers joined NET in
lamenting the direction in which the system seemed to be
moving. In June of 1971 they met in Aspen, Colorado to
develop a response to the infringements on their
autonomy. In a joint letter to Gunn and Macy the six
production center presidents noted "signs that public
broadcasting is moving not toward greater and greater
program diversity and choice, but towards more and more
uniformity; not toward maximum insulation from dictation
of content by the source of funding, but toward
increasing concentration of program decisions in the
hands of a very few people at PBS and CPB; not toward the
creation of a truly different kind of television service

reflecting the variety of experience in our nation, but toward a fourth network in which program content is increasingly influenced by the wishes of the timid and the unimaginative; not, in short, toward what the Carnegie Commission had in mind, but toward something far different."[62]

"We agreed that, if the current trends we perceive were to go unchecked, the worst of all possible worlds for us would result: a system that places all the key funding, programming production, promotion and distribution controls in Washington. This would make the production centers no more than field facilities for the central office."

"In short," the Aspen group concluded, "the production centers looked to the future with gloom. We saw our decision making power eroding. We saw the goal of diversity shrinking to a matter of mere geography, not of judgment." "The Aspen Document" also recounted a number of specific examples of increased program control by the national organizations. The production center presidents "urgently requested" a meeting with the PBS and CPB leaders "for a candid exchange before anyone feels compelled to take an unyielding position."

With the Aspen Document, however, CPB and PBS lost faith in the possibility of working with a national production center system. Such an arrangement, if it were to work, had to be based on mutual trust, cooperation, and responsibility. Aspen made it clear to Gunn and Macy that the system was not ready to work on those terms. Consequently, during the summer of 1971 they began to discuss alternatives to the national production center concept. Since there was just not enough money to support that many autonomous production entities, the Corporation decided to cut down to three the number of major producing stations: two for general programming at WNET in New York, KCET in Los Angeles and one specializing in national public affairs at Washington's WETA. Henceforth, any program proposal from outside one of these three centers would be funded on a series by series basis by the Corporation, instead of through the open-ended block grant system. The change placed considerably more power over program development for the system in the hands of PBS and CPB.[63] Such was precisely the fear of the Aspen group.

Given the increasingly tense relationships between CPB, PBS, the production centers, and the local stations during the summer of 1971, the address by Arthur Singer to a public broadcasting conference in Boyne Highlands, Michigan on June 28 was inevitable, but untimely. Singer, who as president of the Sloan Foundation had helped organize the Carnegie Commission, complained bitterly that public television had not turned out as the Commission had hoped it would. His criticisms sounded startlingly similar to those voiced by the production center leaders at Aspen ten days earlier. He said that Carnegie was "a plea for pluralism, a plea for localism, a plea for breadth of attack, a plea for an escape from the ponderousness and the pedagogy that had afflicted most of educational television." He charged that public television was instead casting itself in a commercial mold and aspiring to become a fourth network under the control of the Ford Foundation, CPB and PBS. "The Ford Foundation and the Washington entities," he declared, "determine program content and make public television just as centralized and dehumanized as CBS or NBC." He argued that the local stations had lost all creative control and had become mere "branch offices for Washington and New York."[64]

After two years of trying to shed its image as a left-leaning, eastern-dominated medium, public

broadcasting was being charged by one of its own creators
with just such biases. Singer's position conformed
closely to the view of public television that had been
forming in the Nixon White House over the preceding two
years. His criticism not only seemed to justify the
developing administration policy, but highlighted the
fact that the public broadcasting community was a house
deeply divided. Rancor, controversy, confusion, and a
chronic shortage of money characterized this fledgling
experiment during the first two years of the Nixon
presidency. From the right, there were charges of
liberal elitism, left-wing bias, and improper Ford
Foundation influence. From the left came bitter
complaints about the trade-off of risk and innovation for
safety and blandness and creeping government control. In
the middle was a group of moderates who were seeking to
build a viable public broadcasting system, with a working
balance between the local and the national entities,
programming of both broad acceptability and diversity, as
well as a respectable, objective voice in news and public
affairs. With more time and particularly more money, it
is possible that such a balance might soon have been
struck, if not for the efforts of the Nixon
administration.

It is ironic that just when advocacy journalism
was being replaced by more reserved -- if somewhat less
daring -- reporting of public events and issues, Nixon
and his advisors became more deeply concerned with left-
wing, anti-administration programs on public television.
Just as the Ford Foundation was trying to ease out of its
formerly predominant role in the medium, with the
administration there were heightened perceptions of Ford
hegemony over political programming. Just when New
York's NET was displaced by the more national and
heterogeneous PBS, the White House began to attack public

television openly for its "New York-Washington orientation." In short, just when public broadcasting was moving on many fronts to gain greater respectability and wider popular acceptance (with fewer programs of controversy), the Nixon administration undertook a concerted effort to undermine its fragile independence.

Within the government from 1969 to 1971 the basic issue was also one of funding: where it should properly come from, and how it should appropriately be used. During this period Nixon and his advisors sought to use the funding mechanism, as well as the powers of executive appointment to the board of CPB, to force public broadcasting further and more firmly down a path which, it is clear, it was already attempting to travel. Because of its newness, its internal strife, and its increasing dependence on yearly congressional appropriations, public broadcasting was particularly vulnerable to such pressure from the White House and its supporters on Capitol Hill. This first stage of the administration's battle with public television is the subject of the next chapter.

CHAPTER TWO

THE VIEW FROM THE WHITE HOUSE

"He who pays the piper calls the tune."

> --Albert Cole, President Nixon's
> first appointee to the
> Corporation for Public
> Broadcasting Board of Directors.

        Richard Nixon became President of the United
States just as the new national public television system
was taking shape. The election of a president with a
long personal history of antipathy toward the media and
toward the "eastern intellectual establishment" boded ill
for an institution which was widely regarded as part of
both. There is no more consistent theme in Richard
Nixon's long and eventful political career than his
antagonistic and sometimes vituperative relationship with
certain segments of the journalistic community. During
his presidency that relationship achieved a plateau of
mutual hostility when members of the Nixon administration
undertook a public campaign to undermine the integrity of
the news media and a covert effort to stifle its First
Amendment freedom. The relationship with public
television was, and remains, an element of the "Nixon
versus the Press" theme that received a good deal less
attention than the battle with commercial networks. But
while all of the media were threatened by the Nixon
administration's activities, public television was in the

most danger. Its editorial freedom stood on the weakest
foundation because of the system's very newness and
dependence on annually appropriated federal money. So
the tremors caused by White House pressure rattled public
television's delicate structure more than those of the
commercial networks and major newspapers. Public
television was, nonetheless, one of the news media; and
it is impossible to understand the motivations behind the
Nixon administration's assault on the news media without
looking back briefly at the twenty-year history of
Nixon's relations with the press that preceded his
election to the presidency in 1968.

According to Richard Nixon, the "eastern
intellectual elite" never forgave him for his early anti-
communist congressional campaigns and, most importantly,
for his relentless pursuit of Alger Hiss. Nixon had
acquired a reputation for rough, re-baiting tactics
during his first run for Congress from southern
California in 1946. But it was his work as a freshman
member of the House Un-American Activities Committee that
brought him to the attention of the national news media.
The young Republican believed that Hiss -- the urbane
graduate of Johns Hopkins and Harvard Law School, veteran
of the New Deal and the 1949 Yalta Conference and current
executive of the Carnegie Endowment for International
Peace -- had lied to the Committee in denying any past
affiliation with the Communist Party and with his
accuser, Time magazine editor Whittaker Chambers. One
criminal trial in New York Federal Court ended in a hung
jury. In a second trial, Hiss was convicted and
sentenced to prison on two counts of perjury. Nixon was
convinced that although the evidence in the Hiss case had
proven him right, the affair "left a permanent residue of
hatred and hostility [towards him] among substantial
segments of the press and the intellectual community."[1]

To those who never believed that the former State
Department official was guilty of espionage or
subversion, Nixon became a symbol, second only perhaps to
Senator Joseph McCarthy himself, of the hysterical anti-
communist purge that was then sweeping the country.
Despite the court verdict that had apparently vindicated
his suspicions about Hiss, Nixon was often portrayed as a
ruthless and opportunistic junior McCarthy. "The case,"
Nixon's longtime friend and press secretary Herbert Klein
later wrote, "had a long-range effect on Nixon's estimate
of the news corps and his emotional distrust of
reporters."[2]

Nixon's campaign biographers, Earl Mazo and
Stephen Hess, claimed that liberal intellectuals were
predisposed to be offended by both the anti-communist
substance and the sanctimonious tone of Nixon's public
utterances. They believed that the famous "Checkers"
speech during the 1952 presidential race, with its
invocations of Pat Nixon's "respectable Republican cloth
coat" and daughter Julie's "little cocker spaniel dog,"
struck "the sophisticated Ivy Leaguers as unctuous and
disingenuous." They felt that Nixon's campaign rhetoric
of "Acheson's Cowardly College of Communist Containment"
and his connection with McCarthy made him the object of
singular animosity among liberals and the news media
institutions which they supposedly dominated. Nixon was
one of the few politicians, Mazo and Hess concluded,
whose very motives were always questioned by his
adversaries in the press.[3]

Nixon believed that The Washington Post
cartoons of Herbert Block (Herblock) were symbolic of the
way in which the eastern liberal journalistic
establishment really viewed him. "Nixon liked to say he
was insensitive to barbs from the press," Herb Klein
wrote. "That was not true." As Vice President, Nixon

"Here He Comes Now"

---from Herblock's Here And Now (Simon & Schuster, 1955)

Dickey

once complained to Block that because of his cartoons, "A lot of people think I'm a prick, but I'm really not."[4] In his Memoirs, Nixon wrote that throughout his public life, Herblock's bitingly cynical caricatures had created an unfairly negative image of him. The Nixons even found it necessary to banish The Washington Post from their home to shelter their young daughters from Herblock's derisive depictions of their father.[5] In Herblock's cartoons, a sinister Nixon was always sneaking out of the political sewer or trumpeting from the partisan garbage can. He held hands with Joe McCarthy and could sling mud right along with the red-baiting demagogue. He wore two faces, at the very least; each had a perpetual unshaven scowl, dark and menacing.[6]

Presidential candidate Nixon fared little better in the press in 1960, or so he believed. After the election Nixon complained that in the final weeks of the campaign "defeatist dope stories . . . churned out by leading columnists" had swayed the public against him. "Despite our best efforts," Nixon lamented, "we were unable to make much of an impression on the press and radio commentators who were spearheading the blitz."[7] It is perhaps impossible to gauge the quality and objectivity of the news media's coverage of the 1960 campaign. Theodore H. White's description of the attitudes of John F. Kennedy's press entourage suggests, however, that the working press had a special relationship with the Democratic candidate that might well have affected their perceptions of the race. Nixon himself quotes White in his Memoirs:

> . . . those forty or fifty national correspondents who had followed Kennedy since the beginning of his electoral exertions in the November days had become more than a press corps -- they had become friends, and, some of them,

> his most devoted admirers. When the bus
> or plane rolled through the night, they
> sang songs of their own composition
> about Mr. Nixon and the Republicans in
> chorus with the Kennedy staff and felt
> that they, too, were marching like
> soldiers of the Lord to the New
> Frontier.[8]

During the campaign Nixon became convinced that there was a conspiracy among some of the reporters aimed at embarrassing him over some equivocal statements he had made about President Eisenhower's handling of the U-2 incident and some mildly critical ones about the position taken by his opponent, Senator Kennedy. In a series of press conferences during late September, Klein wrote, Bill Lawrence of The New York Times, Sander Vanocur of NBC, Phil Potter of The Baltimore Sun and others, including Arthur Sylvester of the Newark News (later a Kennedy appointee as assistant Secretary of Defense) persistently pursued the U-2/Kennedy issue. After one tough press conference in Scranton, Pennsylvania, Nixon angrily snapped out orders to Press Secretary Klein to cancel all further briefings with the press. "I told him," Klein said, "that we already had passed out to the media schedules that listed a press conference in Springfield, Missouri, two days later, on September 21.

"'Cancel that one, too,' he ordered."[9]

Though Nixon later agreed to do the Springfield press conference, it was the last time he met formally with the press corps for the final six weeks of the 1960 presidential race.

Many of Nixon's problems with the news media in 1960 were of his own making. He and his staff gave their press entourage little hospitality and even less candor. As increasingly irritated campaign staff often neglected arrangements for the reporters. The communication gap between candidate and press corps was largely self-inflicted.[10] Klein later admitted, "While Kennedy was wooing the press, Nixon was openly showing his contempt for it."[11]

Campaign aides often followed Nixon's lead in their attitudes toward the press corps. One of them told Teddy White, "Stuff the bastards. They're all against Dick anyway. Make them work. We aren't going to hand out any prepared remarks; let them get out their pencils and listen and take notes."[12] Nixon, however, remembered only the chorus of media predictions in the last weeks of the face of everything from a close Kennedy victory to a Kennedy landslide. In reflecting later on the closeness of the final outcome, Nixon placed much of the blame for his narrow defeat squarely on the shoulders of those in the national news media whose sympathies, he was convinced, lay with the Harvard-educated Democrat. The television network correspondents, Nixon felt, had been unfair to him even in their treatment of his concession speech.[13]

The bitterness and acrimony that had built up between Nixon and the news media over the preceding fourteen years boiled over on the morning after his second -- and, most believed, final -- electoral defeat in two years. Nixon's "last press conference" after the California gubernatorial campaign was one of the most bizarre performances of modern American politics. His emotional harangue betrayed his innermost feelings about the press and shocked both his critics and his closest supporters. To the defeated Nixon, whose patience and self-control had clearly run out, the press conference became an opportunity for a parting shot at his "adversaries" in the news media. He seemed to have felt that they were the ones ultimately responsible for his unusually intense unpopularity in some quarters and for his two consecutive failures at the polls. "Now that all the members of the press are so delighted that I have lost," he began, "I'd like to make a statement of my own." He went on,

> . . . I believe if a reporter believes that one man ought to win rather than the other, whether it's on television or radio, or the like, he ought to say so. I will say to the reporters sometimes that I think, well, look, I wish you'd give my opponent the same going over you gave me.
>
> And as I leave the press, all I can say is this: for sixteen years, ever since the Hiss case, you've had a lot of -- a lot of fun -- that you've had an opportunity to attack me, and I think I've given as good as I've taken.
>
> I leave you gentlemen now and you will write it. You will interpret it. That is your right. But as I leave you, I want you to know -- just think how much you'll be missing. You won't have Nixon to kick around anymore, because, gentlemen, this is my last press conference . . . .
>
> I hope that what I have said today will at least make television, radio, and the press first recognize the great responsibility that they have to report all the news, and, second, recognize that they have the right and a responsibility, if they're against the candidate, to give him the shaft, but also recognize if they give him the shaft, put one lonely reporter on the campaign who will report what the candidate says now and then.
>
> Thank you gentlemen, and good day.[14]

In the eyes of many of his own supporters and, Nixon himself wrote, "virtually all of the press," the

last press conference was a personal and political
disaster. He later described the exultation of his
critics and opponents at what they interpreted as the
ultimate self-inflicted blow. National columns appeared
with headlines such as "Nixon's Political Suicide" and
"Nixon's Rise, Fall, Warning for Americans." In his
Memoirs, Nixon cited Mary McGrory's column, "Richard
Nixon's Last Hurrah," as emblematic of the media's view
of his performance, their desire to write off his
political future. "Nixon carried on for fifteen minutes
in a finale of intemperance and incoherence perhaps
unmatched in American political annals," McGrory wrote.
"He pulled havoc down around his ears, while his staff
looked aghast."

"Barring a miracle," Time declared, "Nixon's
political career has ended."[15] ABC Television broadcast
a program called "The Obituary of Richard Nixon," in
which Howard K. Smith interviewed one close Nixon
associate, Murray Chotiner, and a number of Nixon's past
adversaries, most notably Alger Hiss. There was, Nixon
recalled, a good deal of criticism of the program because
of its strong anti-Nixon tone and because of the national
forum it provided to the man Nixon himself had helped put
in jail.[16]

Nixon believed, however, that the "last press
conference" had served a positive purpose. He told
journalist Jules Witcover that it had given the press "a
guilt complex about their inaccuracy." He felt that a
popular backlash against television network hostility
towards him had made his political comeback possible. As
the 1968 presidential race neared, Nixon began saying
that he "had a lot of friends in the press."[17] Tim
Crouse, author of The Boys on the Bus, wrote, "Nixon had
roughly the same number of friends in the press as he did
in Alger Hiss' immediate family." His feeling about

journalists during the 1968 campaign, Crouse said, was
that they were scum.[18] But Nixon's relations with the
press during his second try for the presidency were much
improved over 1960. One of the major themes of the
media's coverage was "The New Nixon" -- a mellower, more
open and diplomatic figure than the old one.

Despite many claims that the press went easy on
Nixon during the 1968 campaign, never really challenging
him on any of the difficult issues, particularly on his
"secret plan" to end the war in Vietnam, Nixon believed
that the news media was again biased against him. After
the tumultuous Democratic Convention in Chicago, the
Republican candidate held a commanding lead over Democrat
Hubert Humphrey in the public opinion polls. As the
election approached, however, the race became nearly dead
even. Nixon felt that Humphrey's late surge could be
traced directly to the more positive treatment he
received from the press. "Whatever the reasons," Nixon
later wrote, "sympathy for his temporary underdog status;
preference for his liberal view; or simply his likability
-- Humphrey benefited from the favorable press
coverage."[19] Nixon's interpretation was that he was
again "getting the shaft." He later wrote that his
perceptions about unfair press treatment were proved
empirically by Edith Efron in her 1971 book, The News
Twisters. To Nixon, her apparently scientific
conclusions about the news media's coverage of the 1968
presidential campaign vindicated everything he and his
supporters had been saying for twenty years. Nixon
quoted her in his Memoirs:

> If Richard Nixon is President of the
> United States today, it is in spite of
> ABC-TV, CBS-TV, and NBC-TV. Together,
> they broadcast the equivalent of a New
> York Times lead editorial against him

every day -- for five days a week, for
the seven weeks of the campaign period.
And every editorial technique was
employed on the three networks to render
the pro-Nixon side less 'forceful' than
the anti-Nixon side. Indeed, to speak
of a 'forceful' pro-Nixon opinion is
impossible. It does not exist.[20]

However Efron might have reached her
conclusions, The News Twisters did express Nixon's
personal view that in 1968 he won a victory not only over
Hubert Humphrey and George Wallace, but over all of those
in the "mid-town Manhattan, liberal-left news media" who
had tried to assassinate him politically throughout the
1950's and who had presided over his "political funeral"
in the early 1960's. Nixon's actions and recollections
betray a deep-seated belief that he had been bullied by
the news media establishment. His attempt to bully them
from 1969 until 1973 -- including his attempt to bully
public broadcasting -- seemed motivated by a desire for
justice, perhaps even for revenge. Were Nixon's charges
against the news media justified? There is little doubt
that many journalists did not find Richard Nixon a very
attractive figure; but was that reflected in their
coverage of him? Of course, it is a difficult question
to answer. Bias is very much in the eye of the beholder.
What one sees as balanced and fair another can see as
one-sided and unjust. The news media are critical of
every candidate and every president. And few political
figures ever appreciate the probing and questioning.
Lyndon Johnson's one-time press secretary, George Reedy,
wrote that almost any politician refuses to believe that
there are critical or embarrassing stories which find
their way into the press without some partisan help.
Politicians, being both the subject and the source of
journalists' livelihood, expect some sense of obligation

from the media. "In the politician's mind," Reedy said,
"members of the press are always guilty of ingratitude."[21] Nixon not only thought the press guilty of
sins far worse than mere ingratitude, he disagreed fundamentally with its view of American politics and culture
in the late 1960's. Broadcast journalists insisted that
they were balanced in their coverage of political issues,
and that it was their duty to be so. But with such
limited air time -- only twenty-three minutes on the
influential evening newscasts -- the network news
necessarily reflected many crucial judgments about
"newsworthiness." TV news had developed the technical
capability of covering an extraordinary number of events;
what Nixon and critics like Efron objected to were the
implicit priorities of network news programs rather than
their explicit messages. During those years the news
media was, in a sense, biased in favor of giving
attention to the left-wing movements that were agitating
for change. The reason, said Anthony Smith, was that
broadcasters had by and large "accepted the view that
that was the general drift of events." The consensual
news judgment of the media told them that a
"revolutionary student" was "more plausible than a John
Birchite student because he was felt not necessarily to
be taking the correct view, but was probably taking the
historically predictive position."[22]

The Nixon White House and the broadcast
journalism community defined the very terms "balance" and
"objectivity" in programming quite differently. The
administration was striving to shift the public's
attention away from Vietnam and the Great Society, to
peace with honor and benign neglect of divisive social
issues. Almost any television program that tried to deal
with the agony of the Indochinese war or racial problems
at home, no matter how "objectively" it treated the

subject, was, from the White House's perspective, biased. It almost did not matter <u>what</u> television news said about dissent in America, the mere fact that dissenters received attention deeply offended Nixon and his advisors. They wanted only their official view of reality reported. "North Vietnam cannot defeat or humiliate the United States. Only American can do that," Nixon said in 1969.[23] The media, by reporting opposition, by probing into domestic problems or inconsistencies in government policies, were giving aid and comfort to "the enemies" of national security. They, too, became the enemies of the national security in the minds of many in the White House.

If commercial television news had acquired a reputation for liberal bias when Richard Nixon entered the White House in 1969, public television had a reputation for outright advocacy of anti-establishment views. National Educational Television in New York was producing public affairs programs which did not seek to adhere to commercial broadcast journalism's ideology of objectivity. NET took risks. It often challenged a television audience accustomed to the banalities of commercial television with avant-garde theatre and probing critiques of the American system. Such offerings were sometimes found wanting by a public television system that was trying to build its appeal to a wider audience, and its credibility with those who were being asked to pay the bills.

But at the outset of the Nixon administration NET was no longer the sole embodiment of non-commercial television on a national scale. The Public Broadcasting Act of 1967 had established the Corporation for Public Broadcasting to oversee the development of a public television system that was based on the primacy of the local stations. CPB created the Public Broadcasting

Service to reflect the desires of the stations in operating the national interconnection -- the public television network. This somewhat ungainly structure was predicated on the infusion of large sums of money from the federal government, long-term funding not subject to the partisan politics of the moment. When Nixon entered the White House no such legislation yet existed. In its first year of incorporation, CPB was barely scraping by, waiting for the government to fulfill the expectations of the Public Broadcasting Act that had been passed in the last legislative wave of Lyndon Johnson's Great Society. It was left to the Nixon administration to address the issue of long-range financing so vital to the future of the new public television system.

During the 1968 presidential campaign, the Corporation's first chairman, Frank Pace, tried to get a statement from then Republican nominee Richard Nixon supporting the public television initiative that had begun under LBJ. He turned to former ABC Television president Tom Moore who had himself been offered a position on the first CPB board. Moore had become closely acquainted with Nixon in 1960 when he was ABC's vice president for programming and the network handled production of two of the four Kennedy-Nixon debates. Moore maintained his contacts with Nixon after the election. Eight years later, in the spring of 1968, he left ABC and, after the Republican convention, worked for vice presidential candidate Spiro Agnew.

Although of different political parties, Moore and Pace were both Southerners and long-time friends.[24] In the course of conversations between the two during the campaign, as the Corporation for Public Broadcasting was just getting organized, Pace asked Moore to try to get a statement from Nixon on public television. Moore went to campaign manager John Mitchell who turned him down flat.

His attitude, Moore recalled, was "It's not an issue.
We've got too many darn issues now. Why make such a
statement? It won't get one vote." When Moore went back
to Pace and told him there would be no statement from
Nixon, he also said that the Republican candidate was
clearly very negative about what public television had
been doing in their political programming. It was quite
evident, he said, that public television was not for
Nixon. And Nixon knew enough about public television to
be unenthusiastic about it.[25] His antipathy would shape
administration policy throughout his presidency.

Within the Nixon White House the responsibility
for developing public television policy fell mainly to
two special assistants to the President, Peter M.
Flanigan and Clay T. Whitehead. A native of New York
City, Flanigan had grown up in the worlds of inter-
national finance and national politics. His father,
Hap Flanigan, was a successful banker who had been one of
President Eisenhower's closest associates. Peter
Flanigan graduated from Princeton in 1947 and then spent
two years as a foreign service officer in Great Britain.
In 1950 he joined the New York investment firm of Dillon,
Read and Company, where he served as vice president until
the beginning of 1969. In 1959 Flanigan organized New
Yorkers for Nixon and in 1960 he helped build the
national campaign organization, Volunteers for Nixon-
Lodge. He remained close to Nixon after the unsuccessful
1962 governor's race and was instrumental in Nixon's
political comeback during the mid-1960's. Flanigan
served as deputy campaign manager in the 1968
presidential bid and after the election victory joined
the White House staff as a special assistant to the
President. Communications Director Herb Klein described
Peter Flanigan simply; "He was dedicated."[26]

Clay Whitehead -- known as Tom -- also worked with Nixon's 1968 presidential campaign. His background was far less political than that of Flanigan, who became his mentor within the White House. In 1960 Whitehead graduated from the Massachusetts Institute of Technology, where he later returned for a master's degree in electrical engineering and a Ph.D. in management studies. In 1966 and 1967 he served on the MIT faculty as a lecturer while he was completing his work on his doctoral thesis about the behavior of large organizations. During and after the campaign, Whitehead was a member of the President-Elect's Task Force on Budget Policies. "I was working on a number of ideas on how the Federal budget could be used, should be used by the President to put his stamp on the executive branch, to gain control of it -- not in the political sense that we think of, but to gain control of it in terms of what it actually does."[27]

In his early days on the White House staff, Whitehead's responsibilities, as he described them, were "all the drab and uninteresting things that the politicians didn't want to worry about." He developed policy initiatives in such diverse areas as the Atomic Energy Commission, maritime affairs, and some regulatory agencies. He was actively involved in the first decisions about the space shuttle, drafting the President's message on where the space program should go after the Apollo project. He served as White House liaison to the Federal Communications Commission and was particularly interested in policies designed to bring about greater competition in domestic satellite communications. At first, Whitehead devoted only a small percentage of his time to communications issues, but he took on the responsibility of figuring out how the Nixon administration should act on the recommendations of the President's Task Force on Communications Policy. The

task force, headed by former Undersecretary of State
Eugene V. Rostow, had originally submitted its report to
President Lyndon Johnson in December 1968. It
recommended the creation of a new executive agency, a
Federal Department of Communications Policy. The
thinking behind the task force's recommendation of an
entirely new office, The New York Times reported, was
"that authority over communications has become divided
among so many governmental agencies that the net effect
has been a deepening void in national policy
direction."[28] Johnson took no action on the task force's
recommendations and, during the last weeks of his term,
refused to release the report to the public.

In March of 1969, however, the Nixon White
House reversed LBJ's decision and released the Rostow
study. Tom Whitehead undertook the job of translating
its ideas into administration policy. Communications
issues thus increasingly filled Whitehead's agenda during
his first year on Nixon's staff. He quickly developed
into the administration's communications policy
specialist. Almost by default, public broadcasting fell
into his eclectic portfolio. His first memos on public
broadcasting reflected a deep concern about the future of
the institution and vexing problem of long-range funding
for it. Whitehead recommended that the President send a
congratulatory message to the University of Wisconsin on
the fiftieth anniversary of educational radio at the
school. He said: "I think it is desirable for the
President to be associated in an affirmative way with
public broadcasting."[29]

The most important way that the administration
could make an affirmative contribution to public
television would be to propose some kind of long-term
financing plan. To that end, in June, Whitehead wrote to
the Office of Management and Budget's Richard Nathan,

"The point I am trying to get at is that public broadcasting should be relatively self-sufficient in order that it will be independent of the appropriations process (and, therefore, the inevitable political pressures) and so that there will be the appropriate incentives to develop programming that is responsible to the public interest."[30]

Two months later, Whitehead prepared for Flanigan a comprehensive memorandum on the history and current state of public broadcasting, along with some thoughts on the importance and usefulness of administration support and encouragement:

> The Nixon Administration's support of the Corporation for Public Broadcasting will shape the future of public television in America. Since relatively little more money can affect very high visibility when put into broadcasting, the Administration should give the matter thorough consideration.

Whitehead restated a number of difficult questions which public broadcasters were striving to answer. What type of audiences should public television try to reach? What should its programs do: provide cultural enrichment? instruct people in dealing with problems in everyday life? provide a voice for ethnic groups? generate awareness of contemporary events? "Should controversial programming exist for its own sake or to promote understanding and the airing of several points of view? Can an 'honest' documentary always arrive at a conclusion or should it suggest complexity of issues?" What role should CPB play? Should it plan to function primarily as a revenue sharing institution for local stations, or as a selective board, encouraging certain stations and production units to make national programs?

According to Whitehead, the administration had several options. It could continue to give CPB "very small appropriations, on the theory that public television had not generally been an influential, constructive force" and the Corporation had not yet "developed its leadership capacity." The result of this course of action, said Whitehead, would "probably be to perpetuate the disunity and ineffectiveness of the public broadcasting system as a whole, at least for several years."

Alternatively, Whitehead suggested, the government could expand its investment in CPB and the public media. But in that case, the Corporation would have to articulate its role in the system more clearly, and the purpose of public television would have to be better defined. Could the Corporation, Whitehead asked, "coordinate activities of local stations and change the fragmentary nature of the public broadcasting system?" There was still serious doubt, Whitehead concluded, whether the CPB staff was "capable and/or willing to answer such 'hard' questions. Until the Corporation's objectives are clearly formulated, it is difficult to imagine any massive outlay of Federal funds to it." In the meantime, he felt that the administration's most constructive action would be to establish a White House task force on CPB to "provoke answers to these questions" and resolve the issue of priorities.[31]

In late September, Nathan sent Whitehead an interim funding proposal for CPB covering fiscal years 1971-1973, in order to "allow the Administration adequate time to come up with a more permanent solution later . . . ." Albert Cole, a director of Reader's Digest and Nixon's first appointee to the CPB board, also favored greater budgetary support than the $10 million that the administration was currently offering for fiscal

1970. His desire, however, seemed motivated by the
belief that the Ford Foundation was responsible for NET's
anti-establishment programming as its major underwriter.
He succinctly expressed the view that became widely held
within the White House, as well as by many in the public
broadcasting community, that the Foundation's predominant
role was inappropriate because "he who pays the piper
calls the tune."[32] Nixon himself wanted to add $5
million to the administration-sponsored CPB bill for 1970
because he felt "very strongly that public broadcasting
should not be dependent for content on Foundation
supported programs."[33] Qualms about the activities of
the Ford Foundation were not peculiar to the Nixon White
House.

    "What's the easiest kind of target to attack?"
asked one Ford Foundation official in 1969. "An
organization with three billion tax-exempt dollars, run
by people who don't have to get elected, and who are
actively promoting social change."[34] The Ford Foundation
was the object of criticism from all parts of the
ideological spectrum as the 1960's neared their end. It
had not always been known for creating controversy by
promoting "social change." But in 1966 McGeorge Bundy,
for five years special assistant for national security
affairs to Presidents Kennedy and Johnson, was named
president of the Foundation and immediately began
charting a new course. He got Ford money directly
involved in the many divisive, emotional domestic issues
like race relations, poverty and urban decay. In two
years he doubled the budget of the Foundation's Division
of National Affairs from $20-$40 billion. A great deal
of the money went to civil rights and community action
groups like the NAACP, the National Urban League, Martin
Luther King's Southern Christian Leadership Conference
and the Congress of Racial Equality at a time when the

nation was deeply divided on what should be done in the field of race relations. "Foundations," Bundy was quoted in an admiring 1968 _Fortune_ magazine profile, "should contribute in as many ways as they properly can to honest public discussion of issues which are controversial." "Since leaving the White House two years ago," said _Fortune_, "Bundy has continued to generate headlines --and far more public controversy -- than he ever did in presidential service."[35] There were many who felt that Ford's position in such controversies was noticeably one-sided: Liberal, Eastern Establishment.

Only a few weeks after Nixon entered the White House, the House Small Business subcommittee, which, under the chairmanship of Texas Democrat Wright Patman had been conducting an eight-year-long study of tax-exempt foundations, leaked records showing that the Ford Foundation had made grants totaling some $131,000 to eight former aides to Senator Robert Kennedy.[36] The story gave conservative critics new ammunition for their charges that the Ford Foundation was a well-endowed haven for liberal Democrats, a shadow government trying to utilize its tax-exempt income for "social aggression."[37]

McGeorge Bundy was called to testify in the House Ways and Means Committee's hearings on legislation that would change the tax status of the nation's foundations. It was an argumentative session. For four and a half hours Bundy debated with the committee members who saw the Kennedy grants as a perfect example of foundation's unlawful involvement in partisan politics. The ranking Republican, John Byrnes of Wisconsin said, "I wonder whether we don't have to have some kind of restraints" on foundations' grant-making freedom in areas of political and social controversy. "Foundations have no halo," he said. Bundy denied that the Ford Foundation had ever exceeded legal limits in any of its recent

controversial programs and said that he would be "very
wary of imposing a tax burden on foundations in light of
their achievements for the American people." But to many
of those on the committee, the Ford Foundation was not
merely using its vast resources for charitable,
educational purposes. Byrnes said that the grants to
one-time aides of slain Democratic presidential contender
Robert Kennedy looked like "severance pay."[38] Bundy's
testimony did nothing to placate the congressmen and
merely focused attention on the influence that the large
foundations -- Ford, Rockefeller, Carnegie, Duke --were
beginning to play in American life and politics. Later
in the year the conservative journal National Review put
"The Great Foundation Debate" on its cover. In his
article, "The New Class War," editor Jeffrey Hart managed
to criticize the big foundations in general and Ford in
particular, both for trying to insure social stability
for corporate wealth -- as the left charged --and for
financing left-wing revolution. Hart noted that Ford's
$175,000 grant to the Congress of Racial Equality for
"voter registration" in Cleveland in 1967 had resulted in
the election of the country's first black mayor, Carl
Stokes.

While Fortune might write approvingly that "the
foundations have developed into a powerful force for
social change and human betterment -- a third force, as
it were, independent of business and government,"
conservatives like Hart felt that "social change" was a
complicated and ambiguous thing. "Not all change is
necessarily good," he said. "The fall of Troy, after
all, was a 'social change' not much relished by the
Trojans."[39]

With its hostility to all things connected to
the Kennedys, the Nixon administration had a similarly
negative view of the Ford Foundation's activities. Hart

himself was a Nixon speechwriter. Public television, especially National Educational Television, was closely tied to the Foundation. President Nixon wanted it made clear to the Corporation for Public Broadcasting executives that a condition of increased federal support was "the establishment of an independent producing unit" apart from NET and funding of local stations that would turn out different types of programs than those produced by NET. The President was convinced that the Ford Foundation used public television to disseminate its liberal views on American life and politics, views that were quite clearly anti-administration in nature. Although, in Whitehead's view, there appeared "to be little indication that Ford has or wants much influence over program selection."[40] In an October 30 memorandum, Whitehead told Flanigan, "McGeorge Bundy has told me on two separate occasions that he would like to phase out the Ford Foundation's funding in this area once the Corporation becomes the dominant source of money." He was also quick to point out the possible pitfalls of the President's strategy to diffuse liberal bias by creating an alternative to NET. "From the standpoint of the President's objectives," Whitehead explained, "grants to individual stations cut both ways: the people who run educational and public television stations around the country tend to be relatively liberal, but the geographical diversification probably would promote an overall less liberal emphasis than the New York City centralized NET. Funding a separate production unit to 'compete' with NET would not be a bed of roses either, since the liberal bent of people in the performing arts is well known."[41]

On November 3, Flanigan met with Cole and Pace to discuss the President's desire for a more geographically and ideologically balanced public broadcast system. He made it clear to Pace that a $5 million increase was contingent on the creation of a new programming entity on the West Coast, with half of the extra money, and the other half going directly to local stations. Flanigan further described the meeting,

> It was agreed that while NET would be used until the new facilities are in operation, the degree of its funding would not increase: rather the funding would decrease to zero over the next two or three years. Pace agrees with these conditions. He points out, however, that there are limitations on his ability to control total programming and broadcasting policies of non-commercial stations. Non-CPB financed programs produced by NET and others may have anti-Administration content. In addition, non-commercial stations which have received CPB grants may carry anti-Administration programs. . . . I stated our position as being that government funding of CPB should not be used for the creation of anti-Administration programming or for the support of programming-producing organizations which use other funds to create anti-Administration programs. Mr. Pace agrees with this and appreciates the additional support that will be forthcoming for CPB.[42]

The White House made plans to convene a small working group to consider developing an administration position on public broadcasting. Whitehead's proposed agenda for this group reflected a view that the medium could be used to further the political goals of the administration and the personal prestige of the President. On November 4, Whitehead wrote Flanigan, "Since the Nixon Administration will set the tone and pace (no pun intended) for the future growth of public broadcasting, we should give some real attention to how we want to see it develop and how much we are willing to spend." "This is," said Whitehead, "a potentially high visibility area where we can reflect considerable credit on the President at relatively low expenditures." The memo was not only concerned with the public relations value of public broadcasting to the President himself, it suggested the possible utility of public broadcasting as a vehicle of government policy:

> What is the role of Government
> information dissemination in public
> broadcasting; should we make a major
> effort to use public broadcasting as a
> way of achieving social goals; should we
> use it as a way of disseminating
> information about government programs?[43]

After learning that the White House had decided to keep funding for fiscal 1971 at the $15 million level of 1970, CPB President John Macy began his own efforts to conciliate the administration on the issue of program content in order to assure increased funding for 1971 and a permanent financing arrangement thereafter. Following a November 17 meeting with Flanigan and Whitehead, Macy directed CPB public affairs director Bill Duke to send them a schedule of PBS public affairs programs to be aired on Washington's WETA from November 27 to December 7. An accompanying note from Duke to Flanigan said, "Following his conversation with you recently, Mr. Macy thought it would be a good idea to keep you personally informed of programs of particular interest on a regular basis. Attached is our first effort. We will appreciate any comments you might have."[44] Few of public television's producers, however, would have appreciated the White House aides' comments about their efforts. Indeed, such contacts were no secret within the public television community. Producers at NET and some in the press charged that the Corporation was pandering to the administration in order to get a funding bill; and they were not entirely off the mark. One OTP lawyer later said, "You couldn't ask for anyone more compliant than Macy."[45] Macy himself believed that the meetings he and Pace had with Flanigan and Whitehead were merely sensible, if not always successful, attempts at cooperation between the industry and the administration charged with the responsibility for submitting financing legislation to Congress. Pace and Flanigan, Macy said, had known one another in New York before Nixon's election. "Pace tried very hard to keep peace with the administration, and a decision had been made that there was going to be a phasing out of NET. My feeling was that that was sound from an organizational point of view and was not tribute paid to the Administration."[46] One of the other board members frequently involved in the White House meetings was recent Nixon appointee Tom Moore. Like the rest of the board, Moore felt that the hand-to-mouth operations caused by the uncertainties of annual funding prevented the Corporation from executing any kind of plan for developing the potential of public television. But unlike the current majority, he felt that CPB should accept a trade-off with the administration: an end for Corporation funding of politically-oriented national public affairs shows in exchange for White House supported long-term financing legislation that would benefit the entire system. "If public broadcasting were to grow and become a major factor in the country," Moore said, "it could not be a critic of the system itself." Other Corporation board members disagreed with Moore's quid pro quo approach, as did the Public Broadcasting Service and the CPB president. "After we got in," Moore said, "several of us wanted to have more say about the kind of things we were

financing and they [PBS] stiff-armed the hell out of us.
And that stiff-arming took place with Macy's consent."[47]
By seeking compromise with the White House while also
trying to safeguard public television's editorial
freedom, Macy and Pace quickly found themselves at odds
not only with the administration and its appointees on
the CPB board like Moore, but many of those in public
television's production centers. No one seemed willing
to trust the motives of the Corporation under their
leadership. The White House did not trust them to take
tighter control over controversial programming.
Producers, particularly public affairs producers, did not
trust CPB to allow them to keep creative control. Their
failure to achieve an acceptable compromise on long-term
funding would leave them in a political no-man's land.

During 1970, the administration continued to
focus on the issue of funding. How much the government
should grant public broadcasting was less of a question
than where the money should go -- to CPB for its
continued discretionary use or to the financially
strapped local stations themselves. "We felt very
strongly," Whitehead said, "that public broadcasting had
become dominated by a few major centers who had a very
common point of view philosophically, a common point of
view politically, and were very much in the web of the
liberal, intellectual, Ford Foundation view of
things. . . We find that we were frequently sought out by
people at local public stations who were terribly upset
at the way they felt they were being treated by the major
national centers, CPB and the Ford Foundation."

"We felt very strongly that the only sensible
approach was to find a workable compromise between a lot
of people. I suppose, if I had my druthers," Whitehead
said, "I would have said that the government shouldn't be
funding this. Period. But there it was, and the

question was, 'What do you do with it?' We felt that we
needed to find some practical way to let the money flow
into the system, set up some kind of mechanism so that
the checks and balances . . . would come from within the
system rather than from the government."[48]

The financing mechanism, however, was only one
way the President could attempt to affect the structure
and policies of public broadcasting. The other was
through appointments to the CPB board of directors. In
March 1970, the terms of five Johnson appointees on the
board were due to expire. A great deal of time and
effort went into determining how best to use these
openings to secure support for the administration's
position on funding priorities. As Whitehead pointed out
in February, "the board is not particularly visible, but
clearly can have a big influence over the course of
public broadcasting, and it is obviously important to the
President what direction the Corporation pursues."[49]
Throughout the spring Whitehead tried to find five people
whose appointments would reflect positively on the
administration (for example, a "solid minority group
Republican") but who could also be counted on to support
it. The Public Broadcasting Act limited to eight the
number of board members who could belong to the same
political party. In soliciting suggestions on seven
possible choices, Whitehead reminded his colleagues, "We
can name five Republicans without over-balancing the
board politically. The board is one of our primary
levers for assuring that the programming and other
activities of the Corporation do not get overly biased
politically."[50]

In September of 1970, Congress authorized the
creation of the new executive agency which Whitehead had
been developing, the Office of Telecommunications Policy.
OTP's only official function would be to oversee the use

of broadcasting channels assigned to federal government
use. Its primary task, however, would be to advise the
President on public policy for the rapidly expanding
communications field. Whitehead's leading role in this
area was formalized when Nixon named him to head OTP. In
terms of public broadcasting, this responsibility
continued to mean primarily the drafting of a long-range
funding plan. Congress had extended CPB for two years
and provided authorizations of $35 million for 1971 and
1972. Representative Torbert MacDonald, chairman of the
House Subcommittee on Communications and Power, pointed
out, however, in opening his committee's hearings on the
Public Broadcasting Financing Act of 1970, that the
additional years of direct appropriations should not be
"regarded as a grace period during which no progress on
permanent financing need be made."[51] But controversy on
the air made both the administration and the Congress
reconsider their attitudes on a funding plan.

In November the showing of "Banks and the Poor"
caused an immediate reaction within the White House. CPB
board member Cole soon felt the heat from Flanigan to
take some steps with his colleagues at CPB:

> Herewith another example of NET activity
> that is clearly inappropriate for a
> government supported organization.
> Would you do me the favor of letting me
> know the extent to which NET has been
> supported by CPB in 1970 and the amount
> of the budgeted support for 1971.
>
> I am directing this inquiry to you in
> that I think it comes better from you to
> the board and the management of the
> Corporation than from the White House.
> Therefore, I'd appreciate you treating
> this inquiry in that light.[52]

Cole responded to Flanigan by recounting all
the positive, socially useful things that were coming out

of public television -- <u>Sesame Street</u>, <u>Civilization</u>, and
Julia Child. "They have been making educational
television programs for years, and most of them are good,
but every once in a while there is a sour one. . . . But
I want you for the present to accept my statement that
progress is really being made."[53]

Such an optimistic view ran counter to the
administration's increasing sensitivity in the area of
program content. One exchange between Macy, presidential
counselor Daniel Patrick Moynihan, and White House chief
of staff H.R. Haldeman illustrates the effect that even
subtle shades of anti-administration bias had in the
White House: On November 30, Macy wrote to Moyhinan,
telling him that on December 1, one of public
television's most respected programs, <u>The Advocates</u>,
would explore the issue of guaranteed minimum income.
Macy also advised him of who would be on the program:

> Guest witnesses opposing the guaranteed
> minimum income plan will be Mr. Roger A.
> Freeman, economist and former Special
> Assistant to President Nixon, and
> Honorable Ronald Reagan, Governor of
> California, The Honorable Barbara
> Jordan, State Senator from Texas and
> member of President Johnson's Commission
> on Income Maintenance, and Professor
> Theodore Marmor, Associate Director of
> the School of Public Affairs at the
> University of Minnesota will defend the
> need for such a plan.

Macy's letter precipitated a prompt response from
Moynihan:

> I am not only not pleased by your
> letter, I am genuinely troubled by it.
> It seems to me yet another example of a
> persistent pattern of biased treatment
> of the Administration by public

television. I would not say this to
many persons, but I will say it to you.
Consider the implications of the casting
of the forthcoming debate on the
question of a guaranteed minimum income
which will appear on The Advocates.

One President and only one President has
proposed such a scheme. His name is
Richard Nixon. His bill has passed the
House and is now before the Senate. Who
do you choose to oppose the idea?
Naturally, an economist who was Special
Assistant to President Nixon when the
Family Assistance Program was
decided. . . . And now who do you get to
support the idea? A member of President
Johnson's Commission on Income
Maintenance. My respect for President
Johnson is surely as great as yours, but
you know perfectly well the previous
administration would not go near the
subject . . . .

Your audience will be liberal to left in
its politics. They will be for the
Guaranteed Income. They will see it
opposed by an appointee of President
Nixon's and defended by an appointee of
President Johnson's. A Reagan
Republican will side with the Nixon man,
and a Minnesota liberal will side with
the Johnson lady.

I leave the White House every bit as
much a Democrat as when I entered. But,
dear Sir, I also leave profoundly
uncertain of the moral and intellectual
capacity of institutional liberals to
defend the standards of liberal
inquiry.[54]

Moynihan also sent a memo that day to Haldeman:

I enclose an exchange with John Macy
which suggests where some of our
problems come from. Why aren't they
looking out for the President's
perfectly legitimate interests? why are
the Federal funds being spent (as I
assume they are) to distort the facts of

> this situation? and what may I ask is a
> special assistant to the President doing
> opposing his most important piece of
> domestic legislation?[55]

In 1971 such dissatisfaction with public
television programming led to an intensification of White
House efforts to exercise greater control over the
direction of the system. Although the administration
presented a united front, by the middle of the year there
was a growing internal division between OTP's policy
agenda and the more partisan concerns of the White House
staff and the President himself. In a general sense, the
conflict arose between short-term, political and long-
term, structural objectives. Throughout the first six
months of 1971, the OTP staff worked with both the CPB
board and staff members to develop a mutually acceptable
long-range funding bill. In January, Whitehead hired
former University of Virginia Law professor Antonin
("Nino") Scalia as a consultant to OTP with public
broadcasting funding legislation as his highest
priority.[56] Whitehead and his staff aimed to draft a
bill that would further decentralize power within public
television and insulate the system from governmental
influence over programming in the short-term. The bill
would achieve greater insulation for public television by
providing a five-year appropriation. It encouraged a
more decentralized system by specifying the percentage of
federal funds to go directly to the stations themselves,
instead of devoting all of the federal money to the
Corporation's discretional use. The OTP legislation
enunciated a policy that reflected the concern of local
station leaders -- and by former Carnegie Commission
organizer Arthur Singer in his Boyne Highland speech --
that the structural balance in public broadcasting had
shifted too much in favor of CPB, PBS, NET and the Ford

Foundation at the expense of the "bedrock" of the system, the local stations themselves.[57]

The White House, however, had little interest in the long-term structural issues involved in public broadcasting financing. Nixon and his top aides, particularly special assistant John Ehrlichman, Charles Colson and speechwriter and media critic Patrick Buchanan, were concerned about the programs public television put on the air, not who got to produce them. "What I saw," Whitehead said, "was the Nixon people -- that's not fair because I was a Nixon person; the Nixon political people -- who had this very short-run interest in manipulating programming; not only programming, but programs, specific programs with specific people on specific issues."[58] The White House saw the more educationally-minded and often more conservative local stations as their allies in their efforts to get the Ford Foundation out -- and political programs off -- of public television. The President and those closest to him had an unrealistically conspiratorial view of how public television's national organizations operated. There weren't "devils around whispering nasty things in people's ears to make them take anti-Administration slants," OTP lawyer Henry Goldberg said, but in the White House there was a "politician's paranoia" about public television. "It was nutty, the White House attitude. You see, the White House, Nixon, or whoever was calling the shots . . . didn't care about structure, didn't care about localism, didn't care about decentralization or insulated funding. They cared about 'them' and 'us.'"[59]

Goldberg joined OTP in June of 1971, after Scalia's long-term funding bill had already been sent to the Office of Management and Budget, the Department of Health, Education and Welfare and the Federal Communications Commission for their approval. While in

private law practice he had worked with the Carnegie
Commission, assisted in drafting the 1967 Public
Broadcasting Act and helped set up CPB. He, like Arthur
Singer and some other former Carnegie staffers, felt
strongly that the notion of decentralization and localism
had been perverted, or, at least, ignored by the
Corporation in its leadership of public television.
Whether or not CPB was doing the best it could with the
limited resources available by 1971 was a difficult
question to answer because of the tremendous gap between
the amount of insulated Federal funding Carnegie had
envisioned and the yearly appropriations that Congress
had actually provided. Goldberg believed that because
the final version of the 1967 Act had not included the
excise tax financing proposal, the system was not as well
insulated from government pressures as it needed to be:
"What they did in 1968 was to pull the trust fund
financing out and leave the structure there. Well, when
you pull the financing out, the rest of what was created
in the '67 Act makes CPB and the whole public
broadcasting structure very, very susceptible to
political influence and interference, both by the
Congress and by the White House. I was alarmed at that
point. I had Singer's concerns that the vision of
Carnegie was being corrupted, plus the concern that you
had to do something to get insulated or permanent
financing, or restructure public broadcasting or get the
insulation in a different way -- that is, not by
financing, but by getting rid of CPB or giving the
stations money directly . . . ."[60] This is precisely
what the OTP bill attempted to do: remove some of the
Corporation's control by giving more of the Federal money
to local stations.

The Corporation for Public Broadcasting, however, rejected Scalia's draft bill in the summer of 1971. Macy considered it "a sweeping amendment to the 1967 Act, with the intention of reducing the scope of CPB functions and discretion."[61] He was right. But the Corporation's opposition to the proposed legislation made it difficult for Whitehead to argue the case for long-term funding with a White House already opposed to any increased Federal funding for the "anti-administration" public broadcasters. The philosophic concerns that underlay OTP's attempt at a compromise bill got lost somewhere between the White House's well-known antipathy to current programming and CPB's insistence on maintaining the leadership role the Public Broadcasting Act had originally set out for it. The administration increasingly sent contradictory signals, even to its "friends" on the CPB board. The White House encouraged the Corporation to assert greater control over controversial programs, while OTP wanted to remove as much CPB discretionary power as possible. "It wasn't clear to me what they were up to," John Macy recalled. "It was difficult even to get Clay Whitehead to return phone calls. You'd go and talk with him and it would be like talking to that wall. He had a magnificent and cordial 'no response.' And I had a feeling that he wasn't entirely sure what the position of the Administration was himself."[62]

Whitehead's own view reflected the confusing position in which OTP found itself during the summer of 1971: "I don't think very many people appreciate the subtlety of our position. I don't think I appreciated how subtle it was, at the time. The White House folks, by and large, thought that the local stations were their short-term political allies. In some cases, that was true -- but only a short-term view. The public broadcasting view was, 'You ought to give us the money and leave us alone. We do good things and we are somehow endowed by our creator with the judgment to do what's right for the country and you have no business asking us, or holding us accountable.'" Whitehead felt that CPB, PBS, NET and their supporters unfairly saw the "insistence on some accountability and insistence on some level of decentralization as an effort to kill them. The White House saw it as a short-term political lever that they could use."[63]

On June 4, Scalia drafted for Whitehead a "Memorandum for the President," giving a number of reasons to continue efforts at finding a long-range financing plan for CPB. The "Confidential" memo noted that the administration's 1972 budget said, "legislation will be proposed to provide an improved financing arrangement for CPB." The bill had been promised, he cautioned, and "an apparent change of heart at this point would be alleged to be politically motivated." Scalia concluded, "The best possibility for White House influence over the Corporation is through the Presidential appointees to the Board of Directors. These tend to be independent people, however, and failure to submit the previously announced legislation might antagonize them."[64] Indeed, the most notable aspect of the administration's deliberations during the summer of 1971 was the conscious effort to avoid any outward appearance of hostility towards public broadcasting. Nixon-appointed CPB board member Jack Wrather was in constant contact with OTP and the White House, providing them with in-house CPB materials and working to further the President's position. In June, he, too, counseled discretion. "I feel strongly that now is not the time to make quick decisions and changes," Wrather wrote. "The

propitious time to make a move, if such is desired, might
be at a later date, coincident with the new appointments
in early June '72 . . . ."[65]

Nevertheless, Whitehead and OTP disagreed
fundamentally with Macy and the current majority of the
CPB board over the proper role of the Corporation. At
its July 15-16 meeting in Washington, the CPB board
responded both to the criticisms of the Aspen Document
and those implicit in the OTP bill by reaffirming its
leadership responsibilities for public television. The
board not only believed that the Public Broadcasting Act
had clearly intended CPB to guide the system's
development, but also that the White House and Congress
insisted on CPB accountability for the use of federal
funds. Scalia's draft bill reflected a completely
different view. The board agreed almost unanimously that
such legislation would radically alter the intent of the
1967 Act by removing CPB from its position as a buffer
between the stations and the political process. Vice
chairman Killian thought that at the root of the
differences was a concern over a greater degree of
centralization than actually existed. Every opportunity,
he said, should be taken to reduce apprehension over a
highly centralized system. He did not want CPB to be
viewed by anyone as adopting the attitudes and policies
that dominated NET thinking.[66] Macy told the board that
the proposed legislation anticipated an adversary
relationship between the stations and the Corporation,
instead of affirming the position of the Corporation as a
leader in a total system development. CPB, he said, had
a clear record of trying to strengthen a locally-based
system; "before it came on the scene, much of public
broadcasting was a cottage industry."

The board agreed that it was vital for CPB not to forfeit its independence and that the pass-through notion would dangerously involve the federal government in the financial affairs of the local stations. Whitehead himself joined the CPB board meeting in mid-stream to listen to the director's criticism of the OTP bill and its confusion over the administration's equivocal position. The meeting and his discussion with Macy and board chairman Frank Pace convinced Whitehead that the Corporation's current leadership represented a significant obstacle to achieving the kind of structural changes he and OTP envisioned. For its part, the White House simply wanted the Johnson appointees out, and its own men in.[67]

According to Whitehead, the most effective course of action was the redirection of federal support from CPB and PBS "so as to create a structure which will be dominated by those elements in the public television field which are generally most congenial -- namely, the local stations." He mapped out a strategy that would have President Nixon meet with friendly members of the CPB board to obtain their agreement to attempt to reduce CPB funding of NET "to a near-zero level" and to "replace John Macy as soon as practicable with a non-political professional" in exchange for administration support for a new long-term funding bill. But again, the OTP "Action Memorandum" to Peter Flanigan and Charles Colson cautioned that care must be taken "to avoid the appearance of hostility to public broadcasting, both because it is a sacred cow in many quarters and because the President's opponents are already trying to tar him with antagonism towards 'free and independent' media."[68]

Nevertheless, public broadcasting's actions in the field of national news and public affairs production during August and September of 1971 would greatly anger

the President himself and would make it impossible for
the administration to conceal its hostility toward the
medium. They would cause increased tension between OTP's
proposed policies and White House objectives. They would
bring about an intensified effort by the administration
to undermine the integrity of public television and to
crush its editorial independence. They would result in
open warfare between public broadcasters and the Nixon
administration.

CHAPTER THREE

OPEN WARFARE

"There are, I think, serious questions of principle as to whether Federal funds should be involved in funding public affairs . . . ."

> --Clay Whitehead on Bill Moyers'
> This Week program, January 1972

"In spite of what it may seem, no one participating in this exercise has been unclear as to the President's basic objective: To get the left-wing commentators who are cutting us up off public television at once, indeed yesterday if possible."

> --White House staff member
> Jon Rose, November 1971

On August 24, 1971 the future of news and public affairs programming on public television came into sharper focus. On that day, Sidney L. James, chairman of the board of Washington's station WETA and James Karayn, former chief of NET's Washington bureau, announced the creation of the National Public Affairs Center for Television, NPACT. The rationale behind the creation of NPACT, as the next day's New York Times headline -- "Public TV Unit Aims to Centralize New Activities" -- suggested, was that too much autonomy for regional public affairs production centers would lead to wasteful overlap and duplication. And since the vast majority of public television stations lacked either the means or the desire to mount major public affairs programs, NPACT would provide the central control essential for long-range planning and programming of a national scope. According to general manager Karayn, the Center's programs would in no way conform to the traditional formulae of commercial television news. "An anchorman will not sit in the studio and read the news," he said, "he will have to go out and put it together himself."[1]

The centerpieces of NPACT's activities would not be the type of public affairs documentary exposés for which NET had gained such notoriety, but rather, the comprehensive coverage of important political events: congressional hearings, presidential addresses and the upcoming 1972 campaign. The Center's self-proclaimed mission was close to an editorially neutral concept of news and public affairs programming: broadcast journalism of record. Karayn stated at NPACT's formation that the Center would have to be "courageous, intelligent, witty, determined and shrewd. But it must also operate with self-restraint, common sense and fairness and with an understanding of where it fits into the scheme of things in public television."[2]

NPACT's creation represented CPB, PBS and the Ford Foundation's single most decisive and substantive step away from the programming predominance of NET. The entire public system, they felt, would suffer if controversies caused by political programs like "Who Invited Us?" and "Banks and the Poor" continued. Public television leaders Hartford Gunn, John Macy and Fred Friendly saw the creation of a national public affairs production center as a way of maximizing both the quantity and the quality of public affairs programming -- and as a way of distancing the system from past, as well as future controversies.[3]

NET's Jim Day was, predictably, opposed to the creation of NPACT. The Ford Foundation, he claimed, had told him that NET's major responsibility was public affairs. But then, the Foundation -- along with CPB and

PBS -- took away NET's Washington bureau and recruited its director to be manager of the new public affairs entity. Day was powerless, however, to stop the creation of NPACT. In 1971 NET and New York's Channel Thirteen were merged, at the Ford Foundation's behest, into the Educational Broadcasting Corporation.[4]

As founder and chief of NET's Washington bureau, Jim Karayn was the logical choice to manage NPACT. Between 1965 and 1971 he had earned the reputation for producing NET's most journalistically sound programs. Geographically and professionally, he had remained apart from the controversies involving NET's New York-based public affairs production. In 1967 he had pioneered public television's coverage of the President's State of the Union Message and received an Emmy award for the 1968 program, which provided the first in-depth analysis on television of the President's recommendations. Karayn was determined not to repeat the mistakes NET and PBL had made in dealing with the rest of the public television system. In his plan, NPACT would take every opportunity to involve local stations directly in its production activities. At the same time, however, he fought the idea of making NPACT a unit within the Washington local station, WETA. "The problems of stations," he said, "are very different from the problems of production centers. . . . I felt that we were certainly going to have a hard time, not because of the Nixon Administration, but we were going to have a hard time selling public affairs nationally to a system that was not so willing to take it anyway."[5]

Originally, CPB, PBS, and the Ford Foundation imagined the new public affairs center as a division of WETA itself. But WETA was then struggling with an $800,000 operating deficit and the station's leadership was preoccupied with keeping its local programming activities alive. WETA officials feared that a national production center would divert attention and resources away from local concerns; NPACT's creators believed that the relatively weak local station might dilute the energies and efforts of the independently funded public affairs unit. So, like the Children's Television Workshop in New York, which produced Sesame Street, and later, Electric Company and Zoom for national distribution, NPACT would remain independent of the local station to concentrate solely on making television programs. NPACT would use WETA's studios and technical facilities, and the two organizations shared a common board chairman in Sidney James.[6]

From the outset, Karayn planned to make a weekly series on the 1972 election campaign the primary focus of NPACT's regular schedule during its first year. The Center would also take over production responsibilities for two current political programs, Elizabeth Drew's highly acclaimed weekly interview show, Thirty Minutes With..., and the popular Washington Week in Review, a round-table discussion among four of the Capitol's leading reporters on major news stories of the week. NPACT was meant to be an organization that would make every attempt to provide solid, day-to-day journalism, not polemics. It was an important step toward legitimizing the idea of news and public affairs programming on public television. In Karayn's view, there had been "too many false starts in public television's news coverage. This time we're not horsing around -- we're in business."[7]

Karayn felt that to make NPACT into a recognized Washington public affairs presence, his first order of business was to hire one of two nationally known and respected broadcast journalists. For one of the two slots, Karayn intended to hire a former NBC correspondent,

Robert MacNeil. MacNeil, a Canadian, began his career
working for the Canadian Broadcasting Corporation and
Reuters News Service in England. In 1960 he joined NBC
and reported on the wars in the Congo and Algeria, the
building of the Berlin Wall and the Cuban missile crisis.
In both East Berlin and Cuba he had been arrested and
briefly held on spy charges. MacNeil also had covered
American politics and served as assistant White House
correspondent. He covered Kennedy's assassination in
Dallas and Barry Goldwater's 1964 presidential campaign.
Between 1965 and 1967 he worked for NBC in New York, co-
anchoring a national news analysis program, "The Sherer-
MacNeil Report." He then joined the British Broadcasting
Corporation and served as its American political
correspondent. MacNeil covered the 1968 presidential
race and anchored the BBC's coverage of the funerals of
Martin Luther King and Robert Kennedy. While he was with
the BBC he also contributed to several Public Broadcast
Laboratory programs on public television. In 1968, he
wrote and hosted a PBL show, "The Whole World is
Watching," an examination of American network news in the
wake of the Democratic Convention in Chicago. In the
same year he published The People Machine, a book
analyzing the role of television news in the American
political process.[8] Karayn said that he always
envisioned MacNeil as "the toughest and hardest worker"
among NPACT's senior correspondents. But he also felt
that MacNeil had some limitations. He was not very well
known to American viewers and his on-air style was far
more reserved than that of the average television
newsman. Karayn felt that NPACT "needed one major star"
to complement MacNeil. "I wanted Robin, and one
superstar," he said.[9]

The superstar Karayn most wanted as his other
senior correspondent was NBC's Edwin Newman. He told

Macy, Gunn, and Friendly who he was considering for the
NPACT positions and also what he expected to pay them.
The executives of CPB, PBS, and the Ford Foundation,
which were jointly responsible for NPACT's creation, knew
that Karayn was offering Newman $150,000 a year to leave
NBC for NPACT. "They knew it and none of them
shuddered," Karayn said. In the end, however, Newman
decided against accepting the NPACT job.

One of Karayn's other choices for the post was
yet another NBC correspondent, Sander Vanocur. In the
mid-1950's, Vanocur worked briefly in England for the
Manchester Guardian, the BBC, and CBS. He then spent a
year as a local reporter for The New York Times before
joining NBC's Washington bureau in 1957. After covering
the 1960 presidential campaign he was appointed NBC White
House correspondent. He covered John Kennedy's short-
lived presidency and then became a national political
correspondent in January, 1964. In 1965 he went to
Vietnam and was one of the first American journalists to
predict disaster for U.S. policy in Southeast Asia. From
1969 to 1971 he anchored NBC's ground-breaking
newsmagazine program, First Tuesday. Throughout the
1960's he was known as one of the most flamboyant of
network newsmen. While White House correspondent, he had
developed a close association with the Kennedys. His
outspoken criticism of Johnson's escalation of the
Vietnam war had also made him the figure of some
controversy. Vanocur was a loner among Washington
journalists. He was a tough competitor, an intense
personality who did not often hesitate to give his
personal viewpoint in blunt terms.[10] He and the more
retiring MacNeil clearly made a good team. When Vanocur
resigned from NBC to join Karayn's National Public
Affairs Center, he gave up a salary of $125,000 a year as
a local news anchorman. Karayn got him for $85,000. It

was not much money by industry standards, but it would soon help engulf Vanocur, NPACT, and all public television in controversy.

At the September 17 meeting of the CPB board, Frank Pace reported that OTP had formally withdrawn its draft funding bill from consideration by the Office of Management and Budget, although staff level meetings between the Corporation and OTP continued throughout the summer. These conferences, Pace said, were attended with an increasing sense of urgency in the face of the impending expiration of CPB's current authorization on June 30, 1972. All issues seemed to have been resolved, John Macy said, except the most fundamental one: "Should the statute contain a mandatory formula for direct distribution of funds to individual stations, with provisions for possible intervention in this process by other government agencies? OTP still declined to accept the Corporation's position that the pattern of distribution of funds to the stations be determined by the Corporation with the stations." Pace then told his fellow board members that he was momentarily expecting a call from Whitehead about OTP's latest position on new funding legislation.

Macy reported that since the "Aspen Manifesto," Corporation vice president John Witherspoon had conducted lengthy meetings with each of the signatories, and there was now better understanding on all sides. Then he gave the board an update on the plans of the National Public Affairs Center. He told them that in three days, "NPACT would announce the selection of two key on-air national correspondents: Sander Vanocur and Robert MacNeil." The board praised Macy for his success in bringing two such experienced and respected broadcast journalists to public television.[11]

On September 20, at parallel press conferences in New York and Washington, NPACT announced the

appointments of Vanocur and MacNeil as "Senior
Correspondents" and co-anchormen of its election year
series. Karayn pointed out that between them, Vanocur
and MacNeil had personally covered virtually every major
news story around the world in the past decade. Their
hiring, he said, was an important step in the effort to
make public television's news and public affairs into a
recognized element of the national news media. Sidney
James, chairman of the board of NPACT, expressed great
pleasure at the choice of Vanocur and MacNeil, saying:
"We believe that these two outstanding correspondents
will lead the way for public broadcasting to supply an
especially unique service to its viewers. The strength
and experience of Mr. Vanocur and Mr. MacNeil blended
into this enterprise dedicated to a new approach to
interpreting political affairs cannot help but advance
our contribution to broadcast journalism and to the
public."[12]

The President of the United States did not have
quite the same reaction to the appointment of Vanocur and
MacNeil. On the morning after the appointments were made
public, White House staff secretary Jon Huntsman sent a
"CONFIDENTIAL, EYES ONLY" memorandum to Peter Flanigan,
H.R. Haldeman, and Alex Butterfield informing them of the
President's desire to have all funds for public
broadcasting cut off immediately. Huntsman related that
the morning News Summary report of the NPACT hirings had
"greatly disturbed the President, who considered this the
last straw. It was requested that all funds for public
broadcasting be cut immediately." This memorandum
further directed Flanigan to "work this out so that the
House Appropriations Committee gets the word."[13]

Vanocur's name had been underlined in
Huntsman's "High Priority" memo. His appointment as
NPACT senior correspondent, White House aides later

recalled, was like "waving a red flag" in front of Nixon; it made him livid.[14] He and the former NBC reporter had had a history of mutual antipathy and personal confrontation dating back to Nixon's unsuccessful 1960 presidential campaign. Nixon believed, like many others, that one of the most influential factors in his defeat was his performance in the first of the four televised debates with John F. Kennedy. Sander Vanocur was on the panel of questioners for the debate. It was Nixon's view that Vanocur -- whom he called a "well-known Kennedy sympathizer" -- had purposely tried during that first and most crucial debate to damage his image among the voters. As Nixon described in Six Crises, Vanocur asked him a question that "was of no substance really," but one that "was to plague me the rest of the campaign."

> He referred to a statement President Eisenhower had made in a press conference on August 24. Someone asked him, "What major decisions of your Administration has the Vice President participated in?" Eisenhower had replied: 'If you give me a week, I might think of one.' . . . I am sure that to millions of unsophisticated viewers, this question had been most effective in raising a doubt in their minds with regard to one of my strongest campaign themes and assets -- my experience as Vice President.[15]

Clearly, Nixon felt he had a score to settle with Vanocur. Vanocur later said, with some pride, "Nixon hated my guts."[16] The President's visceral reaction to the NPACT appointment demonstrates that Vanocur was probably right. Federal funds, through CPB, provided a little over half of Vanocur's salary. To Nixon, this was indeed the last straw: government money, his government's money paying Sander Vanocur to criticize

him and his administration. On September 23, 1971,
Nixon's war on public television began in earnest.

On the same day Nixon learned of Vanocur's
hiring, Whitehead was working on a rough draft of a
"Memorandum for the President" on CPB. After nine
months, Whitehead was still attempting to push some kind
of compromise long-term funding that would be acceptable
to both the White House and the Corporation. He wrote
that by requiring a significant portion of federal funds
to go directly to the local stations, the administration
could strongly limit the future dominance of public
broadcasting by CPB. "The local stations (NAEB) will
support this action, but only if funds were significantly
increased. CPB may or may not, depending on how far we
go in reducing their discretion in allocating funds."
Whitehead estimated the minimum levels of federal support
required to assure both NAEB and CPB support -- including
the support of White House "friends" on the CPB board --
to be significantly higher than the current $35 million
federal contribution. He proposed a two-year bill,
authorizing $85 million for the first year ($60 million
to CPB) and a $135 million ($85 million for CPB) ceiling
thereafter.[17]

But Vanocur's presence changed everything.
Until he came on the scene public television was merely a
nuisance to the administration. To those in the White
House, public television crossed an imaginary line in the
sand with the hiring of Vanocur. Renowned for being
anti-war and anti-Nixon, he was the catalyst for a
greatly intensified administration drive to control
public television -- or kill it. After all, reasoned
OPT's press and congressional liaison Brian Lamb, "If you
were the President of the United States . . . if you were
popularly elected by the people and somebody was coming
hat-in-hand for you for money, and you knew that the

people coming were fundamentally opposed to you politically, why shouldn't you be the guy that says 'I'm going to stop this train? . . . I think the liberals in public television expected Richard Nixon to do something that they would not expect of themselves if they were in the same position." Vanocur's hiring introduced a very "human element" into the administration's view, said Lamb. "All you had to do was turn on the TV and it was right there for you to look at. . . . They'd be doing another job on [the President] in one way or another, or somebody who had done a job on him in the past, you'd say 'There they go again. Why are we paying public money to those guys?'"[18]

News of the NPACT appointments made the OTP compromise position on increased, multi-year funding obsolete. OTP counsel Henry Goldberg remembered the days immediately following the NPACT announcement: "At that point, I had been there four months. I was still just the new kid, but . . . there was no particular animus toward Sander Vanocur. I mean, 'So what, Sander Vanocur?' But then the word came. I mean the word literally came, in phone calls and copies of memos that Nixon said, 'This is the last straw. Pull the bill. Kill it.' Not only pull the bill and kill the legislation, but cut off all funding. Kill public broadcasting. Murder it."[19]

On September 28, the OTP director submitted an initial response to Nixon's directive. Whitehead attempted to mollify the President and convince him that it would be neither productive nor politically efficacious for him to express his disdain for one reporter with a total cut-off in funds. The memorandum was subsequently redrafted a number of times after being circulated among members of the White House staff for their comments and suggestions. This flow of documents dealing with public broadcasting between September 28 and November 15 (when the final version reached the President's desk) clearly revealed the various attitudes, objectives and policy preferences that would dominate administration thinking over the following two years.

Whitehead's first draft explained that, in the short run, there did not appear to be any way to cut off federal funds, since OMB had already apportioned $30 million of CPB's fiscal 1972 appropriation, and the remaining $5 million earmarked for matching grants to the stations. Whitehead also advised the President that it would be quite difficult to cut back funds for public affairs programming without cutting back for educational and cultural programs as well.

The October 4 version of the memorandum listed four major options for executive action: Option 1 was to negotiate a compromise financing bill "that would increase Federal funds for public broadcasting, but would circumscribe the power of CPB by increasing the autonomy of the local stations." Option 2 was to seek legislation that would drastically cut CPB funds outright and prohibit it from financing public affairs programming. Option 3 was somewhat more benign, to push for a bill that would mandate a new structure for federal funding of only educational and cultural programs at the national level, and for direct grants to the local stations. And Option 4 was similar to number 3, but would include an effort to revise the tax laws "to prohibit foundations from supporting news and political commentary programming, in the same way they are prohibited from lobbying." This additional provision was a direct attempt to undermine the supposed influence and involvement of the Ford Foundation in political programming. Whitehead's recommendation:

> The first option does little but avoid
> controversy and the second is likely to
> accomplish little but controversy.
> Options (3) and (4) would have lasting
> and constructive effect, though both
> would raise a loud liberal howl. Only
> Option (4) stands a chance of achieving
> all our goals.
>
> I recommend you approve Option (4) if
> you are willing to face the controversy
> and that we open the attack in my
> address to the annual convention of the
> local stations October 20.[20]

John Ehrlichman commented that the weakness in all of Whitehead's policy alternatives were that they involved actions not only by the administration, but also by Congress. He doubted whether the legislation route was the safest way to go. "The best alternative," he said, "would be to take over the management and thereby determine what management decisions are going to be made." Charles Colson was concerned that what the administration was actually trying to do might come to light. He wrote to Flanigan and Whitehead of his misgivings about the sensitive content of Whitehead's memorandum to the President. "I don't think you need to put things so explicitly in the first paragraph," he said. "This is a serious mistake for whatever records this piece of paper might ultimately end up in or, perish the thought, should it get out."[21]

In his October 7 reply to Whitehead, White House director of communications Herb Klein supported continued efforts to find a compromise long-range funding bill as the only "doable option." Klein was skeptical about an administration attempt to gain control over public broadcasting. "I believe that the exercise of any of the other three options would fail," he wrote, "and would enhance the viewership of Vanocur and MacNeil

because it would make them major public figures. This
action, coupled with the other serious problems we have
regarding both the networks and stations could turn into
a major public issue which would be damaging to the
President." In summary, Klein felt that there was little
to gain in seeking to control public television, but much
to lose.[22] A few days later, however, Klein changed his
mind and altered his recommendation to go along with
Ehrlichman, Bob Finch, Len Garment, Colson, and Flanigan
in supporting option three: to seek a funding bill that
would itself prohibit the use of federal money for
national public affairs programming -- like NPACT.[23]

In a memo to Larry Higby of Haldeman's staff,
White House aide Jon Rose was, however, far more blunt
than Whitehead in stating the true nature of
administration goals with regard to public television.
"In spite of what it may seem," he wrote, "no one
participating in this exercise had ever been unclear as
to the president's basic objective: to get the left-wing
commentators who are cutting us up off the air at once,
indeed yesterday if possible." To Rose, there was no
equivocating about administration attitudes towards
public television, or what the prospects were for
achieving its objectives.

> Even if we go the Whitehead route and
> succeed in cutting off Federal funds for
> liberal hour on public TV, no doubt Mac
> Bundy will be ready with Ford Foundation
> money to take up the slack. This is
> another battle for which I and a number
> of others would be eager to draft
> legislation if it is desired.
>
> Those are the unpleasant facts. Believe
> me, I do not enjoy watching these left-
> wingers any more than you do, but I
> think it is essential that we know the
> maximum that can be done and do it
> rather than spinning our wheels
> proposing the impossible.[24]

During this crucial period of White House deliberations on public television, the system's most serious and divisive program controversy to date occurred. The problem revolved around the scheduled October 6 season premiere of NET's irreverent magazine program, <u>The Great American Dream Machine</u>. One of public television's most popular and highly praised shows during its first season, Dream Machine was an off-beat amalgam of political and social satire, as well as straight-forward investigative reporting. In 1970-71 <u>The Great American Dream Machine</u> ran a weekly ninety minutes, but its production was extremely expensive by public television standards. For 1971-72 PBS cut the program down to an hour. The first episode of the new season was to feature a twelve-minute exposé by radical journalist and activist Paul Jacobs on alleged FBI attempts to employ three young men as agents provacateurs in the peace movement. Jacobs was not a member of the NET staff, but he had previously produced segments for Dream Machine independently, including one on the Atomic Energy Commission.

In his special report, "FBI Subsidy of Violence," Jacobs interviewed three men who claimed to have served as FBI informants in various anti-war groups, and that they were encouraged by Bureau agents to commit and encourage others to commit such violent acts as arson, bombing, and murder. One of the three, David Sannes, said he had volunteered to be an undercover agent in Seattle. He claimed that under the FBI's direction, he found dissidents interested in bombing and actually persuaded them to carry out a bridge-bombing project. Sannes said that he broke his ties with the FBI after an agent instructed him to booby-trap an explosion to kill the activist who agreed to do the bombing.

Jeff Desmond said that the Seattle Police recruited him as an informer after they had arrested him on drug-related charges. He claimed that as a former duPont company trainee, he knew quite a bit about explosives, and that an FBI agent had given him money specifically intended to buy bomb-making materials.

Charles Grimm, a student at the University of Alabama in Tuscaloosa, told Jacobs that he, too, was recruited by the FBI after he had gotten in trouble with the local police. Grimm said his FBI contact encouraged him to violent acts by telling him that if there was a fire on campus, then they (the government) could "get in there and crush the Communists on campus." He admitted to "burning a few buildings and throwing molotov cocktails" until state troopers finally did come in.

Jacobs did little in his report to substantiate the charges made by Sannes, Desmond, and Grimm. He did show, and quote from, some documents that had been stolen from the FBI's office in Media, Pennsylvania, but his quotations provided no corroboration of the incidents the three men described. All the FBI agents involved, he said, refused to comment on the charges, as did Bureau director J. Edgar Hoover. Jacobs concluded, "Undercover agents do provoke and commit acts of violence -- almost by necessity. The FBI's use of such agents began long before John Mitchell took over as Attorney General. Past administrations, too, have been willing to plant agents and informers inside political organizations with inevitable consequences: Government sanction, if not encouragement, for burning and bombing, all in the name of the law."[25]

NET sent The Great American Dream Machine program which contained the FBI segment to PBS in Washington for review on September 22, 1971. The next day, the PBS programming department, PBS general counsel

Norman Sinel and other PBS executives screened the show.
Although Sinel immediately called NET's general counsel
to discuss possible legal problems with the piece, PBS
did not officially notify NET of any problems until over
a week later. On Thursday, September 30, PBS president
Hartford Gunn called EBC president Jim Day to set up a
meeting to talk about the Dream Machine segment. He did
so only after the closed circuit station and press
preview of the show had already taken place. On the next
day, Gunn and PBS general manager Gerald Slater met with
Day, EBC executive vice president Ward Chamberlin, and
Bill Kobin, vice president in charge of programming for
NET, to discuss various alternatives involving either
recasting the Jacobs piece or changing the context in
which it would be shown. The PBS officials raised
objections about a lack of sufficient documentation,
about Jacobs' personal bias and the unusual freedom NET
accorded him as a freelance producer. Although Day
himself never saw the FBI piece before NET sent The Great
American Dream Machine tape to PBS, he trusted the
judgment of executive producer Al Perlmutter and NET
programming chief Kobin.[26] He later explained, "My
response was that the piece had been delivered to PBS,
therefore it had my sanction, and that I felt that the
piece had sufficient documentation for the kind of piece
it was, and that it should run as it was produced."[27]
Day and the other NET executives came away from the
meeting assuming that Dream Machine and the FBI segment
would, in fact, air as planned on Wednesday evening,
October 6.

Over the weekend, however, NET received formal
denials of the charges from two of the FBI agents named
in Jacobs' film, and immediately decided to revise the
film to include this information. Jacobs' reaction to
the FBI denials was: "Marvelous. At last we've gotten

some response. That's exactly what we were looking for.
Now we could put on a balanced [program] in the sense
that at least there was some denial, instead of bland 'no
comment.' And so I came back into New York to rewrite
the piece and to take into account the fact that they had
specifically denied it." The new version, NET's Kobin
advised PBS, would be ready no later than Tuesday
morning, October 5.[28]

When Jacobs arrived at NET on Monday morning to
rework the piece, however, he discovered that J. Edgar
Hoover, the Seattle police chief, and the third FBI agent
had sent in their own denials of the report. Hoover's
letter threatened to turn the whole matter over to the
Department of Justice for investigation. Jacobs and NET
then told PBS that because of this latest development,
the final version of the FBI segment would not be ready
before Wednesday morning, the day the show was to air.
PBS then decided that because there was no time for the
stations to preview Jacobs' revised version, the FBI
segment should not be included on The Great American
Dream Machine. PBS asked NET to provide an alternative
to the Jacobs piece so that the show could air in its
entirety. But NET refused. On Wednesday evening, PBS
went ahead and broadcast a forty-five minute version of
Dream Machine, with fifteen minutes of music added to
fill in for the empty space left by the deleted FBI
segment. In New York, WNET Channel 13 included Jacobs'
piece in its broadcast of The Great American Dream
Machine.

PBS' decision to drop the Jacobs piece at the
last minute made headlines nationwide. Television
critics who had seen the preview a week earlier, cried
censorship. Many assumed that Hoover's letter had
intimidated Gunn and PBS into cutting the FBI report.
Some saw the incident as another round in the ongoing

personal and institutional feud between Gunn and Day, PBS
and NET. The only question, wrote Chicago <u>Sun-Times</u>
columnist Ron Powers, was "Which Story Makes PBS Look
Worse?"

> The Public Broadcasting Service finally
> put it all together, fans. With the
> impeccable intuitive sense normally
> credited only to the lemming, PBS
> combined the undisputed worst time
> (premiere week), the most unfortunate
> topic (the FBI) and the most acutely
> embarrassing maneuver (yanking a program
> segment off the air hours before
> broadcast time, after having first
> approved it) to effect its first
> pratfall of the new television season.

> Whether it was governmental pressure,
> journalistic caution, or -- as seems
> more likely -- internecine bickering
> that led PBS to pull that 12-minute FBI
> segment off The Great American Dream
> Machine Wednesday, it was most certainly
> unprofessional.[29]

The episode brought criticism of public
television from all ideological perspectives. Marvin
Kitman of Long Island <u>Newsday</u> wrote, "Obviously PBS, CPB,
et al., are quasi-governmental mouthpieces, and it isn't
fair to expect them to get involved in muckraking about
the government. That would be biting the hand that feeds
them. Since they must go to Congress for appropriations,
it would be bad politics."[30] The Indianapolis <u>News</u> saw
the problem of tax money in public television
differently. An October 14 editorial said that the issue
underscored by the FBI piece controversy was not one of
censorship, "but one of the ideological bias that has
become so prevalent in 'educational' TV -- bias
subsidized with taxpayers' money. Programs being piped
out over PBS repeatedly incline in the liberal-left, if
not in fact revolutionary direction."[32]

In order to help clear up the confusion over what had happened and air the professional issues involved, NET decided to begin its new program about journalism, Behind the Lines, a few weeks ahead of schedule, with a rebroadcast of both the original and final versions of the Jacobs piece and a two-hour panel discussion about the entire episode. PBS picked up the program for national distribution so that all of public television's viewers could see the disputed segments and the discussion about them. Joining Day, Gunn, Jacobs, Kobin, and Perlmutter on the Panel were Edward Bliss, former CBS News executive and professor of journalism at American University; Les Brown, TV editor of Variety; Paul Davis, a reporter for the Tuscaloosa News; A.M. Rosenthal, managing editor of The New York Times; Robert L. Shayon, television critic of Saturday Review; and, constitutional scholar Benno Schmidt, of Columbia University Law School. The guest moderator of the unusual premiere of Behind the Lines was James Lehrer, director of public affairs programming at public station KERA in Dallas and editor of its Newsroom program.

The show explored the chronology of events leading to PBS' decision to drop the FBI piece from its showing of Dream Machine, the journalistic merits of both versions of the piece itself and the larger issues concerning the responsibilities of public television's producers and managers. Hartford Gunn denied that PBS had exercised censorship in cutting Jacobs' piece. Instead, he explained, it was an editorial decision made in the best interests of public television as a whole. "It seems to me," Gunn said, "the crucial question is whether our confidence -- or, rather, whether the public's confidence in us would be jeopardized; and we try to look at programming and the problems that programs present in terms of maintaining credibility with the

public. If we lose -- if we were ever to lose that
credibility, then all of what we're trying to accomplish
in public broadcasting goes down the drain."[32]

The guest panel members were divided in their
assessment of Jacobs' work and, therefore, of Gunn's
position. _Times_ editor A.M. Rosenthal said, ". . . in my
opinion this is a most inadequate piece of journalism.
As a matter of fact, without being too rough about it, I
question whether it's journalism at all. It seems to me
to be more of a kind of camera stenography. That is, it
would be the equivalent of our reporter going out,
interviewing three people that he found and thought
interesting and coming back and we putting it into the
paper, textually, and adding a few comments at the
end . . . . If you're asking me whether we would have run
this as it stands, in print terms, the answer would have
been no."

Bliss, who had served as an outside consultant
to PBS on the matter, said he thought the second version,
which included the FBI's categorical denial of Jacobs'
charges, was more balanced than the first and recommended
that, after the changes, PBS go ahead with it. "But," he
included, "I was flat in my rejection of the first
version. I guess I remember telling the program
chief . . . that I'd never put this on at all. I just
wouldn't do it." _Saturday Review_ critic Robert Shayon
and _Variety_ editor Les Brown both thought that although
it certainly could have been better, Jacobs' piece was
worthwhile. "The issue seems to be one of the degree of
documentation," said Shayon. "_The New York Times_ thinks
that it was not good journalism. NET people think it was
good journalism. What is good journalism? It's a
subjective judgment. With all good respect to _The New
York Times_, I would disagree that this was not good
journalism." Though program moderator Jim Lehrer kept

his views to himself on the air, as a member of the PBS
Journalism Advisory Board he had pre-screened the FBI
segment and had wondered aloud to its producers why they
had gotten themselves in a situation to defend the work.
"It was," Lehrer said, "a piece of crap."[33] To those at
both PBS who refused to air the FBI piece, and those at
CPB responsible to the government for all of public
broadcasting, the entire Dream Machine incident was an
embarrassing example of precisely the kind of controversy
they were trying to avoid.

The publicity surrounding the FBI affair served
only to reaffirm the hard line position on public
television that was already developing within the
administration. The press reported that this latest
controversy over "anti-government" programming, together
with the Vanocur appointment, was already having a
chilling effect on the discussions between OTP director
Whitehead and CPB president Macy on long-range funding.
In their contacts with journalists administration
officials made it very clear that they were very
disturbed -- that the President was very disturbed --
about Vanocur, in particular. "Politics has entered the
situation," The New York Times reported on October 13.
"White House aides are known to lack enthusiasm for the
selection of Sander Vanocur . . . as an anchorman of
forthcoming programs of NPACT. They believe he has shown
a consistent bias against the Administration."

Like any administration agency, the Office of
Telecommunications Policy used The New York Times, The
Washington Post and the wire services to make its views
known and to put pressure on the public broadcasters.
But the mechanism did not always work to OTP's advantage
because the journalists found it difficult to believe
that the White House cared about anything other than
getting anti-administration programs off of public
television.

The other mechanism at the White House's disposal for controlling bias was the Corporation for Public Broadcasting's board of directors. John Macy's letter to the board explaining <u>The Great American Dream Machine</u> affair soon found its way into the White House through Jack Wrather, perhaps the administration's strongest supporter on the board. Wrather also passed along to Whitehead a complete set of background materials about NPACT and other national public affairs programs that he had requested from Macy. "I assumed," Macy said, "that everything I was giving Wrather was going to the White House. As a board member, he was entitled to whatever information he wanted. Clearly he was a vehicle for White House infiltration of the board; he was selected for that purpose."[34]

One of the major steps called for in Whitehead's memorandum for the President was a White House-orchestrated public relations campaign aimed at generating opposition to Vanocur and undermining the integrity of public television's news and public affairs operations. Whitehead recommended a number of actions that should be taken to eliminate "slanted programming." The first would be to "induce programmers themselves to keep some balance under pressure of criticism from our friends on the CPB Board and among the general public." The second would be to replace John Macy and Frank Pace by telling them that they had "lost the confidence of the Administration and thereby had become obstacles to the progress of public television." If their resignations could not be gotten voluntarily, then they would be voted out as soon as the White House could gain "firm control of the Board." The third step, therefore, was to "take more effective control of the CPB Board." This would also enable the administration to "reduce drastically the CPB funding of the offensive commentators" by the summer of 1972. Finally, Whitehead suggested that the White House should "build more actively the public case against CPB programming bias through speeches by friends in the Congress, selected columns, and my speeches."

But even with "a loyal Board and top management at CPB," the OTP director cautioned, there were limits to the change that was achievable "within the current structure of the Public Broadcasting Act." He conceded that public television would always "attract liberal and far-left producers, writers and commentators," and since Congress would never agree to eliminate CPB, reduce funds for public broadcasting, or exclude CPB from financing public affairs programming, the administration would be able "to eliminate the worst features" of the medium only by reforming its structure in favor of the local stations. "We stand to gain substantially from an increase in the relative power of the local stations," Whitehead told the President. "They are generally less liberal, and more concerned with education than with controversial national affairs. Further, a decentralized system would have far less influence and be far less attractive to social activists." Whitehead was quite perceptive about the tensions that had been plaguing public broadcasting and how they could be turned to the advantage of the White House. "There is, and always has been," he said, "a deep division within public broadcasting over the extent of national control versus local station control. Many local stations resent the dominance of CPB and NET. This provides an opportunity to further our philosophical and political objectives for public broadcasting without appearing to be politically motivated." The "key to the success of this approach," Whitehead concluded, was the passage of legislation that would remove CPB from the business of national networking, drastically cut the CPB budget, and initiate

direct federal operating support for local stations. He
estimated that "local stations' support could be bought
for about thirty million dollars."[35] The memo was a
thorough, comprehensive declaration of war on public
broadcasting.

Before the final version ever reached the
President's desk, Whitehead had already opened the
administration's attack on public television. On October
20, he addressed the 47th Annual Convention of the NAEB
in Miami. His speech struck one rhetorical blow after
another against the current direction and leadership of
public broadcasting. Over the following year and a half,
the themes Whitehead developed in Miami would become
quite familiar. He emphasized the importance of what he
believed to be the primary ideal of the Carnegie
Commission report: decentralization and localism. He
began sarcastically:

> I honestly don't know what group I'm
> addressing. I don't know if it's really
> the 47th Annual Convention of NAEB or
> the first annual meeting of PBS
> affiliates. What's your status? To us
> there is evidence that you are becoming
> affiliates of a centralized, national
> network.

Whitehead used the occasion not only to
criticize public television's structure, but its
programming and personnel, as well.

> You're centralizing your public affairs
> programs in the national Public Affairs
> Center in Washington, because someone
> thinks autonomy in regional centers
> leads to wasteful overlap and
> duplication. Instead of aiming for
> 'overprogramming' so local stations can
> select among the programs produced and
> presented in an atmosphere of diversity,

the system chooses central control for
'efficient' long-range planning and so
called 'coordination' of news and public
affairs -- coordinated by people with
essentially similar outlooks. How
different will your network news program
be from the programs that Fred Friendly
and Sander Vanocur wanted to do at NBC?
Even the commercial networks don't rely
on one sponsor for their news and public
affairs, but the Ford Foundation is able
to buy over $8 million worth of this
kind of programming on your stations.

Whitehead's criticism, however, went beyond
Vanocur and Friendly. He raised legitimate questions
about the attitudes and objectives of the entire system.
"Is it you or PBS," he asked, "who has been taking the
networks' approach and measuring your success in rating
points and audience? You . . . point to increase in
viewership. Once you're in the rating game, you want to
win it. You become a supplement to the commercial
networks and do their thing a bit better in order to
attract the audience that wants more quality in program
content. The temptation to make your mark this way has
proven irresistible." Some of his comments were
trenchant: "You can program for the Cambridge audience
that WGBH used to go after," he said, "for the upper-
middle class whites who contribute to your stations when
you offer Julia Child's cookbook and Kenneth Clark's
'Civilization.'"
        Whitehead made it clear that the administration
was opposed to a centralized fourth network which, he
implied, PBS had already become. In conclusion, he
dangled what seemed to be a carrot and stick threat to
long-term funding over the heads of the broadcasters.
"Do any of you honestly know," he said, "whether public
broadcasting -- structured as it is today and moving in
the direction it seems to be headed -- can ever fulfill

the promise envisioned for it or conform to the policy set for it? If it can't then permanent financing will always be somewhere off in the distant future."[36]

The message to many in public broadcasting came through loud and clear: there would be no administration plan for long-term funding until the medium became what Whitehead and Nixon wanted it to be. In Variety's graphic prose, the speech signaled a move "Toward Public TV On the Cheap." "What Whitehead wants to do," said one close observer, "is weaken the system to the point of being totally ineffectual on any national basis."[37] To John Macy, Whitehead's address was a shock and a slap at everything he had been trying to accomplish. "I think the Whitehead speech in Miami was when I really saw the beginning of the end," he said. "Because, presumably, we were working with Whitehead. I had had a number of meetings with him. He assured me that before he said anything to the system he was going to discuss it with me. He did not. The speech was a total surprise to me. And clearly, it was designated to negate the efforts I was making to bring about a system. It was clearly contradicting and misinterpreting the direction in which we were attempting to move. We had been trying for a good many months to come up with legislation for financing; and instead of talking about financing, this message was an attack on the system."[38]

CPB vice president John Witherspoon soon sent a memo to all 212 public stations accusing Whitehead of injecting political considerations into public television's news programming and attempting to use the funding lever as a way of pressuring the system to accede to administration demands. Witherspoon listed a number of specific inaccuracies and unwarranted criticisms contained in the Miami speech:

1. The idea that it's time to review the performance of the system when the government has never delivered on its promise of financing. The creation of the present system is not nearly complete.

2. The implication that the Corporation should be carrying out all the principles and mandates of the Public Broadcasting Act and the Carnegie Commission while appropriations are at half their proper level and even though the Act and the Commission report by no means agree on all points.

3. The failure to recognize PBS as a membership corporation or stations as its members.

4. The insistence on ignoring the facts in judging the rationale for the National Public Affairs Center for Television and then pre-judging its performance.

5. The unwarranted and unfair remarks about the Ford Foundation, which has invested two hundred million dollars in public television, and at station management with such statements as the one that Ford is able to buy over eight million dollars worth of public affairs programming on your television stations.

6. The idea that we are becoming hooked on the ratings, noting that if you take a poll you want to win.

7. The notion that you are deliberately programming for an elite, ignoring community needs.

8. The statement that once the Carnegie Commission had its say, the public broadcasting professionals -- station managers included -- disdained its principles.

Witherspoon charged that the statement about permanent financing being "somewhere off in the future," coming from "a man who has been charged by the President to come up with a long range financing plan for public broadcasting, and who speaks for the Administration in telecommunications matters -- says in a straightforward political language that until public broadcasting becomes what this Administration wants it to be, this Administration will oppose permanent financing."[39]

When Witherspoon's charges turned up on the front page of The Washington Post the day after Whitehead met with CPB chairman Frank Pace, the administration's opposition to current Corporation policies intensified. OTP counsel Henry Goldberg thought at the time that it was the public broadcasters who were guilty of turning funding into a political issue. He told National Journal that Whitehead "was not saying anything new," but "what CPB did was to cry 'political foul' and that, to me, was a copout."[40] Goldberg and others at OTP believed that Whitehead had raised important issues in his address but that public television leaders were attempting to ignore the legitimate criticism by claiming that the White House was only trying to intimidate them.

Many local station managers who had been consistently strapped for operating and capital funds were receptive to Whitehead's remarks about the importance of localism. They needed money and he spoke about getting it to them. But for the Office of Telecommunications Policy, said Brian Lamb, the problem was that this group of potential allies often "spoke out of both sides of their mouths. They would come to private meetings with us saying 'We want this thing decentralized. We don't want John Macy or Hartford Gunn to control our lives.' Then when it became a public issue, they wouldn't stand up for what they believed in."[41] Not many stations stood openly with the White House. And among the system's leaders, opposition to Whitehead was even more unequivocal. Though he might have encouraged a few, the OTP director had offended many with his talk at the NAEB convention in Miami.

Robert Wilson, president of KERA in Dallas, wrote to Whitehead, saying, "I was most disheartened by your speech to us in Miami." Specifically, Wilson disagreed that NPACT was a sign of completely centralized public affairs production in Washington and he questioned the meaning of the OTP Director's comments about Friendly and Vanocur. "I suggest the American people could really use more of the type of programs both Vanocur and Friendly wanted to do at their respective networks," Wilson wrote. He called the innuendo about one sponsor "just plain unfair. Fred Friendly and Dave Davis at Ford have never even obliquely interfered with our Newsroom Channel 13 which they fund almost completely. In fact," he told Whitehead, "their example of hands off could well provide a model for any long-range federal financing bill."

On Whitehead's criticism of public television's desire for a mass audience, Wilson said, "Of course, I know if we do the job we're supposed to, we probably won't get a Marcus Welby size audience. (I don't mind telling you I'd like to have a Marcus Welby size audience for some of our programs like Newsroom or Town Hall. Don't you want to see Sesame Street beat Lucy reruns?)"

Finally, Wilson took issue with Whitehead's attack on the power of PBS and CPB over the system. "We desperately need a strong PBS," Wilson told him. ". . . there will never be enough money for 100% locally produced schedules. . . . We need programs national in scope.

"CPB does serve us. Not perfectly but I interpreted your statements to mean megalomania is now CPB's and PBS's chief feature."[42]

On November 4, NPACT general manager Jim Karayn sent his own response to Whitehead's statements about the Center. "I am writing to you," Karayn said, "in hope of eliminating some apparent misconceptions about NPACT's role within public television and its programming plans that were indicated by your references to us in your October 20 NAEB speech." In his letter, Karayn denied that NPACT had been formed to centralize all national public affairs programming for the system. He pointed out that national public affairs programs would continue to come from diverse production sources, including NET (This Week, Black Journal, The Great American Dream Machine), WGBH and KCET (The Advocates), SECA (Firing Line), and KQED (World Press). "The autonomy of these centers," he said, "will not be threatened by NPACT, nor will local station public affairs programming be preempted or diminished because of its creation."

"Secondly," Karayn said, "the Center was not formed to create a 'network news program' patterned on the commercial network nightly newscast model. As you well know, there are just not sufficient resources, in either personnel, facilities or funds, presently available to public television to allow it to consider beginning this type of programming. . . . In addition, I am personally opposed to public television attempting to imitate the commercial networks in duplicating this type of nightly news programming." Karayn made it clear that neither Sander Vanocur nor Fred Friendly had, or would, set any of NPACT's programming policies. "NPACT programming is not dictated by one person or a small group of individuals with a particular philosophical viewpoint or journalistic background." Like KERA's Wilson, Karayn steadfastly defended Fred Friendly against Whitehead's charge of seeking to influence program content. He explained,

> During my years with NET, since 1964,
> and during the past five months that I
> have spent organizing NPACT, I have been
> consistently impressed with the
> unwavering restraint exercised by the
> Ford Foundation in general, and Mr.
> Friendly in particular, in not getting
> involved in public television's
> programming decisions. As one of the
> pioneers and most distinguished
> practitioners of television journalism,
> Mr. Friendly's suggestions are always
> welcome, but they are neither offered
> nor taken as mandates from a 'sponsor.'
> Further, to clarify the record, NPACT's
> funding comes jointly, and in
> approximately equal proportion, from the
> Ford Foundation and the Corporation for
> Public Broadcasting.

In closing, Karayn referred to NPACT's recent
four-day coverage of the United Nations China debate and
vote. He asked Whitehead to speak to United States
Ambassador George Bush about his reactions to NPACT's
work, which included nearly two hours of live coverage of
the critical vote "while the commercial networks were
still tuned to their normal weeknight schedule."[43]

A few weeks later, the Public Television
Managers Counsel of the NAEB wrote to Whitehead of their
disappointment that OTP had "not yet found it possible to
produce the promised and much-needed financing bill, even
in light of your questions concerning our endeavor."
Though the managers agreed with the OTP director's main
point about the importance of localism, they, too, felt
that his criticisms of CPB, PBS, and the Ford Foundation
were not entirely fair and, more importantly, did nothing
to address the fundamental problem of inadequate
financing. As broadcasters, they understood the
financial and technical reasons behind the Corporation's
short-term emphasis on networked programming. "It is
clearly evident," they wrote, "that the Corporation, in

attempting to meet its many obligations could not provide funds for sufficient <u>hours</u> of programs to be produced so that 'alternatives' could be offered the stations by PBS. . . ."

The managers also told Whitehead that public broadcasting in the United States owed an enormous debt to the Ford Foundation. "Indeed, many of us believe that without the dedication of the Foundation to the idea of public television, there would not be any system. . . . We do not believe that any funding source has exerted influence on national public television programming which has abrogated or denied us the right to exercise our responsibilities as individual licensees."

On the question of the balance and objectivity in public affairs programming, the station managers pointed to PBS' refusal to allow the FBI segment of <u>The Great American Dream Machine</u> to run as scheduled. "It was our conclusion," they said, "that the piece as originally submitted constituted irresponsible journalism. As you also know, we were soundly criticized by the press. This example illustrates that the stations do have the authority and mechanism to exercise control over nationally produced program." The NAEB station managers council saw no reason why OTP should delay any further in proposing a long-range funding bill as planned.[44] Indeed, every element of the persistently divided public television industry agreed that nothing Whitehead had said in Miami should stand in the way of increased, insulated federal support. Some felt that much of his criticism was justified. Most felt that he had far overstated his case and more than a few saw his remarks simply as a partisan attack on editorial freedom and an ominous threat to the system's financial survival.

In the press there were many who questioned whether public broadcasting -- already wracked by internal conflict -- could withstand determined pressure from the government. On the morning of Whitehead's Miami speech a New York Times editorial entitled "Season of Discontent" pointed to the difficulties that public television was experiencing and the desperate need for regular instead of "beggar" funding.

A week after the NAEB meeting, a commentary by Bill Greeley in Variety, entitled "PBS and the Plucked Chicken," suggested that there was no reason for the White House to try to censor controversial programming, because public television's leaders were already doing a perfectly good job of it. He recounted that at the convention, PBS board chairman James Loper had presented president Gunn with a rubber chicken. The gift was made in reference to a Time magazine article about Gunn's decision to kill the FBI segment. The PBS logo, Time had said, should not be anything like the proud peacock of an NBC, but rather a plucked version -- a chicken! In criticizing Gunn's proposal that a new board of outside citizens be formed "to guarantee that the public interest be maintained in public broadcasting," Greeley commented sarcastically, "The way things are going in public TV the day may be soon when shows will be aired so that the PBS viewing audience can vote on whether the shows should be aired."[46] As Broadcasting magazine succinctly put it, the fledgling public television system, in its mere four years of existence, had already taken flack from every possible corner:

> If public broadcasting draws large
> audiences, it is attacked for seeking
> the masses; if it programs for small,
> select groups, it is damned as an
> insufferable snob. If it tackles a
> tough issue, it is trendy, left-wing,
> unrepresentative and misusing the
> taxpayers' money; if it presents fine

drama and stimulating discussion, it is
aloof and uninvolved. If it moves
toward centralization, the spectre of
autocracy is raised; if it does not,
there is the accusation that it is
frittering away its public money without
seizing the chance to make an impact on
the national consciousness. Anything it
does, in any realm, is sure to be
attacked by someone as contrary to the
spirit of the Carnegie Commission report
or the Public Broadcasting Act --both of
which mean many different things to many
different people. Meanwhile, the
struggle for federal funding limps
along; federal appropriations increase,
but freedom from annual accounting does
not.[47]

"In television and radio," Broadcasting said,
"there IS no way to be both a Good Guy and a tough,
visible force." Indeed, many public television leaders
were already having second thoughts about the creation of
the system's newest visible force, NPACT. NPACT general
manager Jim Karayn recalled going to Miami and hearing
the director of the White House Office of Telecommunications Policy turn his organization into a cause
celebre. "But even more scary than that," Karayn said,
"was being asked to come to a meeting -- which I always
thought was a kangaroo court -- made up of the station
managers group. It was sort of a shut-door thing, and
[they] asked all these questions about the formation of
this organization. One of the first questions was, 'Jim,
you have been made the vice president, that means there's
a place for a president. What does that mean?' And I
said, 'I don't know what it means.' They said, 'Well, is
it being held open for Fred W. Friendly?' And, I
couldn't believe them. It boggled my mind. Their
hostility towards the formation of NPACT was so
great . . . ."[48]

The Miami NAEB meeting, with the Whitehead
speech and local station suspicion, made it clear that if
there were economic and organizational advantages to
centralizing some of the news and public affairs
production at NPACT, there was also the danger that the
Center would be an easy target for any attack on such
programming. In his address, Whitehead had been quite
explicit about administration attitudes towards the
Center, but White House efforts to purge public
television of its political programs were hardly limited
to public expressions of disapproval. On November 22,
Alvin Snyder, a member of Herbert Klein's White House
Communications Office staff, sent Peter Flanigan a
"Confidential" memo containing several examples of anti-
administration and anti-war, "bias" on the part of
several of public television's leading on-air figures.
Snyder assembled the list, he wrote, "to help document
our case against Frank Pace and the Corporation for
Public Broadcasting. The record is clear and illustrates
mismanagement of CPB under Pace's leadership." Calling
both Vanocur and MacNeil "network rejects," Snyder
maintained, "Vanocur's bias is well documented":

> On the David Frost Show last July he
> said the President has "consistently
> lied" to the American people. Vanocur
> said he is a bit ashamed of his role as
> a transmission belt for those lies. The
> Government, claimed Mr. Vanocur, has
> used classification to cover 'every kind
> of sin, arrogance and obscenity -- and
> there is none greater than Vietnam.'
> Quizzed as to who has the right to
> decide what should be published of top
> secret material Vanocur spoke of the
> 'higher law' that one must adhere to.
> He said the 'higher law' means to accept
> the legal punishment for doing good --
> 'Dr. King taught us that.'

> Last May Vanocur told the Chicago
> Tribune that extending the war into Laos
> and Cambodia was 'stupidity.' Said
> Vanocur: 'Every time you put a
> President on the air about Vietnam . . .
> we have very little chance to say, 'it's
> hogwash,' or 'they're lying to you.'

"Based on Vanocur's set of biases," Snyder
said, "it is clear that we cannot expect an even break
here. Nor can we expect much in the way of objectivity
from Bill Moyers, who anchors the other weekly news
broadcast carried by PBS and produced by NET." A former
press secretary to President Lyndon Johnson, left his job
publishing Long Island's Newsday to host NET's This Week
program starting during the fall of 1971. Snyder
reported that just the previous week "Moyers delivered a
scathing attack on our efforts to end the Vietnam war."
"Moyers," he said, "did not feel it necessary to report
the facts."

Snyder also listed a number of other programs
containing controversial subject matter or with well-
known radical figures as guests: The Jacobs FBI piece on
The Great American Dream Machine; the November 3 Dream
Machine containing an "anti-Establishment song and dance
number by Jane Fonda; a commentary by satirist Andy
Rooney ridiculing the President's concept of an all-
volunteer Army (Variety described as 'sharp and mean
enough to prompt Richard Nixon to veto the next Public TV
appropriation.'); an interview with screenwriter Dalton
Trumbo who pledged himself to work against the reelection of the President (said Trumbo, "Those [McCarthy]
hearings produced a President of the United
States. . . . A freshman member of the committee was
Richard Milhouse Nixon, serving his first term in
Congress . . . . I sometimes think that since Mr. Nixon
was on the committee that successfully sought to throw me

out of my job, I perhaps owe him the favor of -- of a
return engagement, and I intend to join several
committees in 1972 to throw him out of his.')"[49]

Two days later, on November 24, Whitehead
outlined for White House chief of staff H.R. Haldeman
what he and the OTP had been doing "behind the scenes on
the Vanocur/MacNeil situation."

> After Vanocur and MacNeil were announced
> in late September, we planted with the
> trade press the idea that their obvious
> liberal bias would reflect adversely on
> public television. . . . We then began
> to encourage speculation about Vanocur's
> and MacNeil's salaries. . . . We plan to
> do two things in the next few weeks to
> continue to call attention to balance on
> public television, especially NPACT. We
> will quietly solicit critical articles
> regarding Vanocur's salary coming from
> public funds. . . . We will quietly
> encourage station managers throughout
> the country to put pressure on NPACT and
> CPB to put balance in their programming
> or risk the possibility of local
> stations not carrying these programs.[50]

Because of the speculation in the press caused
by administration leaks, Representative Lionel Van
Deerlin of the House Communications Subcommittee, a
California Democrat and a former television news
correspondent, pressed Macy and CPB to release
information on the salaries paid to public television's
on-air personalities. At the November 19 meeting of the
CPB board, Macy said that the Corporation needed a
financial disclosure policy. Without naming Van Deerlin
specifically, he said that the need for such a policy
emerged when a congressman requested information on NPACT
salaries.[51] When Macy went ahead on his own and told Van
Deerlin that Vanocur received a yearly salary of $85,000

and MacNeil $65,000, NPACT board chairman Sid James sent the CPB president a letter protesting such disclosures without the concurrence of the NPACT management and, if necessary, the consideration of the NPACT board of directors. The NPACT board took the view that all requests for NPACT salary information should come to NPACT itself, not to CPB, and that personal financial information should not be given to a member of the press, or even to an individual congressman. It resolved, however, that "Because a portion of NPACT salaries are paid with public funds, salary information should be made available by NPACT upon request to appropriate congressional committees; but such information should, to the extent feasible, be presented in the form of a range of salaries without naming specific individuals, in order to protect such individuals from personal discomfort."[52]

The resolution did not protect NPACT correspondent Sander Vanocur from personal discomfort. In late November, when the $85,000 salary figure got into the press, there was an uproar in Congress and around the country. Whitehead's public relations effort succeeded handsomely. Vanocur had taken a forty percent cut in pay to leave NBC for NPACT and his current salary was far below that of other major network commentators. Karayn would have paid Edwin Newman nearly twice as much as he was paying Vanocur for the same job. But critics were quick to point out that $85,000 was twice as much paid to a Supreme Court Justice, a cabinet officer, or a congressman. The comparison did not endear Vanocur and NPACT to those in the public television system who were constantly starved for funds, or to their patrons on Capitol Hill. Congressman Van Deerlin suggested that CPB might have damaged its chance of winning a permanent funding plan in 1972 because of the Vanocur affair. "I should have hoped," he said, "that this new medium would build up its own on-air personalities, rather than seek to compete in the commercial market. I am afraid that the agency's hope for future success on Capitol Hill has not been improved by these revelations." Even Torbert MacDonald, a strong advocate of long-range federal support for the medium, admitted that he was "a little shocked" by some of the salaries.[53] Though House Democrat Van Deerlin had pressed the salary issue in Congress, OTP reaped the benefits politically. Whitehead had received a great deal of criticism in the press for his threatening statements in Miami. He and his colleagues at OTP felt he had been misconstrued and misinterpreted by critics who were more interested in Nixonian hostility to the media than in the legitimate concern Whitehead had raised about centralization. "The Vanocur/MacNeil thing was definitely used, on purpose," said OTP congressional and press liaison Brian Lamb, "because the press refused to deal with the issues. It was the only way you could get the public's attention."[54] The salaries certainly did get everyone's attention.

Up until that time, no one at CPB, PBS, or anyone else in public television who knew about the salaries paid to on-air correspondents had made any complaints. Before hiring Vanocur, Karayn had spoken to Jim Day to find out what NET was going to pay Bill Moyers, a newcomer to broadcasting. Day told him that NET was paying Moyers $75,000 for thirty-five shows which, Karayn thought, was remarkably high for someone who was totally untrained and untested. "On the basis of that," Karayn said, "Vanocur was a real coup. Because here I am getting him for eight-five, ten more; he is a nationally prominent figure; loved or not loved, he is certainly a trained broadcast journalist, and we have him to do thirty-five, a hundred and thirty-five, a thousand and thirty-five shows."[55]

Karayn also tried to point out to the press that William F. Buckley was receiving $11,000 per program ($3,000 for himself and $8,000 for production expenses) for the production of Firing Line. What was scandalous about Firing Line at the time, Karayn said, was that its research staff was from Buckley's own publication, National Review. "I kept saying, if we were doing a show and the research team was out of the New Republic, there would be a congressional investigation." He told The New York Times, "I wonder what kind of a hue and cry there'd be if we had a program that called for direct payment to The Atlantic, The Nation, or The New York Times." But, Karayn later recalled, "I couldn't make anyone buy that story." For weeks in late November and early December, the press in Washington and around the country focused on Vanocur, his salary and White House anger about both. A bitter Vanocur remembered, "What surprised me was the way the press picked it up and did the work of those who worked for Nixon in singling us out, but especially me. It was almost a glee with which they approached the task."[56]

Bill Moyers said, "The furor over Vanocur amazed me. It amazed me because it was so much ado about nothing. . . . It was unfair, the hostility towards him and the focus he became."[57] Why was Sander Vanocur such a target, not only for the White House, but apparently, for the press as well? Vanocur would be the first to admit that he was never a great favorite among his colleagues. Because of his close relationship with the Kennedys when he was White House correspondent, there were lingering jealousies among fellow journalists. Vanocur was also widely disliked because of his sometimes abrasive manner. "There were just as many Kennedy-ites who hated Sandy as Nixonites," Karayn said.[58] Vanocur had openly criticized the press for what he thought was

its meekly benign treatment of Nixon during his 1968
campaign, and first term, particularly on his handling of
the war. Some colleagues perhaps saw the salary issue as
an opportunity to pay him back. Moyers believed that
both Vanocur's links to Kennedy and his independent and
sometimes contentious nature helped make him the object
of personal attack. "He's not as good a politician as
some of the rest of us are," Moyers said, "and that was a
problem.[59] His partner at NPACT, Robin MacNeil who,
along with Moyers was spared the intense criticism on the
salary issue, felt that the special notoriety Vanocur
received took on the form of a personal vendetta.[60] One
particularly vicious cartoon in the Washington Daily News
pictured a gloating Vanocur looking on as two husky armed
guards strained under the weight of his hefty salary from
the U.S. Treasury.

The cartoon turned up in a group of clippings
that Whitehead sent Flanigan on December 1. "Thought you
might be interested in the attached," Whitehead wrote.
"You can see that the salary issue is beginning to get
hot." Among the clippings were stories by the Daily
News' Dan Thomasson headline, "Public TV Pays High --
mostly tax dollars," and "Vanocur's Fat Salary Angers
White House -- public TV's future clouded."[61]

By the middle of December, the combination of
controversies over the NPACT appointments and the FBI
piece was beginning to have an effect on the daily
operations of public television. Producers of public
affairs programs complained that the standard and
practices guidelines PBS had proposed to apply to their
shows were far too restrictive. Dick Moore of KQED in
San Francisco expressed their generally skeptical
attitude when he told Variety that he knew of a perfect
set of standards -- many copies available -- "It's called
the First Amendment." But many stations received

THE WASHINGTON, D.C. DAILY NEWS, November 29, 1971:

"WHO SAYS WE CAN'T COMPETE WITH THE COMMERCIAL NETWORK GIVEAWAYS?"

criticism from their viewers and supporters about both
liberal bias and the salary issue. New York's Channel 13
received so many letters that president James Day went on
the air in January 1972 to assure viewers that their
membership dollars were not going to pay for such
salaries. Day explained to the New York audience that
NPACT was separately funded by CPB and the Ford
Foundation rather than by viewer contributions.[62] In a
December 10 editorial, "Is Public TV Going Commercial?"
the Christian Science Monitor recognized that the
infamous salaries were, in fact, only a fourth of what
top managers and talent received in commercial
television. Public television fund drives, it said,
"merit widespread public support, which an unfounded
backlash against public TV could undermine."[63] But the
salaries continued to be the source of some undeserved
embarrassment to public television, just as the White
House hoped they would be.

The congressional reaction to "FBI Subsidy of
Violence" and to the Vanocur salary, combined with the
intentional foot-dragging by the administration on a
permanent financing plan, raised serious doubts about
funding for the upcoming season. The effect on
programming could be profound if new funding arrangements
were not soon approved. On December 2, The New York
Times declared, "Public Broadcasting Faces Year of
Serious Budget Problems." One of the most likely
casualties in the PBS schedule was to be the
controversial The Great American Dream Machine, with its
$100,000 per program price tag. The Los Angeles Times'
Jerry Beigel wrote in a column entitled, "Public TV
Future In Doubt," "Enjoy public television while you can.
Enjoy shows like Hollywood Theatre and the Advocates and
be sure your children get some exposure to Sesame Street
and The Electric Company now. Next year, you, and they,

may not be able to."[64] While this may have been
hyperbolic, it was becoming clear the NPACT would not be
able to afford its planned $2 million gavel-to-gavel
coverage of the 1972 national conventions. Indeed, any
project that required any advance planning was
jeopardized by the continuation of annual appropriations
from Congress. PBS president Hartford Gunn admitted when
CPB budget cuts were officially announced that public
television would only be able to "mark time until funding
was clarified."[65] The administration was very clearly on
record against the establishment of a "fourth network"
with federal funds and, in an election year, it was
difficult to expect a new funding plan initiative from
the White House. The press, looking at public
television's bottom line, saw that, while there would be
less of everything, there would probably be much less in
terms of news and public affairs.

Throughout December the administration had been
looking for ways of assuring that news and political
commentary would be completely removed from public
television's national schedule. One strategy that
Whitehead had already outlined was to bypass CPB and give
funds directly to the local stations, "since many of the
local stations cannot afford the talent or attract the
attention to do anywhere near the damage of CPB."[66]
Another possible line of attack was proposed by one of
Nixon's strong supporters on the CPB board, Tom Moore.
He recommended a CPB-centered approach that would have
the Board itself pass a resolution prohibiting the
Corporation and PBS from funding or carrying any programs
of news analysis or commentary. Moore further suggested
that Macy could soon be forced to step down as CPB
president, since the addition of five presidential
appointees in April would allow a Nixon majority to
choose their own executive officers.[67]

On December 7, Flanigan reported to Whitehead and others that the President had approved the "Tom Moore option, with regard to the Corporation for Public Broadcasting."[68] The next day Whitehead again attacked public broadcasting, this time in front of the Hollywood Radio and Television Society. He criticized the drift towards a centralized network structure, after the President had just decided to try to centralize program and policy decisionmaking power in a "friendly" CPB board. At the December 15-16 CPB executive committee meeting Moore's plan was introduced as a request to the CPB management to "devise a plan which will assure insofar as possible the balanced and objective presentation of public affairs." The minutes of the meeting also show that the committee "generally agreed that at this juncture programs involving news analysis and political commentary have a low funding priority and present activity in that area should be phased out . . . ."[69] Administration efforts finally bore some tangible fruit in the subsequent cancellations of both The Great American Dream Machine and NPACT's comprehensive convention coverage because of their relatively high costs and "low priority."

Not everyone in the administration was enthusiastic about the attack on public affairs programming and the plan to "take over" the Corporation through White House appointees. On December 23, OTP general counsel Antonin Scalia sent Whitehead an urgent "For Eyes Only" memorandum warning him about the current administration course. The very idea that Scalia would send Whitehead a formal memorandum signalled the depth of his feelings. Scalia's analysis of the plan being considered for the CPB board "concluded that the most likely eventuality is that the plan will fail and the Administration's role will become public knowledge.

Naturally, this is the worst possible development, but its likelihood argues for exceptional discretion and caution on our part."

Since Scalia's initial recommendation to abandon the "Moore Option" had been rejected, he urged Whitehead, at the very least, to point out to the White House staff all the risks and difficulties outlined in his analysis.

As Scalia saw it, the problems were manifold. If, in the best possible case, the board approved the prohibition on public affairs and the administration's role did not become public knowledge, he felt that the description of forbidden programming would be unavoidably imprecise and susceptible to varying interpretations. Because of this imprecision and the lack of attention the part-time board members could give to CPB matters, it would be extremely difficult to enforce the prohibition, even with a number of friendly board members. Scalia explained that it would take a virtually complete overhaul of <u>both</u> the CPB and PBS staffs to get people sympathetic with the restrictive guidelines in order to make them work. Even assuming all the uncertainties of this approach, Scalia concluded, it would be a very short-term and ephemeral victory since any future board could change this policy against public affairs.

If the board disapproved and the link to the White House became public knowledge, all the above problems would arise, Scalia said, plus a considerable number of additional ones:

> Administration critics in the press and
> in the Congress will have a field day
> embarrassing the President at a time
> when he is most vulnerable, <u>i.e.</u>, at the
> opening of his campaign for reelection.
> The Administration's 'heavy-handed

> hostility to the media' will become a
> campaign issue, giving early momentum to
> the President's opponents.
>
> If the Administration's role becomes
> known, it will be difficult, if not
> impossible, to disassociate the OTP.
> This would in all likelihood have
> serious, adverse consequences for future
> policy development by the Office, not
> only in the public broadcasting area,
> but in most fields in which OTP is
> involved. OTP's efforts would
> henceforth have a political 'taint' and
> its motives would be suspect.
> Congressional funding would diminish,
> and many of OTP's responsibilities might
> be transferred to Commerce.

Finally, Scalia warned, if the plan failed and
the administration's role also became known, "All of the
problems outlined above would be exacerbated, since
criticism for high-handedness would be supplemented by
contempt for failure." He made it clear that any OTP
association with the White House's partisan concerns and
its attempt to control program content through CPB was
not only inappropriate, but threatening to the integrity
of the new telecommunications policy agency. "If, in the
end, you have to go along with this approach," Scalia
counseled, "your acquiescence should be given
reluctantly. I do not think it is an overstatement to
say that OTP's future depends on how you handle this
matter. The more you can do to dissociate yourself from
this particular 'initiative,' the more likely it becomes
that OTP will survive."[70]

Whitehead, however, did acquiesce. Instead of
dissociating himself from the board takeover and from
criticism of public affairs programming, he became the
administration's leading spokesman for the prohibition on
the use of federal funds for their production. His

decision surprised and dismayed both Scalia and OTP
counsel Henry Goldberg, who felt that Whitehead's
position was not only dangerous but also clearly
contradictory to the Carnegie report he so often quoted.
Goldberg remembered that on a Friday evening in early
January of 1972 when the OTP director was to be
interviewed on a National Public Radio program on the
politics of public television, Scalia and his wife came
to his house for dinner. "After dinner, we gathered
around the radio and we heard the interview, and all of a
sudden, Whitehead said, 'No public affairs programming on
public broadcasting,' and Scalia and I looked at each
other absolutely dumbstruck and said, 'Where did he get
THAT?' It was out of the blue. The next opportunity,
the next day, I called him and went into the office on
Saturday and said, you know, 'What do you think you're
doing?' And it was like 'Don't ask questions. You know
public affairs is propaganda.'"[71]

For over two years, the OTP director had
attempted to steer clear of any involvement in program
content. He had consistently sought to emphasize the
importance of long-term, philosophical policy objectives
over those involving more partisan, short-term aims. His
memos to the White House were often tailored to fit --
even pandered to -- the political biases of the President
and his immediate staff. But he had done this, to a
great extent, to present OTP's policy agenda in terms
that the White House would most readily accept. In
public broadcasting, as well as a host of other
telecommunications issues, "the only way he would have a
chance of getting a policy adopted," Goldberg said,
"would be to link it to what was sensed to be the
acceptable objective." Often from 1970-1972, OTP policy
objectives and White House desires for public television

fit together well. Increasingly, as Scalia desperately
pointed out, White House interests and those of OTP were
in conflict.

Top White House staffers, particularly Charles
Colson and John Ehrlichman, often asked Whitehead to take
direct action against specific public television shows
they found offensive. Though there are some memoranda
containing such directives, nearly all such complaints
were made in conversation. "I was suggested a number of
times and I was directed a number of times," Whitehead
said, "to do things about particular programs on public
TV: 'Go talk to so and so and get him to cut that out'
or, 'Do that or that.' There were times I would waffle.
I would say, 'Well, we'll see,' and I'd go off and not do
anything. Sometimes I would say, 'Yeah, but that's
illegal, we really can't do that . . . .' Now I will
confess that sometimes we didn't stand up as strongly as
I would have liked, particularly in retrospect."[72]

Part of the tension of being in any
administration, Whitehead explained, is the tension you
have with the White House. "The White House is where the
power is; the President is where the power is. You can't
lose sight of that. If you want to do your thing, you've
got to maintain a sufficient sense of trust between you
and the White House, that the President lets you do your
thing. He's got to perceive that you are acting in some
sense, in his broad interest." Whitehead decided in the
fall of 1971 that for him and OTP to "keep doing their
thing," it was vital that he solidify his position with
the President and White House staff. At some point after
Miami, he crossed the line between phrasing policy
alternatives in partisan terms the White House would
appreciate, and creating policies that served President
Nixon more than public television, or the public itself.
At only thirty-one years old, and in government for the

first time, Tom Whitehead knew that you had to be a "team player" to stay on the team. And for the Office of Telecommunications Policy, staying on the White House team was crucial. With OTP Whitehead was trying to build a brand-new executive agency in a field of growing importance to the whole society. The office was meant to be a place in government where telecommunications policy was thoroughly studied and developed. "A high motivation," said Henry Goldberg, "was to sustain, nurture and give importance to OTP."

> [The President and his aides] just don't care about structural, regulatory issues in communications. The mere fact that Whitehead could call over to the White House and get Presidential attention, was because he was viewed as a "team player" on the media issue. Whitehead could be relied upon to go out and make a speech in Miami or to get on the radio and say that we shouldn't do public affairs in public television. That enabled Whitehead to enhance the prestige of OTP and get done in cable and in radio deregulation all the other things he really cared about -- to get the White House's attention, and to keep Chuck Colson off his back.[73]

"We had different agendas all the time," said Brian Lamb. "Memos were written to the White House to pander to Bob Haldeman, Chuck Colson and Richard Nixon. . . . We had to get along with the White House or we wouldn't be in being. We'd be thrown out on our ear."[74]

Whitehead's Miami speech had clearly reflected the tension between long-term and short-term, structural and political concerns within the administration. A great deal of work went into it and into other speeches, because OTP had no other public forum to state its views. Many telecommunications issues did not yet come before

congressional hearings. In an area like public
broadcasting, OTP had no official, functional
responsibility. Its job was merely to advise the FCC and
advise Congress about the President's point of view. In
the address to the NAEB in Miami, Whitehead and Goldberg,
who helped draft it, were attempting to crystallize what
they thought the key issues to be. "We were trying to
dramatize them," Whitehead said, "in a way that would
energize an entire public broadcasting system to come to
grips with them." The speech was, however, more
successful in "energizing" the system than OTP expected.
It followed a period of OTP silence after the office had
pulled its long-term financing bill back from OMB --while
the various possible responses to CPB opposition and the
Vanocur hiring were circulated among the top White House
staff. People in public broadcasting were wondering,
Goldberg said, they were calling OTP and asking, "What's
going on? Why'd you pull the legislation? What have we
done?" The Miami speech was intended to be an
explanation of the difficulties that resulted in the
White House's decision to pull the funding bill. It was
supposed to be OTP's philosophical statement of the
problem -- deeply felt. "It wasn't a phony thing,"
Goldberg said, "It was a real concern."

But in the context of the President's well-
publicized antipathy towards Vanocur and White House
hostility to all public affairs on public television,
Whitehead's Miami speech hit public broadcasters like a
baseball bat. Goldberg told National Journal in early
1972 that the speech was never meant to be an ultimatum,
that if it hadn't been so widely misunderstood, it would
be funny.[75] Though he, too, denied any intention to
threaten public broadcasting, Whitehead admitted, "In
retrospect, I think it was an ultimatum and I can
understand why it was perceived that way.[76] In Miami,

White House antipathy and OTP philosophy were in near
perfect harmony. Though OTP's leaders claimed at the
time not to have understood this, the public broadcasters
did. Their opposition to Whitehead, however, pushed him
further away from a long-term funding bill for the system
more toward the White House view of the world. When he
had to choose between safeguarding the fledgling Office
of Telecommunications Policy and the fledgling public
television system, Whitehead pragmatically opted in favor
of OTP.

     Increasingly after Miami, Whitehead pursued
policies that seemed less in line with the philosophy he
had espoused, and more in line with the White House's
determination to get rid of hostile television programs
-- by any means necessary. Scalia warned him about the
dangers of this course: the high probability of failure
and the threat that it presented to OTP. He and Goldberg
were clearly opposed to an attempt to take over CPB in
order to control public television programming. Such an
effort was in marked contradiction to the decentralization of power that OTP had been working for. "The
whole notion of seeking to influence public broadcasting
by board appointments -- by taking this one out and
putting that one in," Goldberg thought, "was naive,
doomed from the outset, and enormously risky to the
existence of an office like OTP. I didn't feel strongly
enough about it to pull up stakes and stalk away . . . I
think that Scalia and I believed that OTP could kind of
lay low for a while. 'Let these guys rant,' It's not
going to work. The real answer to the concern with
having a medium of expression funded by the Federal
government . . . is decentralizing it completely, or
eliminating it completely. If you can't decentralize it,
then eventually, the string would play out in attempting

to influence programming. And then we'd be around to pick up the pieces."[77]

The administration did rant and rave. The election year would see its battle with public television intensify to the point where discretion and diplomacy were forgotten. By June 1972, the White House was more than willing to risk the political fallout from a presidential veto of a public broadcasting bill that had near-unanimous support in Congress. By June 1972, OTP itself virtually demanded such a veto to show both the government and the broadcasting industry that it was a force they could not ignore. And public television in 1972 was the real loser.

CHAPTER FOUR

THE VETO

"In the name of 'public' broadcasting, they are seeking
funds and independence to create a TV network reflecting
their narrow conception of what the public ought to see
and hear. This should not be allowed to happen."

> --Clay Whitehead, recommending
> that President Nixon veto
> the Public Broadcasting Act
> of 1972

In January 1972, Clay Whitehead sent a memo to
Peter Flanigan in the White House recommending a
Corporation for Public Broadcasting budget of only $35
million for fiscal year 1973, the same amount as in
fiscal 1972. He urged Flanigan to make a strong
statement to administration "friends" on the CPB board
that until the Corporation "demonstrated a more
responsible attitude toward funding of controversial
programming and toward highly centralized networking
operations, the administration will be unwilling to
support long-range funding or significant increases in
CPB funds."[1] However, at board member Tom Moore's
urging, the White House increased its CPB request by $10
million, to a $45 million, single year authorization.
Moore felt that it would be very difficult for the
administration to make progress within the public
television community on the issue of news and public
affairs programming unless the President "could show
forty-five million dollars as evidence of his good
faith." The White House, far more concerned with Sander

Vanocur than it was with decentralization, agreed to
Moore's suggestion. Almost all of the additional $10
million would go directly to local stations and for
cultural and educational programming. Those, at least,
were the conditions of the increase that Whitehead
expressed to CPB president John Macy, chairman Frank
Pace, and other Corporation board members.[2]

The CPB board of directors met in Washington on
January 21 and 22. Under the continuing threat that no
appropriation would get out of committee or through the
full Congress unless the Corporation demonstrated its
responsibility for the public television system, the
board's executive committee recommended that the
Corporation staff seek a clearer definition of CPB's role
in the overall program decisionmaking process. In the
area of public affairs, the committee recommended that
the full board resolve to assure balance, objectivity and
fairness in all such programs, and not to fund news or
partisan political commentary by professional
journalists. The board voted unanimously in favor of
these recommendations, but stopped short of an abdication
from involvement in political programming. It rejected
Tom Moore's proposal to adopt a broader prohibition
against funding of any public affairs programs involving
controversial political issues. In other words, although
CPB would not use federal funds to create a nightly
"hard" news program -- something that was never really
contemplated in the first place -- public money from the
Corporation would continue to flow into the production
and interconnection of current series, specials, and
documentaries dealing with important public issues.

Corporation president John Macy told the board
that in response to the executive committee's directive,
the management was attempting to create a "new pattern of
relationship" in which CPB would be more assertive in

exercising responsibility and more involved in the
decisionmaking process throughout the programming cycle.
He cautioned, however, that it would be difficult to
implement the recommendations of the executive committee.
"the imposition of the Corporation in program decisions,"
he said, "will be viewed as interference by a number of
key people within the system and is certain to provoke
outspoken criticism in the public arena.[3]

At the meeting, Macy again raised the issue of
salaries paid out of CPB's federal funds. Many
legislators were rankled by the reports of Sander
Vanocur's $85,000, and Macy realized that the salary
controversy was a potential stumbling block to obtaining
an improved bill from Congress. The board unanimously
approved a motion that any organization receiving federal
funds through CPB program grants should not use those
funds for the payment of salaries in excess of $36,000
per year without their prior approval.

The motion, of course, was meant to head off
the kind of public -- and governmental -- relations
problems that Vanocur's salary had caused. Belatedly,
the CPB board was seeking to protect itself and the
system from charges of financial mismanagement and
irresponsibility for the taxpayers' money. Since
congressional hearings on a new public television funding
bill were less than two weeks away, it was crucial for
the CPB board to show the system's patrons on Capitol
Hill that it had the controversies -- both on the air,
and off -- under control.

NPACT saw the board's actions and Macy's offer
to cut his own salary as an obsequious buckling under the
political pressure over the hirings. They felt it
betrayed the shallowness of the system's commitment to
public affairs and a cowardly lack of support for the
difficult position in which Vanocur, MacNeil, and the

center found themselves. On January 18, NPACT general
manager Jim Karayn provided Macy with an extensive
background memorandum on the hiring of NPACT
correspondents. In it, he reminded Macy that several
days before NPACT announced the hirings, he had sent
advanced notice to the CPB board, and PBS had notified
all station managers about Vanocur and MacNeil. "We
received almost uniform commendation within the industry
on the caliber of our impending appointments," Karayn
wrote. "Likewise, at the time of their public
announcement, the national press coverage of NPACT's
selection of correspondents was extensive and favorable."
He explained, "Although NPACT did not announce specific
salary figures for each correspondent at this time, there
was no attempt made to conceal their general salary
level. An article the following day by Val Adams in the
New York Daily News reported their average compensation
as about seventy-thousand dollars per year. There was no
unfavorable feedback to us from this report." Karayn
pointed out that the controversy surrounding NPACT's
correspondents began over two months after their salary
ranges became public at the time of their hirings. In
addition, he said, the press coverage had left the
erroneous impression that NPACT's full salaries were paid
out of federal funds through its CPB grant, ignoring the
fact that the Ford Foundation provided just under half of
NPACT's budget. The only salient point, Karayn felt, was
whether public television was getting what it paid for
and expected from NPACT and its correspondents.[4] NPACT
was already feeling greatly unappreciated by the public
television system it had been created to serve. When
White House antipathy toward Vanocur became known, Karayn
remembered, "the stations all ran for cover and the best
names in public television ran for cover; boy, none of
the people were around to say 'hello,' or anything."[5]

But public television's federal funding was due to expire on June 30, 1972, and the central concern for the stations and for CPB was financial. Few worried about hurt feelings at NPACT.

*   *   *   *   *

In early February, the struggle between the administration and the Corporation for Public Broadcasting shifted to the public arena, in hearings before the House Subcommittee on Communications and Power. During the February 1-3 hearings on new public television funding legislation White House supporters attacked the "fiscal and political irresponsibility" of CPB. Corporation chairman Frank Pace and president John Macy went to considerable lengths to mollify their critics by increasing CPB's direct funding to local stations from twelve to thirty percent of its appropriations, and by expanding PBS board membership from eleven to nineteen in order to provide for greater representation of local stations. Despite these moves, Representative Clarence Brown pressed for an administration-supported bill that, while extending financing of the Educational Broadcasting Facilities program for five years, would make the Department of Health, Education and Welfare, rather than CPB, responsible for awarding grants to local stations for both capital and operating expenditures.[7]

The Brown bill would circumscribe the Corporation's functions even further by prohibiting the use of funds for coverage of current issues of partisan nature (restricting lobbying, interconnection, advertising and promotion for such programs). Another

provision, aiming to curb alleged Ford Foundation
influence on public television programming, prohibited
the Corporation from accepting grants from any one source
that exceeded ten percent of the federal appropriation.
Such a bill, said The New York Times, "would
substantially undo the work of the Public Broadcasting
Act of 1967," with its drastic alterations in the funding
procedure.[8] Brown claimed that he was acting purely out
of a personal concern for the future of public television
and without administration prompting, but his bill was
well tailored to the White House position. There was no
question, said The Times, that the future of public
television had become an openly political matter when Lyn
Nofzinger, deputy chairman of the Republican National
Committee circulated copies of the Brown bill in the
hearing room with the statement, "The CPB is a victim of
fiscal irresponsibility and partisan non-objectivity in
its hiring practices and programming."[9]

Whitehead's turn to testify came at the very
end of the hearings. His position on the MacDonald bill
might have been predicted, since he had only recently
told Senator Sam Ervin's Subcommittee on Constitutional
Rights that "the establishment of a centralized,
government-funded broadcast voice may be as repugnant to
free speech as an established church would be to freedom
of religion."[10] He opposed the five-year MacDonald bill
as far too expensive in total amounts authorized and too
cheap in the percentage given directly to local stations.
He advanced the administration's proposal to extend the
Corporation for one year only with a $45 million
appropriation. He justified the continuation of the
single year authorization (against the testimony of those
who told the committee that a year was not nearly enough
time to plan and execute the production of a quality
television program) on the grounds that the relationship

between CPB, PBS, and the local stations was still
unclear and that until the directions were better
defined, it was wiser not to "rush forward."[11]

Although he did not actually say that he
"preferred to keep CPB insecure and deferential during an
election year," that was the message conveyed to those in
public television by Whitehead's equivocation on the
funding issue.[12] Whitehead's statements on National
Public Radio and on Bill Moyers' This Week program that
public television should not use federal funds to support
public affairs programs had already drawn a great deal of
criticism. After the Nixon White House had spent over
two years attacking the bias of commercial television
news, Whitehead's remark that the networks did a
perfectly good job in news and public affairs and that
public television should therefore not waste its
resources in this area, struck many as absurdly
hypocritical. "That was hogwash," OTP's Brian Lamb later
admitted. "That was sheer doubletalk. There were a lot
of things that were said during those debates that
obviously wouldn't stand up in any kind of analysis."[13]

Indeed, Whitehead's positions did not stand up
well under the critical analysis of the press. Public
recognition of the "doubletalk," of administration
attempts to control public television, increased
dramatically throughout that winter. Some elements of
the print media, most notably The Wall Street Journal and
the Scripps-Howard newspaper chain, supported the White
House's opposition to increased, long-term funding for
public television. Scripps-Howard papers -- one of them
the Washington Daily News -- ran an editorial which
credited Scripps writer Dan Thomassen with "uncovering"
the story of the "exceptionally high salaries" paid to
"several well-known TV personalities" in public
television and subsequently caused "instant and generally

adverse" reaction from Congress. Though Thomassen's
articles had indeed ruffled some feathers on Capitol
Hill, he had, in fact, "uncovered" nothing. The White
House had leaked the salary information to him and
Scripps-Howard gave the story front-page billing in its
papers.

Many leading newspapers, however, sharply
criticized both the President and OTP director Whitehead
for their partisan antipathy toward public television.
John J. O'Connor pointed out in The New York Times the
glaring inconsistencies in Whitehead's position on news
programs and federal funding, and took the opportunity to
praise the uniqueness of programs like NPACT's election
series.[14] A Times editorial accused the OTP director of
"spreading an electronic wet blanket" over public
broadcasting in an election year by questioning its
ability and mandate to produce political programs.[15]
Television writers at other newspapers documented the
numerous obstacles strewn in public television's path
and, as the Cleveland Plain Dealer's William Hicky wrote,
"how these barriers have prevented the public's outlet
from being the vital and extradimensional communications
and entertainment source it was supposed to become."[16] No
frequent critic of the Nixon administration, the
Christian Science Monitor editorialized, "Public TV has
apparently hit a plateau in its progress into something
like the British Broadcasting Corporation. And
ironically, it is stalled by those from whom it is
seeking support -- officialdom in government, and chiefly
the White House.

". . . [T]he White House opposes the functions
of the fledgling NPACT for much the same reason it has
squared off against the three national networks: its
liberal cast." But public television, the Monitor
reasoned, would not be any less "liberal" if it were

regionalized along the lines the White House wanted. The
pressure to be balanced, to be credible in the coverage
of national affairs, existed chiefly in Washington. And
NPACT, with its wide coverage of the presidential primary
debates not carried by the commercial networks was both
being balanced and serving an important public
function.[17]

In the Indianapolis News, commentator Richard
Schull focused on the essential problem in suggesting
federal government was a strange place for public
television to be looking for support.

> What if Israel had to depend on the Arab
> states for its defense money?
> If the United Auto Workers' political
> action arm was financed by the
> Republican National Committee?
> Absurd, huh?
> Well, that's what's happening in
> Washington right now over public
> broadcasting. The future of public TV
> news and public affairs broadcasting
> depends on the generosity of its natural
> adversary, the elected politicians who
> hold the power of the Congress and the
> presidency.[18]

The St. Louis Post-Dispatch declared, "A
fundamental distrust of national television is reflected
in the current White House attitude toward pending
congressional legislation to finance the corporation for
Public Broadcasting. Using such politically disarming
words as the need for 'diversity' and 'local control,'
Clay T. Whitehead . . . has spoken out strongly against
public television's evolution into a 'fourth national
network'. . . . Translated, the Whitehead position
obviously means that the Nixon Administration does not
want national public television to become involved in the
issues of the presidential campaign."[19]

Chicago _Tribune_ television writer Clarence
Petersen replied to a letter likening government-financed
TV to the "Third Reich's Dr. Goebbels" by saying that
public television's journalism had thus far proved
unsatisfactory owing in large part "to the requirement
that every year public TV goes on bended knee to the
government asking for more funds."

> Now there is a move to set up a system
> of funding that would guarantee
> financing for public TV even if the
> programs at times offend those noble men
> in Congress. . . . This move has met
> noble opposition because politicians
> will not gladly relinquish their power
> of censorship by intimidation. Now the
> White House Office of Telecommunications
> suggests the issue be settled by
> removing news and public affairs
> programming from public TV. This
> suggestion can be most charitably
> regarded as a copout. Less charitably,
> I regard it as an effort to retain
> government control over public TV
> program content. Doctor Goebbels would
> be pleased.[20]

The New Yorker magazine quoted in full
Whitehead's remarks that public television should
probably not carry any news and public affairs since the
commercial networks were doing quite a good job in that
area, and then commented, "What this arrogant statement
implies is that Public Broadcasting news -- an operation
that has been far from perfect, that has been constantly
struggling for money and personnel, but that is the best
alternative available to the inadequacies and
Administration-directed deferences of commercial
television -- is to be dismissed, at the time when we
need it most (in an election year), by a wave of a White
House hand." _The New Yorker_ concluded, "A few weeks ago,
a Republican congressman spoke out on the floor of the

House, charging that Public Broadcasting was leftist.
Now we have Mr. Whitehead, who says that we don't really
need Public Broadcasting's news, because we have such a
wonderful supply of it from the networks, and because any
more of it, presumably, would turn our heads, or, at any
rate, cause confusion, ill feeling and 'mal de siecle,'
among the citizenry. Mr. Whitehead is profoundly
wrong."[21]

On February 20 the American Civil Liberties
Union released a report on the Nixon White House's
efforts to dominate the public medium, entitled Public
Television: A Question of Survival. The author of the
study, Fred Powledge, warned that public television was a
"disaster in the making" largely because of a "cynical
exercise in White House manipulation of a communications
medium that threatens to reduce the medium to even worse
pap than commercial television's diet." He accused the
administration of intentionally trying to keep CPB on a
"starvation diet" with fiscal appropriations that were
meant to "leave national public affairs programming in an
advanced state of poverty." He charged that the
purposeful postponement of long-term financing was
intended to leave the medium "at the mercy of
politicians."[22] The administration, said Powledge, was
further aided in its effort to remove political
programming by many local stations, which had no interest
in such programs and exercised censorship powers through
PBS. The Nixon White House dismissed the ACLU's charges
as "typically polemical and anti-Administration," but in
fact, the report signified what more and more people
concerned with public broadcasting were beginning to
understand -- that "decentralization," on the
administration's terms, would destroy public television.

Supporters of national public affairs programs
began to take their case before Congress and the public.

On February 22, Elie Abel of the Columbia School of
Journalism attacked Whitehead's view on programming
structure and policy before the Senate Subcommittee on
Constitutional Rights, where Whitehead had earlier stated
his position. He said that the OTP director had
seriously misread the Public Broadcasting Act in
interpreting it to proscribe news and national public
affairs. "A public television system," Abel said, "that
is prohibited from examining the people's concern by law,
or Administration edict, or by plain cowardice, is a
system without brains or heart."[23]

On March 1, PBS president Hartford Gunn
publicly answered Whitehead's questions about the
appropriateness of public television's carriage of public
affairs and news analysis, and decried the administration's attempts to use federal funding as a lever on
programming. In an address before the Western
Educational Society of Telecommunications in San
Francisco, Gunn declared:

> Let me say right off raising questions
> about public affairs programming on
> public television -- or about any other
> area of our activity -- is appropriate
> for stations, citizens and all branches
> of the government. Questions, comments
> and criticism are always welcome. What
> is not welcome, or appropriate, is for
> those in positions of real power to
> attempt to influence a public medium on
> the basis of their own personal
> biases. . . ."[24]

Hartford Gunn, the man who -- fairly or
unfairly -- had been given a rubber chicken because of
his reputation for pulling the plug on controversial
public affairs programs, was staunchly defending public
television's duty to produce such political programs. As

the Los Angeles Times editorialized a few weeks later, the issues had been fogged by Clay Whitehead's assertion about public affairs programs. "Public affairs has a place in public television and a national network is essential to its vitality." The Times also made the crucial point that reduced funding would necessitate more centralization of programming, not less. Neither the Carnegie Commission nor Congress wanted an American version of the BBC, said The Times. "But until more money is available, it would be self-defeating to siphon the limited funds away from quality national programming to beef up local station programming. Even the most eager local station manager must acknowledge that the foundation of his programming and the critical audience factor lie with the superb national programs."[25]

It was ironic, Variety suggested, that Whitehead's strategy of trying to set industry moderates and local stations against the more liberal network -- much as Agnew tried to do in commercial television -- may have backfired on him. The local stations did need and want more money and more input into the system, but they, too, were wary of possible executive control over public broadcasting. One result of the White House pressure was that the persistently divergent forces in the public television industry were beginning to join together against a common enemy -- Nixon administration interference. They were, of necessity, becoming more united because of Whitehead's attempts to widen the gaps between them.

For the first time in years, Gunn of the station-centered PBS, and James Day of the New York-centered NET were saying the same thing. The normally conservative NAEB issued a warning against administration attempts to hamper CPB, as many locals began to realize that they would be out of business without a national network to provide them with programs. The shift in attitude was precipitated, at least in part, by OTP general counsel Antonin Scalia's criticism of the local stations for not doing more of their own programming at the same March 1 conference on educational television in San Francisco that Hartford Gunn had addressed. Scalia was highly critical of the NAEB and its president, William G. Harley. "Where were the NAEB Washington representatives," he asked, "when over the past four years, the local stations were being allocated less than 13 percent of the federal funds distributed through the Corporation for Public Broadcasting? Where were they while the diverse community system we once had was transforming itself into a fourth network?"

"Whatever the reason," said Scalia, "the fact that it has to be a government official rather than the stations themselves who raised the alarm about the direction of public broadcasting surely indicates that some sort of atrophy has already set in."[26] His comments, Variety reported, revealed to the local station representatives OTP's lack of understanding that it took a great deal of money to produce local programs; most of the stations were struggling just to stay on the air with the programming they received from PBS. They understood that the low level of federal funding was forcing CPB to concentrate its resources on national programs that the entire system could share. In reaction to the administration's insistence that PBS not be a fourth network, local stations responded to a PBS poll in early March 130 to 2 that the service was providing "about the right" amount of programs. Two stations even felt that PBS was not providing enough networked programs. In response to the administration push to de-emphasize news and public affairs, the PBS board passed a unanimous resolution to affirm their "very deep commitment to

public affairs on public television," and expressed
concern that "there is any discussion, anywhere, of
dispensing with public affairs programming."[27] A month
later, the entire PBS membership voted against a "home-
rule" proposal that would have given editing and cutting
privileges to local stations. The vote, said Variety,
gave "highly significant backing to the national network
and production centers." In short, by the early spring
of 1972 the public broadcasters were finally beginning to
rally together to their own cause.

One action taken by PBS in late February and
early March helped reassure both worried station managers
and skeptical congressmen about the quality of public
television's future national public affairs programs.

On February 22, Hartford Gunn proposed the
appointment of a public affairs coordinator and a twelve-
member advisory panel to evaluate PBS performance in
public affairs. The coordinator would deal with "problem
programs" and see that production units met standards of
fairness and balance, and would act as an "advocate" for
public affairs programming within the PBS hierarchy.[28]
The coordinator and the advisory panel were intended to
act as a heat shield for the stations when they were
attacked for broadcasting controversial programs.
"Working directly with the production agencies," Gunn
said, "the public affairs coordinator should attempt to:
gain lead time and information necessary to head off
program problems before they get so far along the
production pipeline; persuade producers of the validity
of an editorial role with system-wide responsibility
which is not automatically censorship; and better
sensitize both PBS staff and the producers to stories
which should be covered and types of public affairs
programming which should be done." In short, someone in
the national organization would be there to stand behind

producers and journalists, or have some editorial control over them if they did not live up to certain professional standards.

The idea of a coordinator, and particularly the idea of an advisory panel, met with immediate resistance from many advocates of public television journalism. The hiring of a public affairs coordinator appeared less troublesome to public television newsmen than the prospect of the board, principally because the latter's function was less clear to them. What worried many public affairs producers was that the buck would not stop with the coordinator alone, but would consistently pass to the advisory board on all potentially controversial programs. Then, committee journalism might quickly lead to timidity. Said Elie Abel, "Let the coordinator goof a couple of times and the programming he let pass bring down some heat on the stations and the PBS management, and they'll start screaming for greater consultation with the advisory group. We'll then have editing by committee." Bill Moyers felt that "to interpose a sort of journalistic overseer would give the government a good point of pressure that ultimately will be inhibiting rather than liberating." Al Perlmutter, longtime veteran of NET and executive producer of The Great American Dream Machine, was a member of Abel's advisory committee to PBS on journalism standards. He emphatically opposed PBS coordination. "Final authority on all programming," he said, "should rest with the production center, not with anyone at PBS."[29]

Hartford Gunn told the PBS board of directors at their March 6 meeting, "Public broadcasting is being challenged from every side." He noted Scalia's remarks five days earlier in San Francisco which had echoed Whitehead's criticism, and a New York Times editorial accusing PBS of censorship and timidity in the face of government pressure. Public television's difficulties, the PBS president said, persisted in large part because the system did not yet have the formal policies and procedures to deal with the complex problems that confronted it. More than ever before, the staffs of every major public television organization, PBS, CPB, NAEB, NPACT, were preoccupied with organizational matters and political battles instead of producing television programs. Speaking of PBS in particular, Gunn said, "It is all we can do to deliver a program service to our members -- and this would be true if we were spending no time on basic organizational and policy matters. The fact is, the staff is spending most of its time on those matters and our basic job in the programming area is suffering as a result." Gunn urged the PBS board to come to some immediate decisions on the proposed public affairs coordinator and advisory committee and PBS' relationship to the other public broadcasting organizations. He said that The Times' censorship charges were symptomatic of PBS' broader problem. Because the Service was operating in a politically charged atmosphere, every program decision it made, he said, "was subject to misunderstanding -- not to mention the fact that some of these decisions had been exposed to public scrutiny prematurely."[30]

The source of The Times' complaint had been NET's and PBS' last-minute decision to cancel the scheduled showing not of a controversial documentary, but of a comedy show, "The Politics and Humor of Woody Allen." The Allen film included some blisteringly cynical references to President Nixon's past career and current personal life. In it Allen portrayed the Henry Kissinger-like power behind the throne, Dr. Harvey Wallinger, profiled in a mock series, "Men of Crisis." Hitting on the Vice President's attack on the news media,

Wallinger made the point that "Mr. Agnew is extremely
upset about TV since they took off Gilligan's Island."
And he referred to The New York Times as a "commie, left-
wing, Jewish, homosexual newspaper." There was an
extended spoof of the House Un-American Activities
Committee hearings which made Nixon famous in the 1940's.
As committee counsel, Wallinger viciously and tirelessly
probed the "subversive" Boy Scouts of America, much as
Nixon had questioned Alger Hiss. As Mrs. Wallinger,
Louise Lasser described how the pair "used to double-date
with the Nixons." And when Pat wouldn't dance with Dick,
Harvey would.[31] PBS claimed that during a presidential
election airing such harsh satire might violate Section
315 of the Federal Communications Act which guaranteed
equal time for all candidates for office. EBC president
Jim Day himself decided to pull the program after the PBS
complaint. Allen's executive producer, Charles Joffe,
said, "Both Woody and I think it's a shame that a program
that was done entirely as entertainment should be the
source of such controversy. We brought it to public
television because we thought there we would have
complete freedom."[32]

"The only way I see out of this dilemma,"
Hartford Gunn told the PBS directors, "is for the board
to adopt the definitive policies and procedures which
will permit those of us charged with the operation of the
system to understand clearly the rules of the game. Our
decisions -- and the producers' -- need to be made on a
routine basis instead of a crisis basis. . . . [W]ithout
clear policies and procedures, we are not going to be
able to defend ourselves effectively against the current
barrage of criticism." The PBS management felt strongly
that a public affairs chief and an advisory panel were a
vital element in the formulation of just such policies
and procedures for journalistic programming.[33]

The board approved the creation of the new
public affairs coordinator post and the choice of James
Lehrer of station KERA in Dallas to fill it. Lehrer had
been anchorman of KERA's Newsroom program and had also
been a member of the PBS journalism advisory committee.
He was "highly regarded by many in public television as a
tough, resourceful journalist; a solid choice for what
under the best conditions will be a hotseat of
journalistic diplomacy."[34] The Texan had said when his
name was first mentioned for the job, however, that he
had "no intention of being merely an executive secretary
of any group," and had accepted the post only when PBS
agreed to drop the idea of having a six-member advisory
group that would screen all the public affairs programs.
Lehrer said that he could probably live with the twelve-
member evaluation panel that was created, since their
reviews would probably be undertaken only once a year.[35]

"My selection," Lehrer later said, "was a
political decision, I'm sure." Perhaps, PBS thought that
since he was from the heartland of middle America, they
were getting a conservative who was predisposed to
skepticism about "New York liberal" programming. "What
they didn't bother to check out was that in the Dallas
context, I was not considered a namby-pamby conservative.
But that was an irrelevancy. It looked good in the
system to have a guy from Dallas coming rather than, say,
to have somebody who was already on the east coast in
that job."

"They were not going to get a censor," Lehrer
said. "They were not going to get an editor. They were
going to get a coordinator and an advocate on behalf of
those who were producing journalistic programs." Because
of incidents like the Woody Allen show cancellation, PBS
was accused by some critics for buckling under White
House pressure to soften up its programming -- or lose

its federal money. But from his vantage point, Lehrer
said, there was never an instance in which pressure
traveled from the White House through PBS to producers to
actually change or drop a program. But it certainly
could have been that individual producers took it upon
themselves to cut out things which, they thought, might
cause them some problems.[36] As Jim Day put it, it wasn't
Nixon, but fear of Nixon, that killed "The Politics of
Woody Allen."[37] Public television needed federal dollars
to survive, but some asked, Could public television
survive the federal dollars? As Bill Moyers had warned,
"It would be a painful irony if in trying to get out of
the poorhouse, public broadcasters convinced themselves,
privately, of course, not that it's dangerous to take
risks, but that it's wise to avoid them."[38]

Indeed, there were those who believed that
because of Nixon administration threats public television
had decided to simply avoid taking any more risks.
Whether this was true is difficult to assess objectively.
Reactions to public affairs shows varied widely.
Although all the publicity surrounding Sander Vanocur's
salary and politics led some public television managers
to expect liberal bias in NPACT productions, many
programmers and viewers found the new Vanocur/MacNeil
series, A Public Affair: Election '72, was overly safe
and often quite bland. One program manager replied to a
PBS evaluation survey that the shows were dry and "lacked
sparkle." "At times," he said, "I wish that programs had
been as controversial or unbalanced as our worst critics
suggested. If anything, we erred in the other direction,
with too frequent blandness or seemingly uninspired
presentations."[39] Another said they were "too middle-of-
the-road and dull." Variety's review of the series noted
that the correspondents were "perfect lambs" in their

treatment of sensitive issues, and reported that "in more
skeptical circles," Vanocur and MacNeil had been dubbed
the "Lamby pies."[40]

"I think that it's a legitimate criticism,"
Vanocur said later, "not that [the NPACT shows] were
bland -- but that they weren't more daring." With or
without Nixonian pressure, Vanocur maintained, "we'd have
done pretty much the same."[41] MacNeil, however, thought
that the efforts of the administration did have an effect
on the outlook of A Public Affair: Election '72. As he
put it,

> I think we were affected by the
> pressures. . . . I think we were well
> aware of the pressures, and I think they
> colored what we were doing to the extent
> that we were even more conscious of the
> need to be more balanced than we
> otherwise might have been if that
> climate hadn't existed. I think it
> forced us into balance.[42]

Whitehead's April 27 "Progress Report on Public
Broadcasting" reminded the President that the
administration's single short-run goal was to force
public television's coverage of controversial public
affairs to be more objective. His conclusion was that
"Anti-Administration bias, while certainly not
eliminated, has diminished in large part because of
public attention focused on the known bias of Sander
Vanocur."[43] Apparently, Whitehead's efforts achieved
some success. Perhaps NPACT would not have done anything
very differently without the White House-orchestrated
public relations campaign aimed at Vanocur, but if
MacNeil had to be unusually concerned with the
ideological balance of his reporting, then that campaign
served at least part of its purpose.

But with or without administration hostility towards its efforts, no one should have been surprised that NPACT was less "exciting" than commercial network news. After all, its senior correspondents were, by choice, refugees from those networks. In his 1968 book on the influence of television on American politics, Robert MacNeil had been, like many at the time, highly critical of the network news' superficiality, its dependence on graphic, emotional images. Broadcast journalism, he wrote, too often ignored the essential background of important stories. (A Public Affair usually focused on the "background.") Commercial pressures and fear of controversy, he said, make it virtually impossible for network news organizations to come to grips with the vital issues of the day in either their evening newscasts or their all-too-infrequent documentaries. (NPACT made the time and the effort to cover issues commercial television rarely touched.) The very techniques of television news, said MacNeil, took precedence over its content.[44] NPACT's programs did not let form dictate content. Where network news avoided "talking heads" at almost any cost, NPACT programs like Washington Week in Review were all talking heads. A Public Affair covered the story of the 1972 election without hype. To those accustomed to the highly visual, peripatetic style of commercial television news, the program could be quite a letdown. But for the most part, NPACT's election coverage and its other political programs were critical and, by public television standards, popular successes.

A Public Affair: Election '72 began in a somewhat inauspicious manner amid the Vanocur controversy of December 1971 with a program entitled, "Polopoly; the Game of Politics." MacNeil and Vanocur conducted a preview of the upcoming political campaign surrounded by

a giant-sized Monopoly board with the Broadways, Park
Places and Marvin Gardens of American politics. The
correspondents presided over the scene seated on a
similarly elephantine pair of dice.[45] It was the first
and last time the Center bothered with such visual
gimmicks.

A Public Affair: Election '72 began its
regular weekly thirty-minute presentations on February 2,
1972 with a report on one of the most basic, but least
understood procedures in American politics, how the
delegates to national conventions are chosen. The show
greatly improved upon "Polopoly" and The Washington Post
called it an "admirable, honest beginning" to the
election series.[46] Subsequent shows usually focused on
presidential politics at the grass-roots, nuts and bolts
level. The series attempted to get away from the network
news practice of following candidates around the country,
to explore the issues, the people, and the processes
involved in a national election campaign. Election '72
examined the voting behavior and political significance
of specific socio-economic and ethnic blocks of voters;
blue-collar workers in South Milwaukee; young non-student
voters; Jewish voters; black Americans; Hispanic-
Americans at their own convention in El Paso, Texas; the
rapidly changing South; and, in a Vanocur report
entitled, "Will it Play in Peoria?", Middle-America.
Some programs attempted in-depth analyses of certain
aspects of the political process itself: the primary
system; political polling; federal election campaign
financing laws; the role of the political reporter and of
the professional image-makers in campaigns; and, in "Make
Policy, Not Coffee," the changing role of women in
politics. Finally, there were shows pegged to specific
issues and incidents in the course of the campaign: the
Wallace assassination attempt; the political significance

of Nixon's trip to mainland China; an investigation of
the dilemma facing the Republican National Committee in
relocating its convention from San Diego to Miami Beach;
the scramble for delegates; the shape of the major party
campaigns, as well as the minor ones; a conversation with
the McGoverns; the impact of a Nixon visit to Atlanta and
a McGovern stop in a small mid-western town. In its
weekly half-hour, A Public Affair: Election '72
attempted to illuminate the country's political life from
a truly "new perspective" for television journalism. The
shows were not always successful. They could sometimes
be so "educational" in tone that they were just plain
boring. But it was difficult to argue that NPACT's
productions were consistently biased for, or against,
anyone or anything.

Reactions from the public stations ran the
gamut from highly favorable to intensely negative. The
wide range of comments demonstrated only the subjectivity
of each individual viewer's response to this type of
programming. Some perceived the liberal editorial bias
they -- and the Nixon White House -- had expected, while
others were surprised by the lack of any perceptible
ideological viewpoint. A Public Affair, one station
manager said, was the single most important program to
his station's image. One manager commented, "There seems
to be a real conscious effort for balance, especially
since the formation and development of NPACT." But
another felt, "Most programming has a liberal bias and
too much Washington-centered, aside from the fact that
most of PBS/NPACT programs are dull and dreary and
uninspired." If one station executive commented that A
Public Affair was superb and a much-needed alternative,
another complained about "Eastern liberal bias" and "too
much politics."[47] But NPACT's A Public Affair proved
unbiased and insightful enough for the United States

Information Agency to request a large portion of the
series for use in foreign embassy educational programs.
Similarly, the U.S. Air Force Academy asked that NPACT
allow it to use segments of A Public Affair, as well as
Thirty Minutes With... and Washington Week in Review in
its political science courses.[48] NPACT received letters
from some viewers who believed that its election coverage
was biased against, and had purposely ignored, Senator
George McGovern's primary campaign; and from those who
complained of bias in favor of the Democratic candidate.
In short, the reactions from critics, viewers and
professional public broadcasters, taken together, proved
that ideological bias was most clearly in the eye of the
beholder.

In response to a February TV Guide editorial
that criticized public television for hiring two highly
paid correspondents who might express views contrary to
those of the taxpayers who helped support them, the
Seattle Post-Intelligencer's Frank Chesley took up the
issue of liberal bias on NPACT programs. Vanocur's
personal beliefs were well-known, Chesley said. "He is
sometimes imperious, sometimes obnoxious, usually
outspoken. But he is one of the best political reporters
in the country." Chesley called A Public Affair's most
recent program, "The Primary Purpose," "enlightening and,
to us political neophytes, fascinating. I kept waiting
for Vanocur to slip in some 'liberal bias,' but the piece
was quite non-partisan. And so much for 'contrary
political views . . . .'"[49]

A Public Affair continued to have some flaws,
but as Broadcasting magazine reported in the spring of
1972, the program's reception by critics, public
television managers and the public made the controversies
of the previous autumn over Vanocur and the salaries seem
remote. Vanocur and MacNeil, vaguely described as

"liberal," but perceived by some "as a balding Yippie and his icy blond sidekick," had quietly begun to make their mark on public television. "A Public Affair had been enthusiastically received by the critics. Inside public television there is neither wild excitement, outrage or boredom; the series is generally seen as a solid addition to the schedule. . . ."[50]

Despite the growing praise and the relative popularity of NPACT's programming, the Center's entire staff was highly conscious of the ambivalence toward it in much of the public television industry, from the stations to the CPB board. They, in turn, saw the system as generally weak-kneed and soft-spined. Public broadcasters, Sander Vanocur said, "were all nervous to begin with. They suffer from the 'dole mentality' and they're much more anxious to have meetings than ever produce anything. And my coming in and Robin coming in to do serious political reporting . . . scared them even more. They thought, 'My God, what do we need this for? We've got this nice little thing going and now these two guys come up and we're threatened to be cut off from funds."[51] Vanocur thought that NPACT was unfairly bearing the burden of the less professional, "gun-slinging" journalistic programs that had gotten public television into trouble in the past. MacNeil saw that Whitehead's arguments against any public affairs programming had struck a soft spot in the public television system. "Certainly," he said, "there was a large group of people in public television, probably the great majority at the time, who didn't think public television needed to be, or should be, in the news and public affairs business at all, that it should be a cultural tool. And the other networks did 'grubby journalism.'"[52] MacNeil felt strongly that the only way to convince the skeptics and build respect for journalism

in the part-publicly funded institution, in the minds of
all its opponents, within and without, was to "tell it
straight." That meant fairness and objectivity, which is
what he and Vanocur were clearly striving for in A Public
Affair.

Much of NPACT general manager Jim Karayn's
energies went into the institutional and political
infighting that characterized the Center's brief
existence. He tried to keep the correspondents out of
the political battles. Their relationship with him was
often strained because of it. Vanocur and MacNeil
sometimes thought that Karayn became overly "nervous"
from all the pressure over controversial programs. But
Karayn saw it as his job to act as a buffer between the
creative people and the institutional concerns. "I'd
never tell Sandy that they're kicking the shit out of us
today," Karayn said. "It couldn't help but affect them.
No matter how much they said, 'Well, I'm going to be
objective.' I mean, after all, it's their lives; it's
their livelihoods. . . . And, so, you try to keep that
out of their thinking."[53] Yet the public television
stations, faced at the end of 1971 with controversies
over public affairs programming, opposition from the
White House, and the threat of a cut-off in federal
funding, saw a wholly independent NPACT as a menace to
the system. As in the case of the NET-WNET merger,
public television leaders felt that the only way to quiet
the debate was to make the Center a part of a PBS member
station, subject to the same pressures and concerns as
the other 220 stations. NPACT's management strenuously
resisted a merger with Washington's local station, WETA,
believing that their focus on national programming would
be diluted and their energies expended on too many non-
programming issues. At the outset, Karayn had agreed to
form NPACT only on the condition that it not be dependent

on the local station. But those who were seeking to
moderate the tensions and achieve workable compromises
with the government and within the system itself, saw a
merger as the easiest way to tame the beast. By January
1973, NPACT and WETA would both be divisions of the
Greater Washington Educational Television Association.

The proposed merger was only one way in which
public television's leaders reneged on their commitment
to an independent public affairs production center. The
other was on the amount of funding. At its April 17
meeting, the CPB board heard the recommendations of its
program advisory committee, chaired by Jack Wrather. The
committee agreed that public affairs should remain an
area of activity for CPB funding -- thought the
corporation would make no grants for programs containing
"partisan political commentary." But, Wrather told the
board, "It was observed that because of the sensitive
nature of public affairs programming, a concentration of
this kind of production in one of two stations is
undesirable; further decentralization and diversification would be healthy for the system." To that end the
committee recommended one important modification in the
staff's proposed grants: CPB's fiscal 1973 funding of
NPACT should be cut twenty-five percent; the savings --
$400,000 -- should be distributed among local stations
for their own public affairs efforts.[54]

This move clearly contradicted the very logic
that had created NPACT in the first place -- that is, the
need to concentrate limited resources to assure maximum
quality and quantity of public affairs programming. The
cut was due to take effect on July 1, 1972 and therefore
killed the Center's plans for gavel-to-gavel coverage of
the Democratic and Republican national conventions.

A week after the CPB board made its decision,
WETA and NPACT chairman Sidney James sent Corporation

chairman Frank Pace memos prepared by Karayn and WETA president Donald Taverner detailing the profound impact the budget cut could have not only on NPACT's programming, but on the proposed merger of the Center and the Washington station. Karayn's seventeen-page memorandum argued forcefully that the proposal to spread around the money shaved from NPACT's budget would result in less public affairs program diversity, rather than more. Moreover, he said, the cut would make it virtually impossible to cover the start-up costs in combining the two organizations and thereby achieve future economies. "We can continue to do the almost impossible with our limited resources," Karayn concluded, "we cannot work complete magic with even more diluted funds."[55]

A few days later, CPB board member Tom Moore sent Clay Whitehead a copy of the memos from Karayn, Taverner, and James with a note: "Attached is the material that almost brought about a reconsideration [of the funding cut], but I believe the issue is dead, and that Frank Pace will have responded to the effect no reconsideration is possible." Moore included a copy of the most recent NAEB newsletter, directing Whitehead to a small item on page two, "Covering the '72 Election: The Ways and Means." It was good news for the White House. "Fiscal considerations, predictably, are having a major impact on the style and scope of the '72 presidential election coverage, both at the national and the local station level in public broadcasting."

"Faced with a $400,000 cut from its $1.6 million CPB grant," the article continued, "the National Public Affairs Center for Television finds its plans to provide on-the-scene coverage of the Democratic and Republican national conventions effectively blocked."[56]

Despite the severe cut-back in NPACT funding, the White House effort to control public television was not faring well by the spring of 1972. On the long-run objectives of eliminating the use of federal funds for public affairs programming and reducing the influence of the Corporation for Broadcasting by dispersing money and power to the local stations, Whitehead conceded that the results, thus far, had been less than spectacular. He told the President in late April, "We have had little success in convincing most of those involved in public broadcasting (including some of our friends) that coverage of public affairs should be eliminated in the long-run."[57] CPB's decision to cut $400,000 from NPACT's budget was not really much of a victory for the White House forces on the board. Moore's plan had aimed for an end to all Corporation funding for national public affairs. The board only passed a narrowly focused prohibition against the underwriting of partisan political commentary which, in fact, had no effect on any of public television's current offerings. At the same meeting where Wrather proposed the $400,000 NPACT cut, James R. Killian proposed, and the board unanimously approved, a resolution reaffirming its support of public affairs programming.[58] Killian, chairman of the Carnegie Commission, the "father of public television," was not happy with what was happening to his offspring. He was strongly opposed to his fellow CPB directors who wanted to trade-in public affairs for guaranteed federal funding. He felt that some of the board's newer members were not accustomed to "public trusteeship," and were too responsive to the political pressures. Killian thought it simply unacceptable not to have national public affairs programs underwritten by the Corporation and he strenuously resisted the attempts to cut back on their funding. He knew that the White House was greatly displeased by Sander Vanocur and NPACT; Nixon cabinet member George Shultz, a former colleague at MIT, had

personally told him so. But that seemed all the more
reason for them to have the board's unequivocal support.
Killian did not think that the system was more
centralized than his Carnegie report had envisioned and
he rejected as "spurious" the White House's
interpretation of the "bedrock of localism" phrase.[59]
During that spring, a large majority on Capitol Hill were
inclined to agree with Killian. The public broadcasting
financing bill then moving through Congress was a
considerable repudiation of the administration's position
on federal funding.

In his memo to the President, Whitehead pledged
"a strong and emotional fight on the House floor" to
"limit funding to one year and keep funding at the
current level of $35 million or at least no more than the
$445 million requested in your budget."[60] Whitehead was
counting on OTP's ability to work with congressmen
friendly to the White House in stopping legislation
inimical to administration objectives. On the other
side, the entire public broadcasting establishment, CPB,
PBS, NAEB, and Ralph Rogers' chairmen's group, mobilized
to lobby in favor of increased, multi-year funding. In
May, OTP provided Illinois Republican Congressman Bob
Michel with a list of questions regarding the NAEB's
position on funding, the current programming and
structural emphasis on the public television system. The
OTP agenda sought to capitalize on all of the most
potentially damaging issues:

> How do you feel about charges that have
> been made that the Corporation for
> Public Broadcasting and Public Service
> are building a fourth network?

> Are the local station managers happy
> with the job being done by the
> Corporation for Public Broadcasting?

Recently there has been a lot of
controversy in the press about news and
public affairs on public television. Do
you feel that Federal money should be
used for national news and public
affairs?

What is your opinion of the new National
Public Affairs Center for Television?

How do you feel about the salaries being
paid to certain performers on public
television; for example, Bill Moyers--
$75,000 a year, Robert MacNeil--$65,000
a year, and Sander Vanocur--$85,000 a
year? Do we need to pay these kind of
salaries to have a good public
broadcasting system?

Does it bother you that the Ford
Foundation, which has given over $200
million to public television, has so
much influence over the programming that
is done both nationally and locally?[61]

OTP did not get the responses it desired from
the representatives of the local stations. On May 11,
Michel's administrative assistant sent Whitehead's
assistant, Brian Lamb, the NAEB's answers. Testifying on
behalf of the association, Chalmers Marquis refused to
take the OTP-inspired bait and attack the national public
television institutions. He supported CPB's basic
position on almost every point. Were station managers
happy with the Corporation's activities? "The answer,"
Marquis gave, "was a resounding yes." Should federal
money go to public affairs programming? "Yes, and the
Congress itself has expressed its conviction in this
also." How did the stations feel about NPACT and the fat
salaries going to Vanocur, MacNeil, and Moyers? The
system's general acceptance of NPACT programs was
indicated by the large number of stations broadcasting
them. The salary questions, Marquis said, had generated

much heat, but little light. Clearly, the salaries were
perfectly reasonable considering the talent they brought.
Did the Ford Foundation's $200 million worth of
"influence" over programming bother public broadcasters?
"No. Presumably any agency which is provided $200
million for national programming over the last 15 years
has had an effect on the system . . . . But we regard
that effect to have been enormously beneficial to the
American people." What types of programs did the
stations feel that CPB should spend its money on? Number
one, above cultural and children's programs, was national
public affairs.[62]

     Clearly, whatever support the White House had
from local stations in its efforts to de-emphasize CPB
and spread the money around, it was quickly losing
because of its continued opposition to increased funding,
which the stations desperately needed. The Corporation's
offer to provide thirty percent of its federal allocation
directly to local stations and to include more station
managers on the PBS board of directors was, the NAEB
felt, a very good start towards the kind of decentralized
system the stations wanted. The White House and its few
hard core supporters on the Hill stood alone in their
opposition to any increase in funding levels.

     On June 1, the House began debate on a
compromise authorization bill which provided $65 million
for CPB in fiscal year 1973 and $90 million in 1974. The
White House was still pushing for a one-year, $45 million
appropriation. In connection with House consideration of
the legislation, OTP prepared a number of statements
critical of public broadcasting for use by House members.
One such statement, drafted for Ohio Congressman Sam
Devine, talked about NET's leftist programming and
dominance of the prime time PBS schedule. If allowed to
continue its predominance, the statement read, NET would

subject the American public "to a view of 'culture' and current events filtered through the particular points of view represented by New York City program producers." Other OTP statements drafted for Representatives Jim Harvey and Bob Michel questioned the lobbying activities of CPB, NAEB, and individual public television broadcast licensees; the salaries paid to Vanocur and MacNeil; the "expensive advertising campaign mounted by PBS to huckster its network programming"; the carriage of allegedly cultural events "in which nudity is the prime attraction"; the balance and objectivity of specific PBS programs; and the influence of the Ford Foundation in public television.[63] Nevertheless, the June 7 House vote was overwhelmingly in favor of the two-year, $155 million bill, 256 to 69.[64]

When the Senate Commerce Committee reported the bill, recommending its enactment as passed by the House, Senators Howard Baker, Norris Cotton, and Robert Griffin added their own supplemental statement in opposition to the two-year authorization. The Statement called the $155 million appropriation "inappropriate at this time," because the Congress still had no idea of CPB's future needs. The operational experience of CPB, it said, had only served to "raise new questions and new doubts" about the Corporation's role in the system and relationship to the local stations. "CPB," it concluded, "has not stated clearly how it intends to use its increased funding to serve the financial and operating needs of the local station autonomy and independence within the national public broadcasting system."[65] The statement was also drafted by OTP. Despite the best efforts of the administration and its supporters in the Senate, on June 22, H.R. 13919 was passed by a vote of 82 to 1.[66]

On the day of the Senate vote, a conference took place in the office of Norman Cousins in New York.

Cousins and his colleagues on the National Programming
Council (an independent public television advisory
organization) invited Whitehead to the meeting to discuss
the future needs of the public medium. One of those in
attendance was the Ford Foundation's Fred Friendly, who
later recounted that at the last minute, Whitehead could
not attend because of pressing commitments in Washington,
but agreed to speak with the group through a telephone
conference hook-up. As Friendly described it, Cousins
asked, "Dr. Whitehead, if the Congress authorizes more
funds than the $45 million a year the Administration is
requesting, will the President sign it? Will he veto it?
Whitehead's reply seemed unequivocal: "I can tell you
that if the Congress votes that authorization the
President will do nothing to prevent that action from
moving forward."[67]

In fact, Whitehead and Nixon would do whatever
was needed to prevent the Senate bill from "moving
forward." Whitehead and the OTP were implacably opposed
to the two-year funding bill that had emerged from
Congress. "We felt so strongly that two-year funding was
a palliative," Whitehead said. It did not provide the
kind of structural checks and balances that, in his view,
called for a significant government commitment.
Therefore, two-year funding was bad on both counts, he
said. "It was not long-term and public broadcasting
didn't have its house in order to warrant any vote of
confidence."[68] OTP staff members agreed that it was a
bad bill and that the President ought to veto it. The
OTP director must have also known when he told the
National Programming Council that the President would do
nothing to stand in the way of the legislation's passage
that Nixon would be highly receptive to the idea of
vetoing public broadcasting funding legislation. He
might not have been terribly concerned with

decentralization that Whitehead spoke of, but Nixon harbored a very personal antipathy toward public television and its leading lights. He _could_ prevent any more government money from going to Sander Vanocur and friends.

Later that same afternoon another meeting bearing on public television took place in Washington. A select group of thirty independent commercial television station executives met with the President at the White House for almost an hour and a half. Whitehead was present at this gathering, along with Peter Flanigan, FCC chairman Dean Burch and White House Communications director Herbert Klein. The reported agenda included such issues as license renewal and cable television. Part of the discussion that went unreported dealt with the "threat of public television and its use of government and tax-free funds to compete for a share of the viewing audience." Whitehead's notes of the meeting showed that the President had expressed strong personal feelings on this sensitive issue. He told the commercial broadcasters that he had travelled extensively abroad and had seen what government-sponsored television was like; "and in spite of the growing reports of many people that government-controlled broadcasting produces high-quality programming, no commercials, etc., he stated that no one should be fooled -- that was a bunch of crap." He also felt that there was a danger that future presidents might be inclined to use federal support of public broadcasting to their own political advantage. Since "you never know who's going to be sitting in this chair next," Nixon said, "public broadcasting, particularly the use of federal funds, should be kept under the strictest control and not be allowed to become too large."[69] To commercial broadcasters whose viewership was beginning to be eroded in many major markets by the growth of public broadcasting, Nixon's attitude was reassuring. From the President's point of view, it was highly advantageous politically to reassure independent broadcasters in the middle of his re-election campaign.[70]

Four days later, Whitehead's secret memorandum to the President recommended that he veto the public broadcasting funding bill and force Congress to agree to a single-year, $45 million appropriation as the administration had originally proposed. There would assuredly be criticism that the administration was "trying to intimidate the media," and a great animosity towards the White House among professional public broadcasters. Nevertheless, Whitehead said,

> There is not a large viewing audience
> for public TV, nor does the public seem
> very aware of it. The professional
> public broadcasters at CPB and in the
> local non-commercial stations, however,
> are becoming an effective lobbying
> constituency in the Congress. In the
> name of 'public' broadcasting, they are
> seeking funds and independence to create
> a TV network reflecting their narrow
> conception of what the public ought to
> see and hear. This should not be
> allowed to happen.

Therefore, said Whitehead, "I strongly recommend that you veto the CPB financing legislation." Whitehead also looked to the future and told the President what public broadcasters had been hearing from him since October. "Whichever course you choose," he told Nixon, "I believe that we should retract our commitment to the early development of a plan for long-term, insulated financing for CPB. While the goal of insulating CPB from government pressure is sound, the public broadcasting community has not demonstrated the responsibility or maturity to justify such funding."[71]

On June 30, the President vetoed the CPB authorization bill. In his veto message, which Whitehead drafted, he pointed to the serious and widespread concern "expressed in Congress and within public broadcasting itself -- that an organization originally intended only to serve the local stations, is becoming instead the center of power and the focal point of control for the entire public broadcasting system." The problems of long-term funding, he said, were far greater than originally thought, and could not be resolved "until the structure of public broadcasting has been more firmly established, and we have a more extensive record of experience on which to evaluate its role in our national life."[72]

From OTP's point of view, the passage of the two-year funding had been an unqualified defeat. "It was a slap at OTP," said Henry Goldberg, who was highly supportive of the veto. The success of the two-year funding legislation demonstrated to public and commercial broadcasting alike that the Office of Telecommunications Policy could be ignored. It showed, Goldberg explained, that "all you had to do was go around OTP; you never had to invite Whitehead to an NAEB convention anymore. You could go to the Congress and get legislation."

> With the veto, Whitehead took the two-by-four and got everyone's attention again and said, 'you can get it through the Congress, but I still have something to say about it. You're still going to have to come back here to deal with OTP.' The veto at the time was viewed as essential to the workings of OTP. OTP was probably the most ignorable agency in the government. It had no function. It could not deny you a grant, because it did not have the money to grant you. It had no operating power, except for federal government

frequencies. The thing that OTP lived
most in fear of was people getting wise
to the fact that it was completely
ignorable; that it was done with lights
and mirrors and smoke. The legislation
passing the Congress demonstrated that
OTP was kind of a nothing. The veto was
viewed as essential to say, 'We still
have to be contended with.' We just had
to convince the President to veto the
legislation. As it turned out, it
wasn't very hard to convince him because
he hated public broadcasting.[73]

CHAPTER FIVE

WELCOME TO THE NEW PUBLIC TELEVISION

"The politicization of Public Television is complete. . . . It would appear that CPB rather than serving public television as insulation from political influence and control, has opted to serve the Congress and the White House as their insulation from the dangers of public television."

--James Day, November 1972

Reaction to President Nixon's veto of the public broadcasting legislation was immediate and intense. Indeed, White House OTP director Clay Whitehead had anticipated both the "liberal howl" on Capitol Hill and the antipathy of professional public broadcasters. Representative Robert O. Tiernan told his colleagues in the House that there was no better testimony than the President's veto that the threat to localism came not from CPB, PBS, or NPACT, but from the White House, and no better proof of Douglass Cater's assertion that the public broadcasting system was capable of being manipulated by budgetary and appointive pressures from the executive branch.[1] He claimed that the real objective of the veto was to emasculate NPACT and prevent aggressive coverage of Nixon's bid for reelection.

Torbert MacDonald, who had labored the hardest to push through the CPB authorization bill, called the President's action "an incredible sacrifice of the public interest on the altar of partisan politics." "I am absolutely convinced," he said, "that this administration has decided that their interest will be best passed by muzzling the voice of public broadcasting directly."[2]

Representative Harley Staggers, chairman of the House Interstate and Foreign Commerce Committee which had reported the bill to the full House said, "I am shocked and terribly disappointed. This is not a political matter. The entire nation benefits from the Corporation for Public Broadcasting under the able leadership of its president, John Macy. The bill was co-sponsored by three Republicans . . . . It was passed by the House 256 to 69 and by the Senate 82 to 1. Why the President vetoed it I cannot understand." Public television advocate Senator Frank Moss of Utah called the veto "outrageous" and, in an allusion to public television's highly regarded children's programs, said the President "would have Sesame Street and Mister Rogers as his puppets. But without Corporation for Public Broadcasting funding, we will have no Big Bird or Cookie Monster just Oscar the Grouch in the White House using the children of America as his pawns in the funding battle for CPB."[3]

NPACT executive Jim Karayn commented, "either the President is getting very bad advice on public television from his people, or the charges . . . that he and his administration are trying to put a muzzle on are true." He submitted that the veto was actually counter-productive to professed administration goals since it was "fallacious to reason that cutting funds is going to hurt the national service and help build up the local." "The kind of money Nixon is allocating," he said, "will for most stations just about pay the rent."[4]

KCET president and general manager James Loper called the veto "a direct slap in the face to the American people."[5] Chalmers Marquis of the NAEB, which represented the local stations, explained, "If allowed to stand, the President's veto takes away funds desperately

needed by public broadcasting stations. . . . This
decision will cause a real loss in service to the people
of the U.S., including a loss in quality programming, and
represents a major step backwards."[6]

In the print media, condemnation of the veto
was widespread, although some newspapers, like the
Chicago Tribune, applauded it. In a lead editorial, the
Tribune printed a list of public television's yearly
appropriations from $5 million in 1969 to a projected $90
million in 1974 and said, "Even if there were no other
issues involved, it would be hard to justify these
snowballing appropriations for public broadcasting at a
time when the Administration is trying wisely and
desperately to hold down federal spending on other
programs, some considerably more urgent than public
broadcasting."[7] But most major newspapers recognized
that there were other issues involved, far more important
to the White House than controlling the federal budget.
"The record suggests," said the Los Angeles Times, "that
all of Mr. Nixon's reasons for the veto were not included
in the veto message." The Times rejected the President's
charge that the Public Broadcasting Service was an
unnecessary fourth network. Public affairs programs
produced by NPACT, it said, offered "a depth and maturity
and detail rarely available on commercial television."
Congressional support for the two-year funding bill, it
concluded, was overwhelming. "We hope that same support
can now be used to override the veto."[8] Other newspapers
were not as restrained in their criticism of the
President's action. Many regional papers reported the
specific amount of funding that their local PBS station
stood to lose because of the veto. The Louisville Times
said, "All the self-serving rhetoric out of the White
House cannot disguise President Nixon's veto of the bill
providing two-year financing for the Corporation for

"I'll Tell You Everything You Need To Know"

---from Herblock's State of the Union (Simon & Schuster, 1972)

Public Broadcasting as anything more than an effort to intimidate and censor public television."[9] Indeed, most editorial writers, like the public broadcasters themselves, saw the glaring hypocrisy in the White House's "philosophical" objections to a centralized system and its admission that the best programs did, in fact, come from the national service. The Christian Science Monitor declared unequivocally, "The charge that public TV is New York-dominated shows both a phobia over the Eastern Establishment and an ignorance of its nature. . . . To underfund public television out of fear of its partisan political effect is itself a partisan action, whose long-term effect on the quality of American life will be definitely negative."[10]

At the June 30 press briefing, White House press secretary Ron Ziegler, assisted by OTP's Brian Lamb, repeatedly denied that President Nixon's action had anything to do with partisan concerns. Reporters kept after Ziegler for a clear explanation of the veto, but he never did provide one. The President's spokesman was evasive. One newsman asked about Whitehead's statement to the National Programming Council in New York a week earlier that the President would sign the bill then on the Senate floor. "Now he has vetoed it. What happened to change his mind?" Ziegler: "I don't know quite the context in which Mr. Whitehead may have made these remarks."

Question: "Ron, did this subject come up in the discussions and briefings with the television owners and executives in the last two meetings here in the White House?"

Ziegler: "Only in general terms and the discussions at that time really were quite brief in nature, but I think reflected the President's view as put forth at that time and is reflected in the statement you have before you."

Reporter: "Did they reflect their view to him?"

Ziegler: "Well, the individuals that the President met with were not specifically involved with educational television or public broadcasting. . . ."

Reporter: "Ron, does the alleged political affiliation of any members of the Public Broadcasting staff have anything to do whatever with this veto?"

Ziegler: "No, nothing at all."

Reporter: ". . . Does the President object to political themes appearing in programming on what we tend to call educational television?"

Ziegler: "Well, I think this is a question that should be addressed."

"I asked what the President feels."

"My answer to you is that I think I best convey the President's view to you by saying that there is question whether or not tax dollars should be used to fund an extensive national public affairs programming, which is then distributed across the country, whether or not that is the best way for educational television to go, versus funding of local stations for development of cultural and educational programming."

"What is the answer to the question? Does the President object to political themes?"

"I don't quite know what you mean by political themes," Ziegler said. Later, at the end of the press conference, the question was raised again: "Is the President objecting to spending too much money on public affairs network broadcasting that is political [sic] biased or not?"

"You can make that judgment as well as I can."

"I am asking," the reporter insisted, "whether the President has made that judgment."

"The question," Ziegler replied, "goes more to whether or not public broadcasting should devote a great amount of the funding and whether or not the funding should provide for extensive programming of this sort, and networked out . . . in such a great degree.

"In other words, just to conclude the point, should public broadcasting really develop a news and public affairs pattern that is competitive with the commercial television networks, is that the role?"[11]

To most of the press, Ziegler's equivocation merely confirmed that the President's veto had little to do with structure and localism.

In a July 21 New York Times Op-Ed piece, Douglass Cater argued compellingly that the White House's positions on decentralization and single-year funding were inherently contradictory. Cater had been Lyndon Johnson's advisor on public broadcasting and had been instrumental in the passage of the 1967 public broadcasting act. Currently, he was directing the Aspen Institute on Communications and Society, which had commissioned two Stanford University professors to undertake a study on public television financing. Though Wilbur Schramm and Lyle Nelson had not yet completed their study, their preliminary estimates of the probable costs involved in funding a truly effective national public broadcasting system demonstrated, Cater insisted, that the administration's opposition to increased federal funding only increased the system's present difficulties. He wrote that even if all the current level of federal funding were to be parcelled out to the local stations, it would buy only a few minutes a week of low cost local programming. Less money would mean greater dependence on central production sources; not increased diversity.

"The President," Cater suggested, "paradoxically has proved his point; his veto raises legitimate fears of a central system capable of being manipulated by the White House."[12] A week later in the same space, Sunday editor Lester Markel declared that "the government has been involved in an unholy crusade against public television."[13] The Charlotte Observer likewise concluded, "Mr. Nixon's veto seems to us to be one more example of his dislike of television programming, public or commercial, that provide in-depth examination of matters that sometimes are embarrassing to him as a politician. It is the same kind of motivation that has moved him to attack primarily through Vice President Spiro Agnew and other administration spokesmen, the work of newspapers and TV news organizations when they do not present, unevaluated, the views of the government.

"We hope Congress will slap him down on this. Responsible public television, operating without having to kowtow to the government, is more important than Mr. Nixon's politics."[14]

But Congress did not attempt an override of Nixon's veto. Senator Pastore introduced the administration's request for a one-year, $45 million authorization. The Senate passed the measure by a voice vote without debate. In the House, Torbet MacDonald reluctantly accepted the White House version of the funding bill. On August 2, MacDonald said, "Mr. Speaker, it is with easily restrained enthusiasm that I rise to support a bill designed to breathe some life, if only a little, into non-commercial educational broadcasting, for the next year." But he pledged to his colleagues to "continue to oppose, as strenuously as I know how, the naked pressure that the Office of Telecommunications Policy puts on public television by implicit or direct threats, promises or divisive tactics."[15] On August 15

the new CPB legislation passed the House by a vote of 377
to 8. Two weeks later, the President signed into law the
Public Broadcasting Financing Act of 1972.[16]

For the leadership of the Corporation for
Public Broadcasting, the veto was a disaster. It
achieved for Whitehead and the administration the long-
sought resignations of John Macy as CPB president and
Frank Pace as board chairman. On the morning of the veto
announcement, Whitehead met with Pace to inform him of
Nixon's action. At that time, Pace asked the OTP
director to tell the President that he intended not to
stand for reelection as chairman of the board of
directors of CPB in the fall. Pace indicated, however,
that he would nevertheless remain on the board of the
Corporation, and Whitehead "encouraged him to do so."[17]

It was John Macy, the chief operating officer
of the Corporation, who was hurt most by the veto of the
funding legislation he had worked so hard to obtain.
Throughout the spring, Nixon appointees on the board had
hounded him about the criticism that CPB was receiving
from the White House and its supporters in Congress.
Based on the strategy outlined in discussions with
Whitehead and Flanigan, board member Jack Wrather (who
hosted the spring board meeting at California's
Disneyland) set a tone of "no confidence" in John Macy
and his staff. John Golden, then CPB's director of
planning, research and evaluation, remembered that
Wrather had tried "to establish beyond a doubt that John
Macy was a hired hand," and that he had caused the board
great embarrassment by permitting the system to race out
of control.[18] Wrather told his fellow board members that
the program advisory committee, which he chaired, felt
that it had to take the responsibility for reviewing the
management's program recommendations and reporting its
conclusions to the full board for its consideration.

But, Wrather complained, the Corporation staff had failed to provide sufficient information for the committee to make its decisions. Because of this restriction, "the committee was unable to recommend that the board approve funding for the entire program schedule submitted by the management." Consequently, all funding decisions for the rapidly approaching season had to be postponed until a special meeting scheduled for the following month in New York.[19]

John Macy had tried desperately to steer a moderate course by agreeing to some administration demands in order to assure passage of a multi-year funding plan that would finally give public television some kind of independence. Some at PBS, NPACT, and the Ford Foundation felt that Macy's softness on the salary issue was a slap at Vanocur and MacNeil. Many at the national production centers resented CPB's attempts to move into the program decisionmaking area, seeing it merely as an effort to appease a White House and Congress concerned about controversial and political subject matter. Yet, Macy's position on the most substantive point -- that PBS should be a strong center for the national system and the principal beneficiary of Corporation support -- had been in sharp contrast to the administration's view that more funds should be spent locally. Those station managers who had supported the White House push for greater decentralization were sometimes viciously critical of the CPB president. Dr. John Schwarzwalder, president of station KCTA in Minneapolis-St. Paul, reflected their antagonism towards Macy and the other national leaders when he said in June, "The suicide, figurative or actual, of about half of those now in charge of [the public television] movement . . . would bet a net gain to America."[20]

As Sander Vanocur later suggested, Macy was "caught in a terrible position."[21] The criticism came at him from every angle. If public television achieved some great success, PBS usually reaped the credit. If there was controversy, Macy was the man who had to face the Congress and the White House. The CPB president was often in a "no-win" situation. To complicate matters further, at the beginning of the summer, Macy was forced to cease his active duties as Corporation chief executive by emergency abdominal surgery. Later in the summer he would have to undergo a second operation. The veto, one CPB official said privately, was "the last straw" for the frustrated, embattled, and ailing Macy.

On July 24, upon returning to his home in MacLean, Virginia after his first bout of surgery in Phoenix, Macy wrote to Whitehead, "I must confess that the news from Washington on June 30 with respect to the authorization had less than a recuperative effect. In the interests of lowered rhetoric I will not actually report my verbal observations at the time." The CPB president and the OTP director had disagreed sharply over the previous year and the antagonism had grown personal at times. Nonetheless, both tried to be gracious. A few weeks later, after returning to Washington from an extended trip in the South Pacific, Whitehead wrote to Macy, "I returned from overseas to find your letter of July 24 and was happy to learn of your safe passage through surgery. . . . I realize what your feelings must have been with regard to the President's veto, and I'm sorry that it had less than a recuperative effect on your health."[22]

On August 10, Macy officially resigned as president of the Corporation for Public Broadcasting. In his letter to chairman Pace he said, "You are aware of my growing belief that current trends in the development of the Public Broadcasting industry point toward the desirability of a change in the leadership of the Corporation." Macy told his associates privately that Nixon's reelection would be "the death blow to public broadcasting as I envision it," and expressed disappointment that certain quarters of the industry itself had not supported him in his efforts to make CPB a strong national organization.[23] He thought the CPB board's acceptance of the veto, without protest or comment, shameful. "Money came before standing or principal and they [the board] were unwilling to accept the veto as an indictment of their performance. To have that veto, and that veto message on the books, without any challenge from the system, it seemed to me was a complete repudiation. And that therefore, I had no further role that I could effectively play and my presence on the scene was a liability to whatever development was going to occur during the Nixon Administration."[24]

The board members, even those who strongly opposed the veto, felt that it served no purpose to openly antagonize the White House. "I saw no reason to go public with rancorous debate," said Jack Valenti. "It would just harden attitudes. I thought it was much better to work within the board to try to convince people to a point of view."[25] The CPB board never formally discussed passage of a resolution opposing the veto of its own financing legislation. Macy took off for Nantucket Island to recuperate from his operation and from his battles with the White House, its appointees, and much of the public broadcasting system. "It seemed to me," he later said, "that those who had any governance responsibility to the system should have spoken out, but that was not done. The station managers and licensee board of governors saw the veto as a threat to future funding and they decided that the flavor of boots was not as unpleasant as they had thought."[26]

A week after Macy's resignation, John Witherspoon, vice president of the Corporation in charge of television activities, also resigned, citing the "dismally frustrating job" of building a broadcasting system under constant federal scrutiny. "Given the difficult political context, too little money, and our well-known tendency for self-destruction, the building of a system sometimes seems beyond comprehension."[27] Most of the Corporation's top executives would follow suit in the weeks ahead.

Reaction to Macy's resignation was, at times, passionate. Federal Communications Commissioner Nicholas Johnson sent letters to Senator Pastore and Representative MacDonald saying, "I have watched with growing dismay and outrage as President Nixon, acting through his Office of Telecommunications Policy, Vice President and others, has tried at every turn to frustrate the development of public broadcasting, to limit its growth and potential, and turn its programs to its own political ends. Now that the Nixon administration's goal of molding public broadcasting into a domestic Voice of America is clear for all to see, and a great American like John Macy is hounded out of office at a time when he is recovering from surgery," said Commissioner Johnson, "I can no longer remain silent." Johnson concluded by telling the committee chairmen that if the White House was going to start using the CPB as a means of "feeding the American people the Administration's partisan propaganda," he believed that the Congress "should seriously consider full-scale hearings on the disaster."[28]

With the departure of Macy and Pace and a Republican majority controlling the CPB Board, the White

House seemingly held all the cards in its battle with
public television. On August 1, Board member Tom Moore
laid out the scenario for the replacement of Macy and
Pace and completion of the CPB coup in a "confidential"
letter to Peter Flanigan. The objective, he began, was
"to have the Board of CPB adopt a policy devoting all its
non-station appropriations to cultural, educational, and
experimental entertainment programs to the exclusion of
public affairs," and to execute the policy change in such
a manner that would make it permanent and "not altered by
future Boards."[29]

The first move would be to elect new board
member Thomas B. Curtis, former Republican Congressman
from Missouri and current vice president and general
counsel for <u>Encyclopedia Brittanica</u>, as chairman of the
board. There had been much discussion within the White
House in early July about the choice of Curtis.
Whitehead had favored the appointment of conservative
writer and editor Irving Kristol over that of Curtis
because Kristol's agreement with administration policy on
public broadcasting grew from real "intellectual
conviction after some familiarization" with the issue.
He also felt that Kristol's appointment would "reflect
more credit on the President and display less political
motivation."[30] However, on the advice of his close
friend, John Olin, Nixon decided in favor of Curtis and
his appointment to the CPB was announced on July 14.

The election of Curtis as chairman, said Moore,
"should be done with enthusiasm in order to achieve our
basic objectives." After Curtis' election in September
the board's policy committee could be enlarged from three
to five by the new chairman, who would then appoint the
two new members in order to create a Republican majority.
This group would then be able to recommend the policy
change on public affairs and, Moore continued, "with some

opposition, we should be able to pass this with a close majority of the board." He suggested that the President himself meet with board members Cole and Wrather to make clear to them that they would be the vital "swing votes" on this issue.

After the policy change a new CPB president would be chosen who, in turn, would complete the purge by re-staffing the Corporation's professional work force to implement the new policies. The new staff would then undertake the preparation of a strong program schedule and budget requests for the 1974-75 and 1975-76 seasons, Moore hypothesized. "The schedule would be without public affairs, but heavy with music, drama, education, and new forms."

"During his second term," Moore said, "the President could be repeatedly identified with the cultural and educational programming. He can well shape the character of the public television in such a positive way that the public affairs issues will never come up again." Moore gleefully declared, "Welcome to the new Public Television."[31]

The first indications were that, despite some adverse publicity and predictable criticism, an administration takeover of CPB would be a complete success. Through the end of the summer, events corresponded closely with Moore's scenario. And when, after only minimal coverage of the Democratic national convention, NPACT decided to provide complete gavel-to-gavel coverage of Richard Nixon's unquestioned renomination at the Republican gathering, many feared that the White House's message had gotten through to public television even before its appointees could take control of the CPB board.

NPACT had originally planned comprehensive, gavel-to-gavel coverage of both parties' national

conventions, but because of the CPB board's decision to
cut $400,000 from the Center's new grant, these plans had
to be significantly altered. Instead, NPACT would only
be able to provide spot coverage, a ninety-minute
convention preview program, and nightly half-hour
summaries of the important issues and events. The
Democrats' meeting came first, from July 10 until July
13. Critical reaction to NPACT's "Anatomy of a
Convention" and its evening reports was generally good.
Many public broadcasters felt, however, that NPACT's
first effort in Miami Beach had not been very successful
with their viewers. The message from the stations, said
NPACT general counsel Frank Lloyd, was "You weren't doing
something that we perceived, out in the field, as being
different, distinctive and unique in the Democratic
Convention."[32] NPACT chief Jim Karayn and PBS public
affairs coordinator Jim Lehrer agreed that the limited
coverage had not been NPACT's finest hour.

For the Republican convention, to be held a
month later in the same Miami Beach hall, the management
of NPACT and PBS considered going back to the original
idea of unedited, gavel-to-gavel podium coverage.
Thereby public television would provide a true
alternative to the commercial network. Television
critics and political commentators criticized the three
commercial networks for their gavel-to-gavel coverage
because the focus was constantly shifting around the
convention floor, in hopes of locating an interesting bit
of hoopla. What about the business of the conventions,
many asked, up on the podium? Karayn decided in early
August that, despite the budgetary constraints, NPACT
would attempt to provide gavel-to-gavel platform coverage
of the Republican convention in Miami. On August 9,
Variety reported that this "experiment" in broadcast

journalism would be carried by PBS and hosted by the Center's two political correspondents, Vanocur and MacNeil.[33]

But Robert MacNeil and Sander Vanocur flatly refused to participate. "It just seemed to me," MacNeil said, "that for public television not to have covered the Democratic convention and then devote gavel-to-gavel coverage to the Republican convention was inappropriate, when the convention was being called for the purpose of coronating . . . the incumbent President, with all the advantages he clearly had."[34] Both correspondents argued with Karayn not only that the coverage was politically unfair, but that it might be interpreted by others as a complete buckling under White House pressure by a public television system that was still awaiting a funding authorization for the upcoming season. Not surprisingly, that is the way Bill Greeley of Variety saw it. On August 16, Greeley wrote: "The PBS decision to air gavel-to-gavel coverage of the Republican convention in Miami once again confirms the worst predictions inside observers were making about the 'governmental network' back when it was being set up." The podium coverage, he said, would be a purely "White House production, so unjournalistic -- anti-journalistic in fact -- that NPACT's correspondents Robert MacNeil and Vanocur have refused to take part."[35]

Karayn strongly disagreed with his senior correspondents and asked NET's Bill Moyers to anchor the gavel-to-gavel coverage. MacNeil and Vanocur limited their participation to the nightly half-hour wrap-up reports, the same kind of coverage they had given the Democrats. Moyers thought it had been a mistake not to do the Democratic convention. "I thought it was worth experimenting that summer with both of them," he said, "and the fact that we didn't do the Democratic convention was obviously an error. But I didn't think the fact that we didn't do the Democratic convention should deny us the chance, if we could get the money, to do the Republican convention, and simply because I believed in the experiment and wanted to try it, I did it."

Moyers was not concerned about his colleagues' interpretation of the Republican convention coverage as a product of White House intimidation. "No one can intimidate you unless you feel intimidatable. And I didn't feel intimidated by the veto. In fact, I was beginning to feel very good about the fact that the fight was coming out in the open."[36]

The gavel-to-gavel coverage went ahead as planned. Reaction from the public television stations and from the press was generally favorable. Some programmers found Moyers' running commentary on the proceedings brilliant and incisive, while others thought he just talked too much and indulged in frequent hyperbole. Some found him "refreshing," and others, uninspired. Many critics, who had complained throughout the commercial networks' circus-like coverage of the festivities on the convention hall floor, praised NPACT's work. The Christian Science Monitor said that PBS:

> . . . provided a rewarding supplement to the commercial networks, thanks to the National Public Affairs Center for Television (NPACT). Bill Moyers' low-keyed between-speech comments nicely complemented a dial-twister's views of CBS and NBC getting battlefield descriptions from tear-gassed delegates.
>
> Right after the President's acceptance speech Wednesday night, Messrs. Moyers and the commercial network reporters were off and running with reactions. Dialing fast, I found the NPACT commentary not one whit less frank than anyone else's. If anything, Mr. Moyers

sounded the toughest in his metaphorical
brand of phrasemaking, a fact which
should effectively dismiss the
suggestion that NPACT's coverage was an
effort to placate the administration
that supplies its funds.[37]

Newsweek, however, interpreted NPACT's
comprehensive Republican coverage much as Vanocur and
MacNeil had warned:

> The Public Broadcasting
> Service . . . intimidated by the long-
> standing hostility of the Nixon
> Administration, impoverished by
> Congressional cuts in its
> budget . . . gave up any pretense of
> competing with CBS, NBC, or ABC . . . .
>
> The PBS coverage wasn't quite as boring
> as an Andy Warhol movie. The camera did
> cut away from the rostrum for an
> occasional crowd reaction. In the
> absence of MacNeil and Vanocur, Bill
> Moyers provided competent, if uninspired
> commentary. . . . More often than not,
> PBS took the speakers and what they said
> at face value. By any standards of
> modern journalism, its "experiment" was
> a failure. The last thing the viewer
> needed looking in on this vast cave of
> the winds, was an unblinking camera that
> mistook the shadows on the cave wall for
> the reality outside."[38]

Earlier program controversies had once left
public television open to the accusation that it used
government money to be "anti-government." The Republican
convention coverage brought the charge that it was acting
as a government mouthpiece. For public television, there
seemed to be no safe path. The involvement of federal
appropriations made every decision subject to criticism
from some quarter about how it expended public funds. To
somebody's ears, the piper was always playing the wrong

tune. As it had been damned for programming perceived as
anti-administration, public television was damned for
programming interpreted as pro-administration. In such a
politically charged atmosphere, it was impossible to
separate the issues of money, content, and editorial
control. Unfortunately for public television, this
volatile mixture was bound to continue as long as federal
funding for each successive season remained in doubt.

The early September Senate hearings on former
Congressman Thomas Curtis' nomination to the CPB board
were little more than another opportunity for pro- and
anti-administration legislators to air their views on the
growing controversy. As he had done on the Senate floor
in June, Howard Baker supported the administration's
contention that public broadcasting was not yet mature
enough and the Corporation not yet clear enough about its
role to warrant a sizable increase or a long-term plan
for funding. Committee Chairman John Pastore clashed
sharply with Baker and used the Curtis nomination hearing
to warn Clay Whitehead that the committee's patience with
White House equivocation on funding and its veiled
threats to broadcasters was wearing thin. The Rhode
Island Senator said, "There's a gentleman in the White
House who doesn't seem to have his heart and soul in
public broadcasting, and this is no secret. His name is
Mr. Whitehead."[39] Clearly, the next time the OTP
director appeared before the communications subcommittee,
his reception from its chairman would be something less
than cordial.

At its September 15 meeting, the CPB board of
directors elected its newest member, Thomas Curtis,
chairman of the board. At the same time, White House
supporters on the board also tried to rush through the
appointment of deputy director of the United States
Information Agency Henry Loomis as CPB president without

any discussion or debate. Jack Valenti, who was a friend of both Wrather and Moore, resented the fact that his colleagues tried to bring up Loomis' name and immediately called for a vote. He said, "Wait a minute. I know Henry Loomis, but how many of you know Henry Loomis?" "A number of people," Valenti recalled, "had never met him." He then told the board, "We can't be voting for a president that this board hasn't even met, for God's sakes."[40]

Jack Wrather called Loomis at his USIA office in Washington and told him, "The board is meeting right now, could you come right over?" "It was luck," Loomis said, "that I could."[41] After the board held their session with Loomis it was clear that the votes were there to elect him. Loomis was the unanimous choice and the White House had the team it wanted at the Corporation for Public Broadcasting.

For the preceding four years Loomis had been deputy director of the United States Information Agency under Frank Shakespeare. Like John Macy, he had abundant credentials in government service. After receiving his bachelor's degree in physics from Harvard in 1941, Loomis spent five years in the Navy as a radar specialist, attaining the rank of lieutenant commander. After two years at the radiation laboratory at the University of California, Berkeley, he joined the administration of the Massachusetts Institute of Technology as an assistant to the president, James Killian. He soon moved into government, serving as a consultant to the Psychological Strategy Board and a staff member of the President's Committee on International Information. In 1953 he became chief of USIA's office of research and intelligence and then spent three years as staff director of Killian, who had become the first special assistant to the president for science and technology. From 1958 until 1965 Loomis was director of the government's international radio program, the Voice of America. He resigned the post in 1965 in protest over Johnson administration attempts to dictate the nature of VOA's broadcast materials. Though a longtime Republican, Loomis was no ideologue. He resented the politicization of USIA's programs and took a highly visible stand on this principle. After a period as Deputy Commissioner of Education, he left government in 1966 for private business. In the summer of 1968, Republican presidential candidate Richard Nixon asked Loomis to form a group of task forces for easing the transition between administrations. Loomis, who had helped in the late-starting Truman-Eisenhower transition, told Nixon that his would be a bipartisan effort aimed at helping either victorious candidate. Though there were as many Humphrey supporters as there were Nixonites on the transition planning groups, Loomis' efforts were completely underwritten by the Republican National Committee. Therefore, he worked out of the same office building that housed the Nixon campaign. While there he got to know Clay Whitehead, whom he had met previously through their mutual association with MIT. Early in 1972, after the White House decided that John Macy should be removed as soon as possible from the presidency of CPB, Loomis' boss Frank Shakespeare, a member of the White House working group on public broadcasting, brought up the possibility of naming Loomis to head the Corporation. Having worked so long in foreign affairs and having lived outside Washington, D.C., which had only a UHF public station, Loomis had never even heard of the Corporation for Public Broadcasting. When Shakespeare told him about the CPB job, his first reaction was: "What the hell is it?"[42]

During the spring of 1972, when Whitehead planned the changes at the Corporation, he spoke with

Loomis about the president's post. In June, Whitehead
and OTP general counsel Antonin Scalia went to Loomis'
farm in Middleburg, Virginia to discuss the current
situation. Tom Moore also spoke to Loomis on a number of
occasions and invited him up to New York for lunchtime
talk about CPB. As Whitehead and Moore explained it,
"There was a head-to-head fight between the Corporation
and most of the stations, between those who were proteges
of the Ford Foundation and those who felt on the
outside." Loomis decided to talk to his friend and
mentor, Killian, and "began to realize what the problems
really were." Killian urged him to take the job.
Loomis, who was also in line for the directorship of USIA
when Shakespeare retired at the end of Nixon's first
term, was attracted to the "fouled-up" situation in
public broadcasting. "I thought it was pretty good fun
to go in and see if you can improve it." Loomis enjoyed
the role of a permanent, roving undersecretary in
government service -- like a British aristocrat with
noblesse oblige. He was, in fact, something of an
American aristocrat himself, who could afford to serve
his country. Born to wealth, Loomis lived on a large
farm in the rolling hills of Middleburg, Virginia, about
an hour's drive from Washington. His hobbies were
hunting and riding and, as Broadcasting magazine put it,
he was a man "in whom wealth and experience have bred an
immense self-assurance that sometimes comes across as
simple abruptness: he is a man accustomed to command."[43]
One story about Henry Loomis described how, for over two
years while director of the Voice of America, he never
even bothered to cash his federal paychecks. This, the
story went, gave the government's General Accounting
Office fits in trying to close its books. When GAO
officials appeared at Loomis' Washington office while he
was abroad, they found the two years' worth of pay

envelopes piled, unopened, in his desk drawer. Loomis claimed that the story was purely apocryphal.[44]

Loomis told Whitehead in the spring that he would be equally pleased with the job as USIA director as he would with the CPB presidency. He told the OTP director that he was a civil servant and that he would go "where the President thought [he] could make the greater contribution."[45] At the time, however, Loomis did not know that CPB was supposed to be independent of the government and that the President did not officially control its staff appointments. He assumed that the White House would simply tell him which job they wanted him in, when the time came. Of course, neither the President -- nor the White House -- should have been in charge of Loomis' hiring as CPB president. The administration's role was legally confined to choosing the membership of the CPB board of directors. It was perfectly understandable for the White House to use its appointive power to populate the board with individuals sympathetic to the President's viewpoint. In its June 1972 nominations of Neal Freeman, conservative radio commentator, editor at the conservative publishing company, Arlington House, and producer of William F. Buckley's Firing Line program, and conservative critic and teacher Irving Kristol, the administration used this power well. But the White House -- often through board members Moore, Wrather, and Cole -- interceded directly in the affairs of the Corporation board. President Nixon himself had decided that Curtis should become CPB board chairman and the White House ordained that Loomis should become Corporation president. OTP even sought to fill open slots on the CPB staff with its own choices. When Wrather needed Loomis' resume for the CPB nominating committee, he called Whitehead's office for it.[46]

Whitehead himself did not feel that there was any contradiction between his oft-stated belief that the government should not become involved in programming matters and his active involvement in the deliberations of the CPB board. The only contradiction he did recognize was in the need to centralize power in order to decentralize it. "You had to take power in order to disperse it," he later said. "The system as it was, was not going to do that by itself." Whitehead felt that CPB and PBS were really like a single organization and that they were not going to respond to local station needs, or to OTP's demand for decentralized control without a firmer push. "Independence from government control meant doing the exact opposite of whatever the government said. So we felt -- I felt -- that we really did have to take control . . . that this was altogether proper."[47]

"People in public broadcasting itself expected that what we were about was taking control so that we could decide what the programming was, from the White House. And," Whitehead admitted, "I think there were some people in the White House who thought that's what we were doing." Because of the President's renowned antipathy towards public television, few could believe that the attempt by the administration to take over CPB was motivated by anything other than the desire to get Vanocur, Moyers, and all the other "liberal" commentators off the air. Whitehead had purposely sold his decentralization philosophy to the White House in these partisan terms and, by the summer of 1972, it was impossible to distinguish his loftier objectives from those of the hostile White House. Tom Whitehead wanted to distinguish between policy and programming, between structure and content. He was willing to control one, he said, but not touch the other. But as a practical matter, there was no distinction. To the President, getting rid of political programs, anti-administration programs, was the ultimate objective. It therefore had become Whitehead's objective, too.

Yet the veto and subsequent leadership changes at CPB, which seemed like administration victories, worked against White House efforts in the long run by revealing the superficiality and hypocrisy of its pro-localism position. For almost a year, Whitehead had been criticizing the public broadcasting industry because of its supposed drift toward centralization of power over programming. Decentralization and local station power had then served the administration's desire to rid the medium of news and public affairs by allowing the most conservative elements within the industry a greater voice in programming and policy. Under the new circumstances, the White House effort to remove controversial national political programs from the schedule would be best served by centralization of control in a Nixon-dominated CPB. Public broadcasters and their supporters simply believed that Whitehead had traded in his tactic of hiding behind the rhetorical smoke screen of localism, for a direct frontal assault on enemy headquarters: CPB, and the national programming service, PBS. It was not difficult to see the contradictions inherent in the White House's past decentralization thrust and its current support for complete CPB control under its hand-picked Corporation leadership. OTP counsel Henry Goldberg agreed with administration critics that centralizing power so that you could decentralize it later was ironically reminiscent of American policy in Vietnam: "We had to burn the village to save the village."[48]

The newly-elected president of the Corporation seemed to be a man with not only little knowledge about, but also little sympathy for, public television. Loomis' appointment, though true to Tom Moore's scenario, caused

a revival of fears and warnings that the administration
was out to control public broadcasting and create a
domestic version of the USIA. Loomis certainly looked
like the right man for the job. And just as certainly,
the White House staff wanted finally to have their say
over what went on public television. The President's top
aides, H.R. Haldeman, John Ehrlichman and Charles Colson,
constantly pressured Whitehead to take an active role in
determining actual program content. For example, Brian
Lamb recalled, "Bob Haldeman called him and said that the
President wanted his Russian speech -- the speech that he
had given to the Russian people -- run on PBS again
during the election."[49] The day after Curtis' election,
and two days before Loomis was finally approved,
presidential special assistant Charles Colson fired off a
memo to Al Snyder of Herb Klein's communications office.
"How did we miss the fact that National Educational
Television ran the full McGovern speech to the Security
Analysts in New York?" Colson asked. "Not only do they
run it once, but they re-ran it a second time. Somewhere
along the line we're not watching these things carefully
enough. . . . The Corporation for Public Broadcasting
also never made known to us that this had happened, so we
would of course have found out about it only by
monitoring. They damn well, as a public corporation, had
an obligation to tell us and I would like you to take
this up with whoever you deal with there . . . ."[50] The
White House did not understand, or did not care, that as
a public corporation, CPB did not have any obligation to
tell them what was going on public television. That was
not yet clear to the man they had chosen to run the
Corporation for Public Broadcasting, Henry Loomis.

Thomas Curtis had stressed after his election
as CPB board chairman that a shift to greater localism in
public television was imminent. Henry Loomis indicated

at the time of his hiring, however, that he and the
Corporation would soon become actively involved in
programming decisions and "take full responsibility for
programs distributed by the Public Broadcasting Service."
As many had predicted, Loomis seemed to be the
administration's hatchet-man at CPB, justifying greater
centralization on the grounds that it was responsive to
local needs.[51] On September 20, Loomis met with the PBS
board of directors and with the system's station managers
over a closed-circuit interconnection. His initial
encounter with the leaders of public television's 220
stations seemed to go well. Though he did not pull any
punches with his personal reactions, he was more than
candid about the fact that he did not yet know much about
his new job. "When I was asked to take this job," Loomis
said, "I was totally dumbfounded and a little confused, I
didn't know what it is. Unfortunately, I live fairly far
from Washington, and Washington's educational station is
UHF, and I haven't got [a UHF antenna], so I have never
seen an educational television or a public television
show, so if innocence is a virtue, I am very virtuous."

He then fielded questions phoned in from around
the country. From the ETS board: "What would be your
prediction for long range financing legislation in 1973?"

"An honest answer is, 'damned if I
know.'. . . My guess is that probably we will be
concentrating on other things this first year, and that
it would be better to try for that one in a couple of
years from now, but that is just a personal feeling
without knowing too much about it."[52]

Though Loomis' tone was not exactly meek and
mild, he did not think he had said anything that could be
construed as intimidating to the public broadcasters.
Yet, some of them saw Loomis' remarks in their most
threatening and offensive light. Under Loomis, the

Corporation for Public Broadcasting sounded a lot like
the old NET: A central organization with total control
over national programming in which the stations
themselves had no representation. There was, of course,
one crucial difference. CPB was not run by a group of
intellectual broadcasters with Ford Foundation money, but
by White House appointees with federal funds. Loomis had
been told by the White House that the Corporation was
really no different from any other government agency, and
he had yet to learn differently. Many of the public
broadcasters felt that his emphasis on CPB responsibility
masked an administration-inspired grab for programming
power. The danger of a domestic USIA, a voice of the
White House, sounded very real.

The press picked up on the fact that some of
the station leaders had been insulted by Loomis'
admission that he had never seen anything on public
television. Money-starved programmers and managers could
not believe that the new CPB president wanted to wait "a
couple of years" before proposing long-range, increased
federal financing for the system. Congressman Lionel van
Deerlin characterized Loomis' appointment as CPB
president as "the same as selecting to coach the
Washington Redskins someone who detests football." The
complete lack of familiarity with the situation had not
prevented Loomis from stating categorically that there
should be no national news show, and that there should be
no "instant analysis" after public events on PBS. He had
yet to see a PBS program. Loomis also said that he had
not yet met with officials of NPACT, but he remarked
sarcastically that he had "heard of those initials
before."[53] The hard-edged wit did not strike many of the
broadcasters as particularly funny. They had just
experienced a year in which their worst fears about
government funding and political pressures had been

realized. They naturally tended to hear his remarks in their most ominous tone. Loomis claimed that he was no creature of OTP's. But OTP was responsible for his selection and when he explained his views on public affairs to the system, he sounded unmistakably similar to Whitehead. "I think it would be an improper use of our limited funds to do the type of programming that is done well by the commercials, and as you know, the commercials do a great deal of public affairs programming," the new Corporation president said.[54] The inescapable inference at NPACT, correspondent Robert MacNeil recalled, was that Loomis "had been stuck in there to do us in. I assumed that when Henry Loomis became president of CPB that he was a White House appointee, in effect, and that he'd been appointed, in part, to get rid of public affairs programming."[55]

The White House, after all, had made the same assumption. Whitehead and Flanigan intended to remain closely involved in the deliberations of the Corporation board and the actions of its professional staff now that their own men were in control. On October 6, Whitehead sent Flanigan a memo proposing a presidential meeting with Curtis and Loomis. The purpose of the meeting, as MacNeil and others might have expected had they known of it, would be to "impress on Curtis and Loomis the necessity of dumping NPACT and withdrawing CPB support for news and public affairs programs, particularly preventing all current efforts to make public broadcasting a 'network of record' a la New York Times."

A tight White House rein over its new appointees would be needed since, as Whitehead said, "past efforts to do this through 'friendly' Board members have been unsatisfactory apparently because these Board members do not appreciate the depth of the President's personal concern. There should be no confusion on this

point at present." The OTP director further suggested to
Flanigan that one of the most important Curtis/Loomis
tasks would be "to clean house at CPB and staff it with
reliable people." "They should be open," he said, "to
suggestions from OTP on staffing." Finally, as an
"incentive" for the new chairman and president of the
Corporation to enforce stricter priorities in the use of
CPB programming and networking funds, the administration
would keep fiscal 1974 funding for the Corporation at or
near the current $45 to $50 million level. "Thereafter,"
Whitehead told Flanigan, "if progress is being made,
funding will increase."[56] The hope clearly was that
public broadcasters could, in the ACLU's words, be
"starved" into submission and then forced into line under
the White House controlled CPB.

During the fall of 1972 it very nearly
happened. Throughout October and November, Whitehead met
with Loomis and Curtis and had close contact with various
other members of the CPB Board. There was admittedly
improper cooperation between the White House OTP director
and the president of the supposedly independent
Corporation on the proposed shifts in CPB policy.
November 7, Loomis sent Whitehead the 276-page "National
Program Profile," which contained initial CPB staff
recommendations for major series support in fiscal year
1974. Attached to the document was a note which said,
"Tom--This is our 'burn before reading' document. No one
knows you have it. HL." Whitehead added his own
handwritten cover sheet which warned White House OTP
staffers, "DO NOT REPRODUCE. We're not supposed to have
this."[57]

Of course, the cover note, "Burn before
reading," was absurd. Loomis was making an old foreign
service officer's joke about over-classified documents.
But the note also had a serious side. If Loomis' close

cooperation with the White House became public, whatever
credibility he had with the public broadcasters would
automatically disappear. He was already having a great
deal of difficulty convincing people that he was not the
administration's mercenary.[58] Exposure of his attempts
to mediate between the hostile White House and public
television camps would make his already tenuous position
with the broadcasters untenable. Most of them felt their
system was on the verge of total collapse from too little
money and too much politics.

Public broadcasters were understandably
suspicious of Henry Loomis. The assumption among PBS
executives was that Loomis' marching orders from the
White House were, simply, "Control it or kill it; but if
you kill it, don't get caught doing it."[59] Nevertheless,
the system's leadership worked hard to cultivate him as
an ally in the battle with the administration over
funding and programming. In late September and early
October, the PBS staff compiled a number of hefty
briefing books for the new CPB president. The most
important of them contained a documentary history of the
institutional relationship between CPB and PBS. Its
emphasis was on the gradual increase in rational PBS
control over programming and the interconnection and on
its affirmative partnership with the Corporation on
funding decisions. It provided models and explanations
for a number of possible structures for national program
decisionmaking, but encouraged Loomis to continue
Corporation support for PBS' primary role as the
legitimate voice of the local stations.[60]

Similarly, NPACT counsel Frank Lloyd compiled a
book on the Center's original concept, its programming,
and activities during its brief year of existence.
Naturally, Lloyd aimed to present NPACT's efforts in
their best possible light, but he included almost as many

critical comments from the system as he did positive
ones. He also collected a sample of videotapes of the
Center's most successful -- and balanced -- efforts to
date.[61]

Bill Moyers, whose This Week program became
Bill Moyers' Journal in the autumn of 1972, began to
develop a close working relationship with Loomis. "I
tried to educate Henry as to what journalism was about,
and he listened," Moyers said. "He was amenable."
Loomis was not merely a front man for the White House,
Moyers believed. He had his own pride and his own sense
of integrity.[62] But Loomis began what would become a
successful tenure as president of CPB under the
assumption that it was like any other government agency,
rather than an independent entity. Having worked solely
in the executive branch, or completely outside of
government in a university and private business, he did
not immediately grasp that the Corporation was supposed
to be independent from the White House, despite the
presidential appointments to the board and the federal
money. "I was not as aware as I became very quickly,"
Loomis admitted, "about the First Amendment's domestic
impact. I was thinking of a comparison between the
Corporation and the Voice [of America], which is very
superficial. There is a vast difference between them.
It took me a while to recognize that."[63]

Before Henry Loomis came to recognize that CPB
was not a domestic Voice of America and that the presence
of federal dollars need not preclude the treatment of
sensitive political issues, he managed to antagonize and
alienate most of the public broadcasting establishment.
Salvatore Fauci, chairman of the board of station WSKG in
upstate New York, met Loomis in early October in New York
during a gathering of the public television station board
chairmen's committee. Fauci questioned whether Loomis

was at all inclined to support a system that precluded
CPB from some sort of program control. Loomis appeared
to Fauci to be "rather dogmatic" and represented a
"polarity with the standards enunciated by the PBS." In
a letter to Hartford Gunn relaying some of his misgivings
about the new CPB president, Fauci quoted from the PBS
program standard paper: "'The journalist does not deal
in absolutes, neither absolute truth nor absolute
objectivity.' Henry Loomis is an absolutist, so much so
that I found myself vigorously defending 'Banks and the
Poor' after he strongly denounced it as 'dishonest
programming.' I frankly thought the program was an
attempt to represent a view not often adequately
represented: the poor -- that the program richly
deserved to be aired despite its technical flaws. I
presented the analogy of a flea trying to take a healthy
bite out of an elephant. After much further discussion,
it came out that he never saw the program, but centered
his whole opposition on the dishonest [sic] methods
utilized in producing the show."[64]

On October 24, Gunn wrote back to Fauci: "I
cannot honestly say that I know where Henry Loomis will
come out on these issues after he has had a little more
time to think about them."

". . . [H]e does bring years of experience with
the USIA and the Voice of America where those in charge
had absolute control over program selection, production
and distribution. To construct a parallel arrangement
for public television would be to introduce, it seems to
me, the conditions for a domestic propaganda
chief . . . ."[65]

Despite the delicate political situation
surrounding public television in the fall of 1972, Loomis
did not tread as lightly as he might have during his
first weeks on the job. He criticized the industry's

strategy in seeking long-term funding from the government
as politically naive. Loomis felt that once the public
broadcasters found that Nixon was trying to hold down
funding and was unhappy about programming, they said,
"'Forget the executive branch and get it from Congress.'
Well, you don't have to be a very astute student of
civics to realize it takes two branches . . . to
accomplish what you're after. . . ."

   "It was absolutely stupid," Loomis thought.
"The public broadcasters were arrogant and rude and non-
communicative with the executive branch. They were the
enemy. 'The hell with you all, we're going to get [a
funding bill] from our friends on the Hill.'" Loomis
also believed that too much money coming into any
organization too quickly led only to unnecessary
wastefulness. He drew on his past experience as deputy
commissioner of the Office of Education where, during his
tenure, the budget had doubled three years in a row.
Inundated by funding and without enough staff to cope
with it, Loomis said, the education office hired "anyone
who walked in off the street who appeared to be alive."
The budget far outpaced the agency's legitimate needs and
so, Loomis recalled, "you couldn't shovel the money out
of the window" fast enough. The new CPB president was
hesitant to commit himself to seeking large funding
increases for public television until he was sure that
the system could sensibly absorb them.[66] But his "go-
slow" attitude rankled public television's other leaders.
Operating on the same $35 million appropriation for the
second consecutive fiscal year, they could not readily
accept Loomis' view that there could be such a thing as
too much money in public television. The three-year-old
national system was supposed to be growing, moving boldly
forward, but with funding at a standstill at a time of
rising inflation, its performance was instead sliding

backward. Public television, the system's professionals said, was _not_ like any of the government agencies that Loomis had known. James Loper of KCET complained, "All of Loomis' analogies relate to the Voice of America. He knows more about Laos than he does about Kansas City."[67] Given his opposition to political programs, his ambivalence on the issue of long-range, increased financing, _and_ his professed intention of making national programming decisions wholly within CPB, it was impossible for most observers not to surmise that Henry Loomis was, after all, just doing the dirty work for the Nixon White House.

On the program production level, both at the local stations and at NPACT, the veto of increased funding and the proposed CPB policy changes meant that production could continue only on a shoestring budget, if at all. "The fact of the situation is this," Hartford Gunn told the PBS board on September 20, "we are no longer moving forward in the quality of service we are providing to our member stations. We have begun to reverse our progress, and the rate of decline threatens to accelerate."[68] In a late September letter to the NAEB, KCET's Loper projected that in the coming year public television would be weaker than in the past, with many stations "in the most precarious financial position ever." "I would question," he wrote of the recent shifts in direction at CPB, "whether public broadcasting . . . can survive another period of 'temporary readjustment.'" Besides the simple problem of a lack of sufficient operating funds, it appeared to Loper that with all the purges that had taken place, it would be "extremely hard to attract good people into what have proved to be impossible jobs." He quipped, more bitterly than jokingly, that public broadcasting had "all the elements of the play, 'Ten Little Indians,' in which, one by one, each of the presumed enemies is eliminated until there is simply no one left in the entire institution."[69] Months later, Loper's predictions were borne out by Newton Minow, chairman of Chicago's public station WTTW and former chairman of the FCC, who said that "the veto, and the reorganization of CPB and PBS, has left us without the means to perform our service to the public. We no longer have any resources to do any programming."[70]

The Aspen Program on Communications and Society published their Schramm-Nelson study of public television financing in October of 1972. It starkly illustrated what the broadcasters themselves had been saying for months: the public television system, particularly at the local level, was rapidly deteriorating for lack of money. The situation could not be improved, Schramm and Nelson wrote, merely by spreading around the money currently available, as the Nixon administration was suggesting. "The Corporation for Public Broadcasting, which is now the largest single source of program support," they wrote, "had roughly ten million dollars for programs and five million dollars for station support in 1971. Even if this entire fifteen million were divided among two hundred stations for local programming, it would provide only approximately <u>fifteen hours of local programming per station per year at five thousand dollars an hour</u> -- the present cost of a starkly simple panel discussion program produced by station KQED in San Francisco. Or, at the most, it would provide one hour a week of very low-cost programming."[71]

The system was increasingly centralized by national program production because "a dollar spent on a national service will raise quality a great deal higher for more audiences than the same dollar divided among stations for local programming."

> If there is a strong trend towards
> 'centralization,' it seems clear to us
> from conversations with a variety of
> station managers that the primary reason
> has been one of financial necessity
> rather than design. At present stations
> can, and occasionally do, decide not to
> carry a particular program provided by
> the national service. In reality,
> however, most carry nearly all that is
> offered through PBS because little else
> is available from other sources at costs
> which the stations can afford. With
> local programming severely limited by
> budgets, and with other 'outside'
> materials too expensive to purchase, a
> station manager who does not want to use
> a PBS-supplied program has but one
> realistic alternative: a shorter
> broadcast day.[72]

The study estimated that the total yearly
operating cost involved in bringing the program service
up to a minimum standard -- with a better balance between
nationally and locally produced programs -- was $432
million. This represented an increase of $266 million
over the current expenditure of approximately $166
million for public television in 1971.

The nation could well afford such a system,
Schramm and Nelson believed. For an annual public
television budget of about $400 million in the United
States, they wrote, the costs would be less than $2 per
capita. "It would seem difficult indeed to argue that
such an expenditure would create a national hardship,
faced with the fact that the Canadian government provides
close to six dollars per capita annually for public
television, and the British government over three dollars
per capita. The 1971-1972 CPB federal appropriation
amounted to seventeen cents per person, a figure that
suffers in comparison not only with the support levels in
other countries but also -- and perhaps even more

dramatically -- with the close to fourteen dollars per person which U.S. commercial television costs annually."[73]

The study concluded that a close look at the current situation clearly demonstrated that the local and regional components were sadly lagging in terms of effectiveness and in terms of the overall goal of program balance. Schramm and Nelson's report showed that the White House's position that there should be greater localism before there was greater federal funding was simply unattainable. This was so patently clear to the broadcasters -- including the aching local stations who had supported Whitehead's push for local funding before the veto -- that their only conclusion was that the White House was seeking to destroy public television.

The fears and frustrations of NPACT were particularly intense. The staff was understandably on edge. They sensed that there was a conspiracy against them and tended to "see shadows down every hallway." After all, recalled production manager Al Vecchione, "It was a brand-new organization. Many of us had moved in a fairly mature phase of our careers -- with families -- to another city and taken on a brand-new job with a fledgling new company, and that causes some human concern, too. You get shook about who's going to pay the rent the first of the month. . . . They were difficult times."[74] General counsel Frank Lloyd thought that it was extremely difficult, at first, to convince much of the system of the danger in what the Nixon administration was trying to do. Many station leaders were perfectly willing to give up public affairs and shut down NPACT if that would insure future federal funding. There was a bunker mentality in the White House, said Lloyd, and so NPACT looked for conspiracies. There was certainly enough evidence around them in Washington -- with the slowly emerging story of the break-in at the Democratic National Committee headquarters in the Watergate hotel by men employed by the Committee to Re-Elect the President -- to indicate that such conspiracies were indeed taking place. "The problem," he recalled, "was with the station managers; when you went out to Iowa or someplace else they would say, 'Aw, that's silly.' People outside of Washington just didn't have this sense of what was going on in this city and what the Nixon Administration was like."[75]

Robert MacNeil and Sander Vanocur both wondered whether they were being overly paranoid about administration attempts to get them. MacNeil described the insecurity and confusion this way:

> When you are being plotted against and persecuted -- when all of it's mysterious -- you never know how much value to put on your own perceptions of it. We wondered often, 'Are we, were we being paranoid? Were we imagining conspiracies and plots that weren't there? Was there a perfectly rational and honorable construction that could be put on the actions of various people at the time?'. . . It was hard to know what was paranoia in our minds and what was justifiable concern.[76]

"Even members of my family," recalled Vanocur, "thought I was being paranoid about it, but I knew what was being done to me and I couldn't do a damn thing about it. . . ."[77]

Vanocur was disgusted and disillusioned by the lack of support given him by most of the public television system. He quietly left his position as senior NPACT correspondent when his infamous contract expired at the end of 1972.

Perhaps the most frustrating part of the battle
to those who remained to fight for public television's
independence from attempted White House control was the
fact that many within the public system had no desire to
antagonize the President with public affairs programs
which would threaten his approval of federal funding.
Most local station managers were nervous about funding to
begin with, Vanocur said. There were still many who
felt, as they had before Whitehead's first attack a year
earlier, that there was no place for news and public
affairs on public television. Some wondered out loud why
they needed all the aggravation of a threatened funding
cut-off. They had a good thing going with their popular
and critically acclaimed educational and cultural
programs; "why," some of them asked, "risk it all for a
few controversial journalists and their controversial
programs?" Therefore, MacNeil later wrote, "many
stations seemed willing to buy the Corporation plan to
eliminate public affairs." He said,

> Not everyone saw the danger represented
> by the scheme of Corporation president
> Henry Loomis to restructure public
> television. They just wanted all the
> trouble out of the way so that President
> Nixon would not veto any more bills and
> the lovely Federal money would start
> rolling in again.[78]

The autumn of 1972, with Nixon's landslide
reelection, seemed to be a time when the future of a
whole range of constitutional freedoms hung in a
precarious balance under White House pressure. But it
was the future freedom of public television which seemed
to hang most precariously in November of 1972. People
were justifiably worried and they doubted whether the
system could withstand the heat. TV Guide said in early

November, "Last Days Loom for Public-TV Network."
Hartford Gunn had told the NAEB convention in Las Vegas
that first-run programming would largely run out by
January; by April, after a heavy round of repeats,
perhaps five to six hours a week would have to be turned
back to the stations -- who probably could not fill in
the gaps anyway. "We're in the right place, all right,"
a harried station manager grumbled at the Las Vegas
convention. "This whole business has become a big crap
shoot." Henry Loomis told TV Guide that the whole public
television structure was "under review," including
whether PBS was to survive as the vehicle for national
programming. "Indeed," TV Guide reported, "PBS' broad
prerogatives in the choice of programming already are
being taken over by the CPB board of directors, which
even now is deciding the amounts and categories of PBS
fare for the 1973-1974 season. Asked if this did not
represent greater centralization of public TV control at
a time when the administration has been calling for more
'localism' in the medium, Loomis responded that in his
view such control is essential if CPB is to be
accountable to Congress and the White House for what goes
on PTV."[79] From Nairobi, Kenya, speaking at the
Commonwealth Broadcasting Conference, EBC president James
Day assessed the dismal situation: "The politicization
of public television is complete," he declared. "It
would appear that CPB, rather than serving public
television as insulation from political influence and
control, has opted to serve Congress and the White House
as their insulation from the dangers of public
television."[80]

November 1972 should have been the very darkest
hour for public television. The November 8 meeting of
the CPB board was the first opportunity for the Nixon-
appointed majority to solidify its grip over the

Corporation and the system with preliminary program proposals for the following season. But mid-November also saw the beginning of a shift in the momentum of the battle with the first of a surprising series of events that would culminate six months later with a new, friendly partnership agreement between CPB and PBS, and public television's coverage of the hearings before the special Senate Committee on Watergate. It was, in fact, a truly dramatic turnaround, which began when Henry Loomis tried to take his power as CPB president too far, too soon.

Loomis might not have meant to play the villain in the continuing melodrama of public television, but his actions in the late fall of 1972 gave most observers the impression that he was well-rehearsed for the role. At the November 8 board meeting, he brought up the idea of public television coverage of the last planned moonwalks of the space program, during the Apollo 17 mission. Loomis, a physicist by training who had served as staff director to the President's advisor on science and technology, naturally had an interest in the moon landing. The commercial networks planned only minor coverage of the flight. NASA, the space agency, offered CPB a free video feed of twenty-one hours of the moonwalks. "It seemed to me," Loomis said, "that this was the kind of broadcast for the record, similar to public hearings, that was an entirely appropriate thing to at least consider."[81] The CPB board agreed that Loomis should go ahead and determine whether the stations themselves were interested. Two station presidents, Jim Loper of KCET and Robert Schenkkan of KLRN in Austin, Texas, were attending the Corporation board meeting ex officio. After official business concluded, Loomis asked them what they thought of the Apollo idea and whether he should go to the system with it. They said yes, that it seemed like a pretty good idea.

Time was already short, however, with only a month before the Apollo flight. Instead of asking PBS to conduct a poll of the stations, Loomis decided to cable the system's 142 station managers himself from the Corporation. The next day his message came over the teletype system:

> The National Aeronautics and Space Administration (NASA) has informed us of its desire to provide coverage of a substantial portion of the Apollo 17 mission on December 11, 12, and 13. In order to be responsive to this offer we need to know whether or not stations are interested in carrying this programming.
>
> . . . NASA is anxious to emphasize the scientific aspects of the mission and has offered to help assemble a special group of scientists and science reporters under the supervision and editorial control of a public broadcasting production unit.
>
> The programming would originate in Houston and be fed to the entire system. NASA will contribute all pool and feed costs. CPB will underwrite national advertising. The time available for planning and production is short. Therefore, we would appreciate your immediate reaction to this suggestion . . . .
>
> We want to underscore the fact that no commitments have been made to NASA. This is a suggestion only. The decision belongs to the stations.[82]

The next day, The Washington Post reported simply and straightforwardly that the Corporation for Public Broadcasting was interested in doing Apollo coverage "aimed at the real space nuts" in the television audience, and had begun a poll of the stations to gauge the feasibility of such a project. The Post quoted a CPB official who said that "early returns indicated a positive response to the proposal, although coverage would wipe out three straight nights of Public Broadcasting Service offerings."[83]

PBS officials were stunned by Loomis' unprecedented action. The system had never received such a message directly from the Corporation president. This, perhaps more than the proposal itself, demonstrated to PBS executives the intention of the White House-appointed CPB leadership to take over the entire public broadcasting system. In his first weeks as Corporation president, Loomis had made few concessions to diplomacy in his relations with public broadcasters and his public statements. Now he had clearly gone too far. The Apollo idea looked like the proof positive that he was seeking to create a domestic propaganda agency. PBS leaked the cable to The New York Times, which interpreted it, as PBS had, as an audacious attempt to seize the initiative on national program selection. Henry Loomis got burned, and badly.

On November 11, the Apollo story hit the front page of The Times looking very different from the previous day's Washington Post item. "Dispute on Program Authority Splits Public TV and Fund Arm," characterized Loomis' action as a breach of standard procedures and an ominous "opening wedge" in his drive for CPB control over program decisionmaking. The Corporation's move, The Times reported, was viewed as a dangerous precedent, "as a case of one government agency carrying 'propaganda' -- an event financed, conceived and controlled by another government agency, NASA." An "anonymous PBS official," -- PBS public affairs coordinator Jim Lehrer -- was quoted in the story, saying "This would be like letting GM underwrite and produce for public television a program about car safety."[84]

"If there is any doubt," _Variety_ declared a few days later, "that this is a propaganda spread in the interests of a government agency for the 'Nixon Network,' the CPB wire dispells the notion." Though Loomis was careful to stress that the Apollo coverage was merely a suggestion, _Variety_ insisted that such a suggestion to the stations, from the organization that funded them, was a "heavy suggestion indeed."[85]

The entire episode quickly turned into a complete embarrassment for the new Corporation president. As it turned out, NASA decided that it would not underwrite any part of the production costs for the coverage. Criticism from key station management representatives in Washington, substantial numbers of affiliates themselves, and the PBS board forced Loomis to back down by saying that time was actually too short to produce quality television coverage by the public system and that the commercial networks were doing more than originally expected. On November 21, PBS and CPB jointly announced an agreement to limit the coverage of Apollo 17 to highlights only. Thus, said _Variety_, Loomis' first program project "fizzled on the launching pad."[86]

The Apollo affair reinforced the fear that Loomis' intention to bring the Corporation into a larger role in programming represented a legitimate threat of a government controlled broadcasting system. "It brought home to me as nothing else did," Loomis recalled, "the paranoia on that side of the fence and that my experience in USIA was clearly a problem."[87] Given the signals coming from the White House, the paranoia seemed entirely justified. Loomis' hesitation about long-term funding and public affairs programs, combined with the issue of programming authority, encouraged hostility and suspicion towards him within the system.

In mid-November, after the Apollo incident, he
appeared on WNYC's <u>All About TV</u> program with James Day;
David Ives, president of Boston's WGBH; Robert Wilson,
general manager of KERA, Dallas; and Fred Powledge,
author of the ACLU reports on White House intimidation of
public and commercial television. When Loomis said that
a perfectly good case could be made for ending all
federal funding of public affairs programming, Day
quipped, "I can make a much better case than I can a
budget, unfortunately." Loomis' yet-to-be formed
position on whether CPB should allow any non-federally
funded political programs to be sent over the CPB-
underwrited interconnection system sounded like
censorship by Catch-22. His support for public affairs
productions that would appeal to specialized audiences
and for non-editorial, "network of record" broadcasts of
government and special commission public hearings did not
impress skeptics like Powledge. "It seems to me,"
Powledge said, "that, in the past year, let's say, that
Public Television has gone tremendously downhill. I
think what -- what used to be a very venturesome --
adventuresome medium -- is now devoted almost exclusively
on the national level to -- to pap, the transmission of
pap.

"It looks as if we're going to get more of --of
a sort of sanitized version of what seems to be
happening. . . . As I understand it, the Public
Broadcasting Act of 1967, which is your guiding -- your
founding document, says that you're going to operate in
ways that most effectively assure the maximum freedom of
public television . . . 'from interference with or
control of program content or other activities.' Now, it
seems to me that this is exactly what you're doing. You
are influencing program content yourself, which I'm sure
that the Congress did not mean for the Corporation for
Public Broadcasting to do."

Later in the discussion, Powledge said, "It sounds like centralization is going to occur, doesn't it?"

"No," Loomis replied. "I think talking to all the stations couldn't be more decentralizing."

"Maybe," Day chimed in, "look upon the moonwalk as a local show, with an origination on the moon."

Station managers Day and Ives concluded their remarks on <u>All About TV</u> with fairly sharp words, obviously directed at Loomis and the direction in which he was trying to move CPB. "Well," Day said, "I recall that my predecessor as President of NET, Jack White, warned four years ago in a speech before the stations that we were in danger of building in public television a domestic USIA. I think we're too close to it right now. Mr. Loomis' predecessor in his job, John Macy, said in a speech a couple of weeks ago that there comes a time when freedom is more important than federal money. And I think we've probably reached that point."[88]

Although his efforts had certainly misfired, one positive result of Loomis' Apollo gaffe was the beginning of serious discussions between CPB and PBS on the institution of a more formal division of responsibilities. Four days after his fateful Apollo message, Loomis again cabled the stations to say that he had met with Hartford Gunn for four hours "to discuss at length CPB-PBS relationships." They had agreed that the CPB and PBS staffs would work together to develop precise draft language spelling out Corporation responsibilities, PBS responsibilities, and agreed procedures.

The meetings between PBS vice president Gerald Slater and general counsel Norm Sinel, and CPB president John Golden and general counsel Tom Gherardi revealed only what had been increasingly clear over the preceding two months: there were practically <u>no</u> areas of agreement between the two organizations. CPB believed that the system would work best if CPB was responsible for all decisionmaking relating to the selection, review, acceptance, distribution, and scheduling of programs, whether or not those programs were supported by federal funds. PBS would thus revert to the status of a "wholly owned subsidiary" of the Corporation, responsible only for the purely technical service of interconnection.

PBS, on the other hand, indicated that all functions pertaining to the distribution of public television programming must be conducted by an institution directly controlled by the station licensees, not by political appointees. The PBS board, management, and membership did not believe that the Corporation was able or willing to be responsive to the desires of the local stations. "It is clear," Slater and Sinel told the PBS board, "that the basic issue in those meetings [was] not merely one involving PBS and CPB. The basic issue involves the local stations and their ability to guide their own affairs in a way that best serves their communities and insures the maximum independence for public television."[89]

The draft papers submitted by each staff on December 15 constituted two fundamentally antagonistic statements of principle. The CPB document stated that the 1967 Public Broadcasting Act had vested all authority and responsibility for public television in the Corporation's board of directors.

> Except as that Act or other pertinent
> law may otherwise specify, the CPB board
> has complete discretion as to the manner
> or manners in which its authorities may
> be exercised and its responsibilities
> met . . . .

> . . . The CPB board may not, and would
> not if it could, permit PBS to make
> final decisions on interconnection, a
> matter within CPB responsibility under
> the Act.

> . . . The CPB board may not, and would
> not if it could, permit PBS to make
> final decision on proposals for program
> support of acquisition matters within
> CPB responsibility under the Act.

> . . . In making these determinations,
> the CPB board will insure the most
> efficient allocation of CPB resources,
> which are principally taxpayers'
> dollars, by seeking to reduce
> unnecessary duplication of effort by its
> own staff and that of its contractors or
> grantees.[90]

The PBS document, on the other hand, rejected the notion of complete CPB authority over the system, saying, "PBS functions as the national organization with primary responsibility for all policies and activities concerned with the national distribution of programs. It is unwilling to delegate these policy and decisionmaking functions to any organization not under direct station control. . . . PBS views any movement by CPB from a leadership to an operational role for CPB as a violation of the letter and spirit of the Act which would render CPB incapable of satisfying its mandate to create a free, decentralized public television system, based on the strength of the local stations."[91]

The debate here was over what the "public" in public television meant. The Corporation was saying that "public" meant supported by tax dollars. Therefore, it, as the government's chosen agent for the use of these tax dollars, was responsible to the public through its elected representatives in Congress and the White House. PBS was saying that what made public television different from the commercial networks was the fact that it was built upon the principle of decentralization, wherein the <u>local station</u> was responsible to the community interest directly. CPB was not just a creation of the Congress, but of the stations themselves; and PBS was not merely a figment of the Corporation's imagination, but the representative of the collective interest of those local stations serving the public interest.

The unstated issue in the emerging struggle for power between CPB and PBS was the role played by the White House and Nixon's appointees on the CPB board. Was the Corporation acting as the surrogate of the administration in attempting to take control of the public television system? It certainly appeared that Loomis and CPB were doing the White House's bidding. They were centralizing decisionmaking power, they said, in order to disperse it from the clutches of PBS. "You had to take [power] from PBS before you had anything to give," Henry Loomis said. "You had to take it and be trusted that you would, in fact, give it." But no one trusted the Corporation to give the power back to anyone. Already, CPB was making decisions contrary to the wishes of the local stations. The specter -- if not the reality -- of White House influence hung over the takeover fight. The prime focus of White House concern, however, was not structure, but programming. And during the winter of 1972-1973 both CPB and PBS were trying to formulate program schedules, based on three possible federal appropriations for the coming year. Which programs were funded and which canceled added the most controversial and political element to institutional debate.

The CPB staff and program advisory committee of the board had postponed funding decisions on every important public affairs program for the 1973-74 season. There were, perhaps, two very different reasons for this

action. One was simply that the CPB staff did not yet
have the competence of experience to run the entire
system without PBS guidance. Hartford Gunn told a
December 15 telephone conference of the PBS board
executive committee, "Internally, I gather that there's
now some concern on the part of some of the staff members
at the Corporation that they're in over their head and
that they are not able to keep up with the work load and
they haven't got the expertise to do it." But this
difficulty, Gunn explained, did not seem to deter the CPB
board. The board itself, more specifically, the Nixon
appointees to the board, were intent on making the final
programming determinations themselves. Administration
supporter Jack Wrather was in firm control of the
Corporation's program advisory committee. With the
backing of the Republican board members, he was pushing
for an end to CPB support for all political programs.
"As near as we can find out from our own sources, I guess
who had better remain nameless," Gunn told the PBS
executive group, "the actual program decisions are being
made . . . by Jack Wrather himself and more or less
rubber stamped by his committee . . . and then in turn
that's pretty much rubber stamped by the full board; so
that I gather Jack has become essentially the program
director."[92]

The December 15 PBS conference was called to
discuss the Corporation's request for joint meetings of
the two staffs in order to pare down the old $70 million
CPB draft budget to the $45 million level which the White
House was willing to grant for fiscal 1974. The CPB
board was demanding that it have sufficient lead time to
consider the staff's budget recommendation before its
January 10 meeting. The Corporation staff needed PBS'
help if it was to submit its report to the board before
the Christmas vacation period. PBS leaders, however,

were wary of the Corporation's intention with this
request. The organizations were in outright competition
for program decisionmaking power. Their institutional
jealousy was tremendous. Some PBS executives considered
the CPB staff generally second-rate. PBS general counsel
Norm Sinel felt that there were inherent problems in the
relationship between the "operations people" of PBS and
the "grant-making people" of CPB. They were a different
breed. The programmers considered the grant-makers
"stoppers" instead of "movers," endowed with a talent for
keeping projects from coming to fruition, but not for
doing anything original or creative themselves.[93]

The Corporation's new management viewed the PBS
organization with near-equal disdain. Loomis and
Gherardi thought the past business practices of the
Corporation under John Macy ludicrous and the informality
of the CPB-PBS relationship absurd in managerial terms.
Likewise, they felt that the PBS people had not exercised
fiscal responsibility or rational management
techniques.[94] The new regime believed in prudence in
dealing with the taxpayers' money. "The real problem,"
Loomis maintained, "was that PBS' accounting, for a long
time, was total anarchy . . . [because of] incompetence
and lack of concern." Loomis did not think it a
deliberate lack of concern, but merely a lackadaisical
attitude towards details beyond the creative endeavor.
He characterized their view about their CPB-granted money
as, "'We'll spend it as we want. We're too busy to worry
about this paperwork; just get on with the good program.'
On the one hand," Loomis said, "you sympathize with that.
But on the other hand, you have to have somebody who
worries about the chits and what belongs to which."[95]

PBS officials did not view themselves as
fiscally irresponsible and resented repeated CPB audits
of their organization aimed, they thought, at proving

them as such. They considered the audits as efforts to
find evidence to justify a Corporation takeover of PBS
functions. They saw CPB's request for help on
programming decisions at this late date as a potential
trap. The CPB board, Gunn said to the PBS executive
group, "had it set up so that they've got all the hot
ones undecided." He said it could very well be that
since CPB had never tried operating the system, this
confusion was simply "a product of their ignorance.
They're doing a lot of very strange things that don't
make any sense," he said, "and in some cases, I think
it's not a plot, it's just that they don't know how to
operate the system now that they're in the process of
taking it over."

"They've got all the press now on their back.
Jack Anderson is ready to come out on Monday with a blast
and Newsweek is ready and The Washington Post had been
hitting them every day now for three days in a
row. . . . Certainly, in public relations terms it's a
total disaster."

The Corporation had begun to receive a great
deal of criticism from the press and the local stations
as its preliminary funding decisions became known.
Approval of all NPACT funding, Bill Moyers' Journal, The
Advocates, William F. Buckley's Firing Line, Tony Brown's
Black Journal -- the entire national public affairs
schedule -- had been withheld. PBS, the stations, and
the press interpreted this as a triumph of White House
efforts to end all national public affairs programming.
The PBS group, the producers and supporters of these
programs, began, in December, their own countermeasures
to CPB's takeover of the system. The PBS executive
committee decided during their December 15 telephone
conference to add an extra day to the planned meeting of
the full board on January 5, devoted solely to

the programming questions. The rest of the meeting would focus on what to do about CPB's move to assume PBS functions. Gunn clarified these arrangements for the group: "We put the programming maybe in on the 4th, which would give us at least a majority of the board and then we take up on the 5th the future of public television."

"If any!!!" someone chimed in.[96]

The six-month period that began with the Apollo controversy and the commencement of the CPB-PBS debates saw an extraordinary turn-around in the battle over the future of public television. It saw a tremendous outpouring of financial and moral support for the system from the general public. It saw Ralph Rogers, the wealthy, respected, Republican leader of public television's board chairmen, whom the White House had once considered for an appointment to the CPB board, fight relentlessly not only for public affairs programs, but for the overall independence of the system from political control by CPB. The President's most prominent --perhaps most notorious -- media advisor would unabashedly reveal on national television the true motivations behind the White House's public television policies. And two weeks after his shocking performance, the Senate Communications Subcommittee would hold yet another round of hearings on yet another proposed funding bill for public television, during which administration attempts at intimidation and obfuscation would receive a sharp bipartisan rebuke. The President's hand-picked chairman of the board of the Corporation for Public Broadcasting would dramatically resign from his post charging that the White House had interfered with the decisionmaking process and compromised the independence of the CPB board. Finally, there would be public television's closely contested decision to provide

nationwide, prime-time, gavel-to-gavel coverage of the
hearings before the Senate's Select Committee on
Presidential Campaign Activities -- the Watergate
hearings. This almost inconceivable succession of events
had the cumulative effect of assuring the first passage
of a multi-year funding bill for public broadcasting and
the future of national public affairs programming. The
first six months of 1973 saw the administration's battle
against public television turn into something of a
wintertime Russian campaign for Richard Nixon, on his way
to Waterloo.

CHAPTER SIX

THE SLIPPERY SLOPE

". . . despite our strongly held wishes to the
contrary . . . it will be impossible for us to 'kill' the
Corporation either through direct legislative action or
through suffocation by stringent cutbacks in appropriated
funds."

> --OTP General Counsel
> Henry Goldberg, April 20, 1973

Although 1973 would prove to be the pivotal
year for both public television and Richard Nixon's
presidency, it began pessimistically for the former and
victoriously for the latter. It could hardly have been
foreseen that in six months' time the positions would be
completely reversed. At the outset of 1973 Richard Nixon
was inaugurated for his second term after a landslide
reelection victory over George McGovern. At the same
time the Public Broadcasting Service and its member
stations were in a state of financial exhaustion and
threatened with an imminent takeover by the
presidentially appointed Corporation for Public
Broadcasting board of directors. Despite the
embarrassment of the Apollo affair and objections from
the system itself, CPB was moving ahead with its plans to
take upon itself all national programming authority for
public television.

The system quickly reached the conclusion that
CPB should keep its hands off the program decisionmaking,
which should remain in the hands of the stations through

their agent, PBS. The lines in the battle for public television were drawn.

At its January 10 meeting, the CPB board of directors adopted a resolution calling for greater local station involvement in programming decisions, but under the aegis of the Corporation, instead of PBS. As part of the process of "expanding access" to national program decisionmaking, the board said it would reappraise CPB's relationships with PBS, the NAEB, National Public Radio, local station boards, citizen advisory groups, and any others who shared its "devotion to excellence and diversity in public broadcasting." The board said it was "particularly concerned about the dilution or confusion of decisionmaking responsibility between CPB and PBS and would therefore try to negotiate a formal contract to govern their future relationship." Specifically, the January 10 resolution stated:

> This board has reviewed its Project Grant to the Public Broadcasting Service and pertinent legal, legislative, and administrative materials. This review has demonstrated the inclusion within PBS of activities and functions which should be lodged within CPB, and the possibility of unnecessary duplication of staff and other resources in both corporations.[1]

The board directed Loomis to submit, as soon as possible, a plan "to establish, solely within the Corporation, the staff and resources necessary" to exercise what it believed was its responsibility under the Public Broadcasting Act; that is, control of national programming.

"Thus," wrote the Los Angeles Times' Cecil Smith, "the long-predicted emasculation of public television has begun."

The presidentially appointed directors of the Corporation for Public Broadcasting were taking over the public television system. Although its stated objective was greater local station control, many observers believed simply that, under White House direction, the Corporation was finally moving in for the kill against its politically uncontrollable rival, PBS. To Smith and others, President Nixon was finally "reaching for the 'off' switch." "The way things are going," said Smith, "you figure the President is capable of anything, no matter how petty, to put television right where he wants it -- under his thumb."[2] CPB chairman Thomas Curtis stubbornly maintained the Corporation's independence and desire to keep public broadcasting from being the voice of any administration. But privately he was increasingly angered by the frequent informal contact between the White House and certain members of the Corporation board and staff. The president of CPB did not, however, share the chairman's concern.

Henry Loomis stated at the January 11 announcement of CPB actions that he was interested in closer cooperation between public broadcasting and the government. He suggested, for example, joint funding of programs with federal agencies like the Office of Education and the National Science Foundation. Loomis saw nothing wrong with direct contact with the White House or the Office of Telecommunications Policy in dealing with the governmental issues that affected public broadcasting. While the PBS board was meeting to plan its strategy to keep the system out of CPB hands, OTP's Brian Lamb arranged a lunch date for himself and Whitehead with CPB counsel Tom Gherardi. The day after CPB's board of directors met, Gherardi supplied Henry Goldberg with the full text of the resolution to take over programming from PBS, and Whitehead met with board

member Irving Kristol at the Century Club in New York.
Later in the month, Lamb, Whitehead, and Goldberg had
dinner at Gherardi's and they began a series of weekly
luncheons, which included Loomis and CPB vice president
Keith Fischer. On January 31, Fischer sent Brian Lamb
drafts of proposed CPB policies on use of the federally
funded interconnection and on public issues programs.
These were in their very first stages and, as Fischer
advised Lamb, the CPB board itself had not yet seen the
draft documents. "We will keep you advised as these are
formulated into more formal documents," the Corporation
vice president told the assistant to the OTP director.
"I enjoyed meeting you the other day and look forward to
our second weekly lunch next Monday."[3]

Disagreement over the propriety of such
meetings was one cause of increasingly strained relations
between Curtis and the management of the Corporation.
But the CPB leadership was apparently united in its
commitment to a take-over of PBS functions in the very
near future. The Corporation, Curtis and Loomis
announced, would assume all responsibility for the pre-
broadcast acceptance and post-broadcast review of
programs to determine strict adherence to objectivity and
balance. Asked if Loomis would be the chief editor under
such an arrangement, Curtis replied quickly, "Oh, yes."[4]

The administration, of course, had an abiding
interest in the power struggle between CPB and PBS. The
intramural battle had been envisioned and, at least in
part, inspired by the White House. But the clash between
the Corporation and the Service was also a bureaucratic
tug-of-war with a dynamic all its own. To the competing
power centers the desire to control the program decisionmaking process was as much a driving force as partisan
politics. Though some of the original members of the CPB
board like Jack Valenti and James Killian had always

opposed the Corporation's involvement in programming,
many board members supported the takeover as a way of
demonstrating the Corporation's fiscal responsibility and
thereby assuring future funding from the federal
government. In January 1973, the real conflict was
rooted in the fundamentally different perspectives that
the two national organizations and their boards of
directors brought to their stewardship of the public
television system. PBS was an organization dominated by
professional broadcasters, while CPB was directed by a
group of concerned laymen. Both were interested in
building a strong system and obtaining long-term federal
financing, but between them, there were significant
differences of approach and opinion.[5]

Some board members who were not necessarily
strong Nixon supporters were, nonetheless, very much
affected by the White House's opposition to public
affairs programs. Those who were not used to Washington,
said Valenti, "didn't understand the political process,
and found it compatible with their views to say, 'Let's
get rid of this controversy, let's assure ourselves of a
two-year or a three-year appropriation and if the price
we have to pay is dumping public affairs, it would be a
worthy price to pay.'"[6] The CPB board was highly
sensitive to the administration's position on new
financing legislation and the White House certainly tried
to manipulate this concern to further its own objectives.
Whitehead and Flanigan stayed in close contact with the
Republican members of the board and with "loyal"
professionals on the Corporation staff. Curtis revealed
several times during the January 11 press conference that
the board was under White House pressure on the news and
public affairs programming issue. "The Nixon
Administration," he said, "or some of its spokesmen are
very worried about this area." And, he admitted, CPB had

to be "concerned about the constituency in the White House as we go through their budgetary process."[7]

At the time, Henry Loomis was not completely aware of the amount of contact between the White House and his board. His own efforts had received only a mixed reception from within the administration. President Nixon and his advisors clearly expected Loomis and Curtis to get rid of the offensive public affairs programs once and for all. Individually and collectively they were a great disappointment to the administration. White House communications director Herb Klein wrote that although the White House itself had chosen the former USIA executive for the CPB post, "In office he proved less pliable to White House demands than had been anticipated by the President."[8] Whitehead and OTP hoped that the new Corporation management would take steps to decentralize the system as quickly as possible. But Whitehead did not feel that Loomis and Curtis were any more "professional" than John Macy and Frank Pace had been. He did not get along with Curtis, who resented the OTP directors' effort to influence him. Whitehead found also that Loomis was just not as "effective" in the CPB presidency as he had hoped he would be. Henry Loomis did not pursue the administration's objectives, though he certainly tried to appease them as he went about constructing what he thought should be a more rational, organized system. "The problem as I saw it," Loomis said, "was partly to try to reduce the emotions and the knee-jerk reactions on both sides and one of the things I had to try to do was to reduce the reaction in the White House staff. I came in with an advantage there because they had known me and I think they were aware of my record at USIA and they basically thought my head was screwed on right, that I wasn't some crazy liberal guy." But Loomis recognized that an asset with the administration could be a serious

liability with the public broadcasters if his ongoing
relationship with the White House became public. He and
his staff did keep Whitehead and OTP well-informed about
CPB's direction and convey the impression that the
Corporation was making progress in the areas of White
House concern. Loomis' basic message to the White House
was, "For Christ's sake, give us some support and stop
nitpicking the way [you've] been doing in the past, which
would only screw up the works that much more."[9] He, like
his predecessor, was viewed with suspicion when trying to
placate both the White House and the public broadcasters.
He could never much satisfy either one, and certainly
never both at the same time.

In January 1973, the objectives of the
administration and those of CPB appeared, at least, to be
in perfect harmony: to halt the use of federal funds for
so-called controversial public affairs programming.
Though a simple cut-off of CPB funding for these programs
would not necessarily mean their cancellation, the
Corporation's refusal to allow such programs financed by
other sources on the national interconnection would
effectively block their distribution to the system. In
December, CPB had released a list of shows for which
funding decisions for the 1973-74 season had been
"deferred." The Corporation had based its decisions, not
on the $70 million appropriation that both PBS and
Congressional Democrats were expecting to pass, but on
the administration proposal of only $45 million.[10] The
White House version was not made official until the
President's budget message in late January. But since
Loomis and his staff had been working in close
consultation with Whitehead and OTP, they knew what to
expect. As Whitehead had suggested during the fall,
holding funding at a constant $45 million level created

an "incentive" for the Corporation to redirect its
priorities in program funding; that is, away from news
and public affairs.[11]

Although deferral was not a final verdict for
cancellation, the list certainly reflected the White
House's professed desire to remove all programs of
national politics from the schedule. Approval was
withheld for William F. Buckley's Firing Line, Black
Journal, Bill Moyers' Journal, The Advocates, Washington
Week in Review, as well as NPACT's two new projects,
American '73 and For the Record. Loomis justified the
possible cancellations on the grounds that CPB ought to
be putting its money into programs that "would stand up
timewise in six months or a year." He argued that it was
not "efficient" to use a lot of money for shows on
politics that would quickly become dated. He felt that
public service programs, like VD Blues -- which combined
information and entertainment to warn young people about
venereal disease -- which could be used over and over
again were more appropriate and efficient.[12] Though he
was not inclined to see Henry Loomis as a "conscious
agent of a Machiavellian plot to destroy public
television," the Chicago Tribune's Clarence Petersen
decried the "blandness boom" that CPB's new priorities
ushered in. "It appears," he wrote, "as if the blandness
boom will continue, as politically appointed corporation
directors take the job of programming away from
professional programmers."[13] Clearly, if public affairs
programs on contemporary political issues were to
survive, public broadcasters, viewers and supporters
would have to fight for them.

To guarantee the continuation of news and
public affairs and, more broadly, to preserve public
television's independence from the increasingly
aggressive encroachment of CPB, PBS, the stations and the

Ford Foundation began making plans for alternative means of funding the interconnection and providing a national program service. While calling plans for a "survival network" premature, Fred Friendly had said in December that the Ford Foundation had a "moral obligation" to support public television as long as it was needed. "We will do whatever we have to," Friendly declared. "We're two hundred fifty million dollars into public television and we have to figure out what we can do best."[14]

Normally, as Friendly remarked, public television "rejects unification the way the human body rejects another ear." But in the face of the CPB threat, the various other groups within public broadcasting strove toward unaccustomed unity at the beginning of 1973.

Newly-elected PBS board chairman Robert Schenkkan of station KLRN in Austin, Texas said at a January 5 news conference that it was a crucial time for the future of non-commercial broadcasting in the United States, amid indications that the Corporation was moving "in the direction of centralized control of the medium, counter to the intent of the Public Broadcasting Act."[15] Schenkkan and PBS president Hartford Gunn later replied to CPB's January 10 resolution by declaring, "We do not consider the action of the CPB board to assume operating control of the national program service to be the final decision regarding the future structure and organization of our public television system. We believe that there are several alternatives to turning over control and operation of the interconnection to CPB.[16]

A final appeal from a representative of the stations came on the morning the CPB board met, at the Maryland Center for Public Television in Owings Mills, Maryland. Frederick Breitenfeld, executive director of the Maryland center and board chairman of the Educational

Television Stations division of the NAEB, urged the board
members to defend public broadcasting, not control it,
though he acknowledged that "the issue may be academic at
this point." Anticipating the board's resolution to
centralize programming control in its own hands,
Breitenfeld said, "that means, in all likelihood, that
two distinct public broadcasting instrumentalities will
soon be operating. One will be the Corporation and the
other will be the stations. This is probably not healthy
pluralism, but dangerous division. Meanwhile, you will
be called upon not less but more to defend and to account
for national television series, individual programs,
particular personalities, perhaps even specific scripts.
It may well be an American precedent."[17]

Breitenfeld's appeal fell on deaf ears. The
Corporation's direction had been determined. "Cool
reserve to outright hostility," the Los Angeles Times
reported, "could best describe the range of initial
reactions of local public television station managers
around the country to the Corporation for Public
Broadcasting's announced intention to take direct control
of national programming on public television."[18]
O. Leonard Press, director of the Kentucky Authority for
Educational Television and chairman of the NAEB board,
said the Corporation had "arrogated to itself powers of
program control that properly belong only to stations.
It has taken from those stations the power that was
theirs under a membership corporation, replacing it only
with a general right of access of CPB decisions. . . . I
do not believe that the station community will quietly
accept that decision."[19] Station leaders supported PBS,
both with their opposition to the CPB takeover and their
disagreement with the Corporation board over funding
public affairs programs. The director of the University
of Alaska's public television station wrote to CPB

chairman Curtis to express his "extreme dismay at the
actions announced at yesterday's CPB press
conference. . . . I cannot emphasize strongly enough my
belief that an organization like the Public Broadcasting
Service . . . is necessary to provide a buffer zone
between the politically appointed board of the
Corporation, which receives federal dollars for
programming, and the using stations and their viewing
public. . . . I am particularly alarmed at the thought
that a network controlled by the Corporation would
examine every program before it was put on the
interconnect to determine whether or not it would even be
offered to the stations, thereby depriving the stations
of their ability to choose from the widest possible
sources of programming for their community. I sincerely
hope that the Corporation board will reconsider its
decision, or at least for the moment defer it, so that
further study can be made of this matter, and that some
strong, viable station-controlled organization remain in
charge of the program selection and distribution process
for public broadcasting."[20]

On January 15, Indiana University's public
station manager cabled Schenkkan in Austin with a
complete battle plan for the fight against the
Corporation:

> STRONGLY ENDORSE PBS BOARD POSITION AND
> YOUR SUBSEQUENT STATEMENT OF CPB ISSUE.
> I REGARD THE CPB RESOLUTION OF JANUARY
> 10 AS A DECLARATION OF WAR ON STATION
> MANAGERS AND THEIR NATIONAL ORGANIZA-
> TIONS. WE MUST RECOGNIZE THAT THE CPB
> HAS BECOME A DANGEROUS ADVERSARY, AND
> THAT IT MUST BE SCUTTLED OR CURBED. WE
> MUST NOT LET OURSELVES BE DELUDED BY
> SOOTHING RHETORIC OR MINOR CONCESSIONS:
> THIS WILL ONLY RESULT IN OUR FIGHTING
> OUR BATTLES ON GROUND CHOSEN BY LOOMIS

> AND COMPANY, TO OUR DISADVANTAGE. WE
> MUST MOVE AGGRESSIVELY TO TAKE COUNTER-
> MEASURES BEFORE LOOMIS CAN FURTHER
> CONSOLIDATE HIS POSITION AND WEAKEN
> OURS.

He called CPB a "dangerous institution," and even suggested that the stations oppose increased federal funding for the Corporation because "we dare not strengthen an agency which threatens to become a federal dictatorship in public broadcasting."[21]

In somewhat more measured tones, Gordon Tuell, general manager of Washington State University's KWSU, wrote to Curtis, "It is difficult to believe that so much turmoil could develop in so short a time over, around, and within the public broadcasting world. Up to the moment of the totally unexpected presidential veto of the MacDonald bill last year, confidence was very high that at long last the almost twenty years of struggle to keep our heads above water was nearing an end. The shock wave of that veto action has been ricocheting with devastating results throughout the public broadcasting domain. As a result, the stations seem to have been forced to set up camp to do battle against the new hierarchy of CPB . . . ." Tuell rejected the idea that the CPB staff could do any better, fairer, or more responsible job of program selection than that of PBS and concluded by asking the CPB chairman, "Is the goal service to the people according to their expressed needs through decentralization? Or is it control based on governmental dictates through centralization? The stations are willing to work cooperatively with the Corporation, but they are not willing to become 'subjects' of the Corporation."[22]

Tuell sent this letter to Washington Senator Warren Magnuson, chairman of the Senate Commerce

Committee, whose subcommittee on communications handled
public television matters. "Administration pressures on
the broadcasting industry are in many ways becoming even
more stifling to the nation's public broadcasting
stations than they are to our commercial counterparts,"
he told the long-time advocate of public television:
"However, these pressures can be exerted more directly on
those of us in the non-commercial branch of the
business . . . ."

> If public broadcasting . . . is to be
> rescued from a damaging setback at the
> hands of a new group of administration-
> inspired leaders, there is going to have
> to be support from those of you in our
> government whose voices command
> attention, and who represent the needs
> and wishes of the people.[23]

PBS had support for its position from House
Communications Subcommittee chairman Torbert MacDonald.
On January 3 he had written in Variety that the Public
Broadcasting Act did not give CPB authority to produce
programs, but only "to contract or make grants to program
producing entities . . . ." That wording, MacDonald
said, "was inserted in order that no grounds would exist
for suspicion that CPB would become a mouthpiece for the
Administration -- any Administration." He rejected the
White House's and Loomis' contention that there should
not be political programs, saying, "Certainly, the
legislative history of the origin of public broadcasting
leaves no doubt that the Congress intended public
broadcasting to deal with current issues . . . ."[24]

The NAEB reacted strongly to the Corporation's
attempt to take over programming power. Association
president William Harley sent Curtis a statement, saying,
"only an agency that is directly responsible -- and

structurally responsive -- to the licensed stations should determine the selection and scheduling of programs for national interconnection distribution." Harley's objection was that "Under Federal law the line of accountability at the Corporation for Public Broadcasting ultimately leads to the government, not the stations." CPB, he told Curtis, "should therefore have no operational role in the national programming process."[25]

Public television seemed to be battening down the hatches for a long, hard fight against the White House, CPB, and Henry Loomis. By January 23, both PBS and the Eastern Educational Network were seriously pursuing plans for non-CPB funded "survival networks." On that day, PBS convened an emergency joint meeting with the Educational Television Stations division of NAEB in San Diego to explore "alternative means of funding a national interconnection, which would be directly controlled by the stations."[26] At the same time, EEN, the oldest regional network in the system, announced plans to create its own survival network out of its thirty member stations from Bangor, Maine to Buffalo to Baltimore.

These actions seem, in hindsight, to have been important demonstrations of renewed vigor, spirit, and unity within the public television community. But many observers in January 1973 were pessimistic about the ability of PBS and the local stations to withstand the CPB offensive. The New York Times described the "survival network" activities as mere "outgrowths of an elaborate dance of death," in which CPB was bent on dismantling PBS and replacing it with its own structure to produce programs and feed them to affiliates.[27] John J. O'Connor lamented that public television was being "drawn into steadily increasing political control." "The picture for public television in this country," he wrote on January 24, "has grown alarmingly dim."[28] The

conservative Chicago Tribune advised that such were "the
perils of public subsidies." "Public Broadcasting . . . is taking quite a beating at the hands of the
Nixon Administration," the Tribune said in its lead
editorial on January 19. It was a shame to see
government trying to influence what was broadcast, but
what, the editorial asked, did the backers of educational
television expect when they dumped their financial
problems on Congress' lap in 1967? "Did they really
believe promises made at the time that federal money
would guarantee 'maximum freedom' and 'objectivity and
balance' and would 'ensure the autonomy of local stations
and insulate them from government pressure'?" Such
federal subsidies, the Tribune concluded, invariably led
to federal interference.[29]

The bleak outlook was echoed that week by a
seemingly embittered John Macy, both at the Columbia-
duPont Broadcasting Journalism Awards in New York and at
the Center for the Study of Democratic Institutions in
Santa Barbara, California. "At this point," he said,
"the endeavor to establish freedom of expression in non-
commercial broadcasting must be deemed a failure." He
summed up the current situation by saying,

> Personalities who have probed vigorously
> or offered unfavorable assessments of
> administration actions will not receive
> continued funding. Commentaries
> following Presidential statements are to
> be eliminated. These developments lead
> to the sorrowful conclusion that the
> heat shield has been penetrated and
> video journalism, public style, severely
> burned.[30]

Variety's pessimistic conclusion was that
"barring an uprising of the troops or congressional
intervention, both unlikely, the CPB is going ahead with
plans to remove all program decisions from PBS."[31]

To the surprise of many, however, there was an uprising of the troops. By the middle of February it was becoming clear that public television viewers were not only vast in numbers, but deeply concerned about the future of news and public affairs programming. This concern was reflected by an unprecedented outpouring of financial support from the viewing audience. In many major cities memberships climbed fifty percent over the previous year. Donations from the public in New York, Boston, Chicago, Los Angeles, and Dallas reached record sums.[32] Jonathan Rice, program manager at KQED in San Francisco, said, "I think we're seeing a strong response to the publicity about the government trying to control television. People seem to want to help us stay independent." Local stations were able to capitalize on the growing consciousness of efforts by the White House and CPB to dominate the public medium. In New York, Channel Thirteen's pledge week pitch was, "We can't depend on the government or foundations, we need you;" and it was achieving notable results.[33]

In December, when it first became apparent that Washington Week in Review might not return the following season, moderator Robert MacNeil asked viewers to write in to express their views. By the end of January, NPACT had received over 13,000 letters. Of those, he said, twenty were against the program. MacNeil quoted from a few of the favorable letters in a January 26 speech to the Consumer Federation of America in Washington, D.C. He did so, he told his audience, to highlight the reaction of Henry Loomis. "At his press conference on January 11, he [Loomis] said: 'The number and emotional content of letters is not necessarily a good measure of audience size or interest.'" To which MacNeil declared, "I think that translates as: 'To hell with what the public wants.'"[34]

MacNeil's address was not only an indication of the increasing willingness of those concerned with the future of public television to speak out about the White House threat to PBS. It was also emblematic of a rising tide of outrage over Nixon administration attempts to intimidate all of the national news media. The winter of 1972-73 was filled with the "White House versus the Press" controversy. More and more it seemed as though the freedom of speech guaranteed by the First Amendment was in legitimate danger from the White House. Indeed, as White House communications director Herb Klein wrote: "With the self-confidence generated by the landslide vote for Nixon over McGovern, some felt the time was right to drive the critics of the Administration to their knees, to humiliate them publicly."[35] Or as legal counsel John Dean put it in a staff memorandum, those months following Nixon's reelection were a time when the President and his men began in earnest "the use of the available machinery of government to screw our enemies."[36]

The battle for public television seemed to be only one aspect of a much grander scheme within the White House to crush opposition in all quarters. As former CPB president John Macy said, "public television's agony" was shared by "other practitioners of the information cult." For nearly four years the administration had been publicly challenging the honesty and fairness of television network news and newspapers like The New York Times and The Washington Post. For the first time in American history the government, in the Pentagon Papers case, sought to impose prior restraint on the publication of news. The President ordered that the telephones of unfriendly journalists be wiretapped. The acting director of the FBI complained that American journalists were "too much a part of the culture of disparagement which threatens to destroy all respect for established

institutions." White House aide Charles Colson warned
the three television networks that they might be subject
to antitrust prosecution if they did not "move
conservatives and people with a viewpoint of middle
America onto the airwaves." In a December address to the
Indianapolis chapter of the journalism fraternity Sigma
Delta Chi, Clay Whitehead denounced commercial television
news as "ideological plugola" and "elitist gossip." He
stated ominously, "Station managers and network officials
who fail to correct imbalances or consistent
bias . . . can only be considered willing participants,
to be held fully accountable . . . at license renewal
time."[37]

The administration's strategy for taming the
power of the commercial networks sounded very much the
same as it had been for public television prior to the
summer of 1972 and the management changes at CPB. The
idea was to divide and conquer by using the argument for
"localism" and greater diversity of viewpoint. A
commercial broadcast license has been characterized as a
license to make money and without one, a local station
would be out of business. Local affiliates were thus
more conservative and more manipulable than the New York
centered networks -- which needed no government license
to operate. But the networks might be rendered harmless
if their outlets could be incited to rebellion.
Whitehead had not only held out a threatening stick, but
the carrot of an increase in the licensing period from
three to five years -- if the stations had "balanced"
news coverage. What most broadcasters saw was a very
deliberate attempt to strip the networks of their ability
to criticize official views. To strengthen the stations'
leverage on the network schedule, as The Washington Post
contended, was "to blunt the critical inquisitiveness of
the network news organizations -- with the threat of

government reprisal at the end of the line. Under the pretext of eliminating bias, and in the guise of our First Amendment rights, the Administration is proposing to set the local affiliates or, failing that, itself up as the ultimate arbiter of the truth to which the public is to be exposed."[38]

"The view on the part of the Administration," John Macy said, "was that the only way you achieve balance was to have that journalism be a cheering section for the Administration; not just neutral broadcasting, but really to have those that would beat the tub for the Nixon Administration." The best illustration that the White House was not merely interested in ideological balance, was the case of William F. Buckley. Perhaps the country's foremost conservative spokesman, Buckley, Macy recalled, "became as much an anathema [to the White House] as some of the allegedly liberal reporters" when he criticized the President on Firing Line.[39]

"They did not believe in a society of dissent or even of conversation, unless it was one-sided and assenting," said Bill Moyers.

> I can understand their not wanting direct, barbed criticism. But the mentality that did not want TV to educate, in the best sense of that word, was mentality to be feared. Not for what they might intimidate in you, but for what they might do to the country as a whole. Their attitude toward public television was a harbinger of their attitude toward society as a whole . . . .[40]

And the press was not the only target. After his reelection President Nixon undertook what Richard Nathan called "The Plot that Failed": an attempt to create a "super-presidency" by arrogating to the White

House alone the powers of the Congress and the federal agencies.[41] The President said he was building a "New Federalism," decentralizing and dispersing power back to the states but was in fact seeking to centralize all power and authority in the White House. The parallel to the administration's approach toward public broadcasting is clear. The White House impounded congressionally appropriated funds when it disagreed with their use, as it held down CPB's federal funding because it did not like the way that money was spent. The White House imagined that the federal bureaucracy was hostile to its program, so it sought to create clear lines of authority leading to loyal Nixon appointees at the top of the agencies, appointees who could be held directly accountable by the White House. The attitude toward public broadcasting reflected the very same desire for clear lines of authority controlling a hostile agency -- public television -- through those at the top appointed by and responsible to the White House. Corporation for Public Broadcasting directors were supposed to be independent leaders of an independent corporation, but the White House believed they should act as other appointees in the executive branch. John Ehrlichman's characterization of the ideal Nixonian bureaucrats was "When we say jump, they will only ask how high." In taking over PBS and cutting public affairs programs in the name of localism, CPB under Loomis and Curtis seemed to be jumping pretty high in January of 1973. The contradictions between the White House's professed goals and actions seemed increasingly and frighteningly clear.

Nixon's subordinates, Robert MacNeil claimed in his speech to the consumer federation, had been "running roughshod over the public interest." "Their claim for fairness," he said, "is as phony as the conservatism they have been preaching." "Bias in their minds is apparently any attitude which does not indicate permanent genuflection before the wisdom and purity of Richard Milhous Nixon."[42] Apparently, much of the viewing public agreed. By the end of February, CPB itself was flooded with mail deploring attempted government control of public television and squelching of news and public affairs. The Corporation was swamped, Variety reported, with "literally thousands" of complaints specifically against White House maneuvers aimed at undermining the editorial independence of public television.[43]

At its February 6-7 meeting in Washington, the CPB board of directors finally made some program funding decisions for the upcoming season. Loomis had decided that the Corporation should proceed with its planning under the pessimistic -- but nonetheless realistic -- assumption that it would have to survive in fiscal 1974 with the same $35 million appropriation as in 1972 and 1973. This represented only half of the $70 million that the system was hoping for and $10 million less than even the White House-sponsored CPB authorization bill. But Loomis felt that no government-supported agency should budget or hire personnel on "aspirations" or even on congressional authorizations. He thought that the public television stations that had hired people and made program plans based on their aspirations were idiotic, and he was not shy about saying so. "An authorization isn't worth a nickel," he said. "You've got to hire on an appropriation which is passed and signed."[44]

The board decided to approve funding at fiscal 1973 levels for two of the public affairs programs that had been at issue, The Advocates and Black Journal. No decisions were made on the other public affairs programs that depended on CPB support. Loomis liked The Advocates because its liberal versus conservative debate format assured that each program would be ideologically balanced. <u>Black Journal</u>'s host and producer Tony Brown had undertaken a concerted public relations campaign in late 1972 when he got wind of CPB's intention to cancel the program. Cutting the only public affairs program dealing with black issues was a touchy matter. Amid a great deal of press criticism and pressure from black groups, CPB backed down on <u>Black Journal</u>.

The Corporation also announced on February 8 that it expected to reach the rest of its programming decisions in consultation with the Governing Board Chairmen of Public Television Stations, headed by Ralph B. Rogers, pending the outcome of the recently initiated discussions between the two organizations.

The chairman's committee was the newest public broadcasting organization, but it quickly became pivotal in the first months of 1973. Rogers had assisted in the group's formation a year earlier at the request of the system's top professional managers. A respected, lifelong Republican from Dallas, Rogers was a highly successful businessman who had often put his own forceful managerial skill at the disposal of non-profit institutions like the Dallas Symphony and the city's public television station, KERA, as chairman of their boards of directors. The coordinating committee became his personal vehicle for negotiating on behalf of the entire public television system in its battle with CPB. The Corporation had refused a PBS request for a joint meeting of their board, but did meet with Rogers and nine other lay representatives of the licensees at its February 6 gathering to discuss national program decisionmaking and the operation of the interconnection. The stations and PBS had agreed at their emergency meeting in San Diego in late January to let the Rogers group represent them in negotiations with the Corporation on the structure and control of the public television system. In the weeks prior to CPB's February meeting, the Rogers group conducted a number of open meetings with station executives around the country to discuss the institutional controversy. Three CPB directors, including Jack Wrather had participated in one or more of these meetings. Feeling among the station people was running high and the gatherings were sometimes intensely emotional. Many of the station leaders were openly hostile towards Loomis and the Corporation.[45] Rogers began his prepared remarks to the CPB board on February 6 by admitting that it was "certainly possible that some individuals, in the heat of the moment, may have made some intemperate remarks." But he made it clear that none of the governing board chairmen themselves "questioned the integrity, competency or concern" of the Corporation board and staff. These were soothing words to cool the rhetoric -- but the integrity and competence of CPB was indeed the key issue to a large part of the public television community.

Rogers told the CPB board that the licensees were strongly opposed to CPB control over the interconnection and national program schedule. To the stations, the Corporation's threat to deny programs underwritten by other sources like the Ford Foundation access to the interconnection smacked of outright censorship. Their argument was simple. Each local station was responsible under the law for what it broadcast. The law safeguarded the public. Only the individual station knew whether any particular program on the interconnection fit its local needs and complied with its responsibilities to the public interest. In a reference to the popular public affairs programs which CPB had yet to approve for 1974, Rogers said, "No legitimate sponsor or donor can be put in the position of making vast expenditures for programming -- and then having the interconnection denied to those programs when a substantial majority of the licensees want them."

Rogers asked that CPB withhold specific commitment for programs until they were approved by properly constituted representatives of the stations. This was purely good business, he explained. "Since it is through the licensee that programs reach the public, you certainly do not want to spend the precious programming dollars without assurances that most of the licensees want them." On the all important issue of CPB control over the national programming, Rogers told the Corporation board that his group was "opposed to any elaborate advisory system such as has been proposed by your staff. Not that we reject the opportunity to receive or give advice -- we applaud it. Unfortunately, the advisory system for program grants is a return to the dark ages of NET. We had virtually the identical system there -- the licensees gave advice, but the decision was made by the staff. It did not work then --and it won't work now."[46]

Rogers' discussions with the Corporation went well. On the day after the meeting, ETS chairman Breitenfeld and PBS chairman Schenkkan sent a message to the stations: "We are greatly encouraged by the progress that has taken place, and we are eager that this new dialogue proceed in the best possible atmosphere." Accordingly, the station organization leaders urged their colleagues to refrain from any public comments on the CPB negotiations. At that point, as the NAEB newsletter pointed out, "the negotiations [were] the whole ballgame" for public television. In short, as of February 8, all bets on the future programming, structure, and control of public television were off, pending the outcome of the Rogers-CPB discussions.[47]

Throughout the remainder of February, the Corporation's preliminary program choices for the fall season and the White House's influence on these decisions continued to be a hot issue in the press. "One of these days," Edwin Diamond wrote in the <u>Boston Globe</u> on February 22, "it looks as if they'll be burying the body of public television."

> The immediate cause of death will be the decision of Mr. Nixon's Public Television appointees to cut off funds for a number of national public affairs programs . . . .
>
> But Bill Moyers, one of the most incisive minds on television, is getting the ax. <u>Washington Week in Review</u>, which provides sharp political insights for viewers beyond the Potomac, is also being dropped. Elizabeth Drew, one of the best interviewers on TV, is in limbo. Even William Buckley will be going.
>
> If Moyers, <u>Washington Week</u> and <u>Black Journal</u> are considered too 'liberal' -- whatever that means -- by the Nixon Administration, then Buckley is judged too 'conservative.' It seems he fell into disfavor at the White House for criticizing Mr. Nixon's China trip.[48]

The programming changes, said Diamond, mark "the transformation of public television into government television." The new public television bosses, as Bill Moyers said, were not concerned about duplication but about dissent. "They only want the official version of reality." Curtis, Diamond wrote, had acknowledged as much in a recent interview. He was not sure that he had seen "any of those programs," he said, but added: "Certain people in the Nixon Administration have clearly expressed [dissatisfaction] and . . . put pressure on . . . ."

Indeed, earlier in the month, on February 5, Whitehead had met with the President, H.R. Haldeman, and Charles Colson. The President opened the meeting by saying how much he admired and appreciated the way Whitehead had been handling his job, particularly with respect to the problem of the networks. A number of communications issues were discussed: license renewal, cable television, and public television. Nixon reaffirmed his view that the administration should oppose the funding of controversial public affairs programming with tax dollars. Whitehead expressed his own concern about the feud among various parts of the public television industry over future directions and federal dollars. Perhaps in a bid to gain the support of White House hardliners Haldeman and Colson, Whitehead himself warned about the "strong proclivity of public TV to produce one-sided political affairs programming as an instrument of social change and the danger of CPB becoming a mouthpiece for a future, less restrained Administration." The OTP director said that this might make it necessary in the future to eliminate any use of federal tax monies to support public television.[49]

And yet it was not some future administration that might threaten the independence of public television, but the current one. The Nixon White House was itself proving Whitehead's point about the potential for political control. In the face of an apparently successful White House effort to dictate programming Whitehead's continued public support for an approach rooted in structural concerns was perverse. His credibility was further undermined by his own foray into partisan criticism of network news.

On February 20, the Senate Subcommittee on Communications conducted hearings for its overview of the activities of the Office of Telecommunications Policy.

Whitehead was raked over the coals by committee members
for his role in the administration's intensifying battle
with the media in general, and public television in
particular. Whitehead's December disclosure that the
administration was drafting legislation which would hold
individual commercial stations accountable, at the risk
of losing their licenses, for the content of network
material they broadcast, had brought him intense
criticism. He sorely regretted his criticism of network
news as "ideological plugola" and "elitist gossip."
While he was villified by the press, he gained respect as
a "team player" from the President and his top advisors.
The Indianapolis speech showed Charles Colson that the
OTP director was definitely "on board." But to those in
the White House concerned about the frequent charges that
the President was trying to crush the news media, the
Whitehead speech was an embarrassment. It exacerbated
their mounting public relations problems just as bits and
pieces of the Watergate scandal were beginning to seep
out.[50]

"It was," said Whitehead, "one of the more
disappointing aspects of my tenure at OTP."[51] The Sigma
Delta Chi talk had been planned as an important statement
of policy. It was given purposely on a Monday --
typically a slow news day -- at noon so it could easily
make the evening news. The Associated Press was called
over the weekend with advance word on the speech so
overnight editors at the network news bureaus in Chicago
could pick up the story and send their crews down to
Indianapolis. "The only thing that didn't work," said
OTP's Brian Lamb, "was that the AP guy's lead on it was
not right and we've been suffering for that ever
since."[52] Instead of signaling the government's desire
to allow for more freedom and diversity in television,
Whitehead's remarks came off as an obvious threat. His

interest in applying the philosophy of decentralization quickly foundered on the same shoals as his public television policy. In the context of clear and present White House hostility towards the media, almost no one in the industry, the press, or the Congress could accept Whitehead's "structural" arguments at face value. Whitehead himself was simply another White House agent in the battle against the news media.

The senators conducting the OTP review, especially public television advocate and subcommittee chairman John Pastore, and Vance Hartke of Indiana, were justifiably skeptical about Whitehead's intentions and were sometimes openly hostile. Pastore repeatedly criticized the administration's opposition to increased or multi-year funding for public television. "The point is," Pastore said, "you cut [public television's appropriation] down from forty-five million to thirty-five million dollars and as I pointed out, when we enacted the law, there were only a hundred stations; now there are two hundred thirty-three."

> You begin to split up this pie of $35 million among 233 stations, and I mean, isn't this all counterproductive? What can they do with it? Their share will be so small. They can't program. . . . They ought to be given more money but what you have done is put the squeeze on the money, the squeeze on the authorization period and what you are doing is suffocating the whole industry.
>
> What you have done is you have built a wall between the Corporation and the local licensee. You come here and say we don't want much money and we want to constrict the time but we want everybody to program their own -- produce their own programs -- it is almost impossible.

Whitehead replied, "Mr. Chairman, we have never stated that the local station should produce all the programs. We agree that there are expenditures, very worthwhile programs that should be done at the national level."

"That is right," said Pastore. "But they can't do that out of the thirty-five million so that cuts down the pie even more. You are expecting people to do something big with only a little and it is impossible in this industry. You know that." Later in the hearing, Pastore repeated the same theme. "For the life of me," he said, "I cannot see why you keep resisting the two-year authorization. . . . We would all be better off for it . . . and you understand these things. It ought to be done."

"Mr. Chairman," Whitehead answered, "I certainly agree with the concept, there ought to be a longer range funding. But I think there is more involved here than just the planning horizons of the Corporation."

Of course there was, Pastore believed. "I know what it was," he said, "Sandy Vanocur and so on. I know what started all this. It is politics."

"We think there are--"

"Politics, that is what it was."

Senator Hartke objected to the numerous inconsistencies in the administration's broadcasting policies and to Whitehead's reinterpretation of the communications act fairness doctrine, which Hartke himself had authored. He called the OTP director's regulation philosophy "one of the best smoke screens that I have ever seen in the political world," for the White House's partisan antipathy towards public television and commercial network news. "You mentioned words like the 'rip and read' ethic of journalism and you talk of wire service copy." He asked Whitehead, "Have you ever worked in a newsroom at a newspaper, or radio room, or news room? Do you understand what really happens there?"

"I think I have some feel for it," Whitehead replied, "although I have never worked there."

"Have you ever worked in an area of how this all comes together?" Hartke continued. "Do you really believe a person in a small community should go back through and analyze every news broadcast to see whether or not it had elitist gossip -- and what is that other word?"

"Ideological plugola," Pastore offered.

"Ideological plugola?" said Hartke.

After sparring further with Whitehead on the substance of the Indianapolis speech and the political implications of OTP's proposed commercial license renewal bill, Hartke concluded, ". . . you want centralized control of public broadcasting, local control of commercial broadcasting, and in between all of this we will come up with a five-year extension if everybody can stay in line politically, right?"

"I think you misunderstand what we are trying to do," Whitehead said.

"I think I understand too well, thank you. . . . I would hope we have time to come back to this at a later date."

"We will," chairman Pastore added. "Further questions? If not, we want to thank you very much Mr. Whitehead. I look with great anticipation to your next speech, the title of which will be 'Mea Culpa.'"[53]

During March, Ralph Rogers, Hartford Gunn, and Fred Friendly sought to transform the temporary alliance between the chairmen's coordinating committee, PBS, and ETS into a single new entity to represent the stations and manage the interconnection. On March 14, Variety disclosed that the three organizations had agreed "in principle" to join together. <u>Variety</u> also revealed that the Ford Foundation stood ready with $15 million to finance the proposed "super group" if the battle with CPB continued.[54] On March 28-30 the representatives of the public television licensees would meet in Washington to consider the proposed merger. On those same dates, the Senate Communications Subcommittee scheduled its hearings on the new public broadcasting financing legislation. And, simultaneously, the negotiations between Ralph Rogers and the Corporation were nearing their preliminary conclusions. The battle for public television was reaching its climax.

At its March 7 meeting, the CPB board voted to seek a two-year, $140 million funding bill from Congress; authorized the subcommittee of directors James Killian, Jack Valenti, and Tom Moore to begin its consultations with Rogers' station group regarding their plans for the use of the interconnection; and adopted a 1973-74 national schedule. As expected, the popular but "controversial" <u>Bill Moyers' Journal</u>, <u>Washington Week in Review</u>, and <u>Firing Line</u> were left out of the schedule for the coming season. To some critics, the board's support for two-year funding was more surprising. Their resolution noted that the Corporation had been operating for two years with only the $35 million provided under the continuing resolution. The directors asked for relief in the form of a special appropriation and called for the officers of the Corporation to support legislation at the Senate hearings calling for two-year authorization at the level of $60 million for fiscal 1974 and $80 million for 1975.[55]

This was a far cry from the administration's bill -- providing only $45 million for the single fiscal year, 1974 -- which Loomis and Curtis had still publicly supported in January. The Corporation's March 7

resolution characterized the increased, multi-year
financing as "basic to sound planning" for public
television activities and "essential to the maintenance
of a pattern of deliberate growth in public
broadcasting's quality and quantity of services." Henry
Loomis noted that CPB, <u>like other independent
organizations</u>, was entitled to appeal the
administration's proposed budget, if it felt strong
arguments could be made for increases.[56] In January,
Loomis had received a letter from Office of Management
and Budget deputy director Frank Carlucci, advising him
of the administration's plans for a single year, $45
million authorization bill for CPB. "The President,"
Carlucci concluded in his letter, "expects each and every
official in the Corporation for Public Broadcasting to
actively support the budget set forth in this letter and
its enclosures. This support should be given in
testimony before congressional committees, in informal
contacts with Members of Congress and their staffs, and
in speeches and meetings with outside groups."[57]

White House opposition to any multi-year
funding showed Loomis that he had not "gotten as far on
that side of the fence" as he had hoped. He had come to
the view that the public television system desperately
needed the stability that a two-year authorization could
begin to provide. He also recognized that successful
Corporation support for the two-year bill would give him
a great deal more freedom in working out the system's
difficulties -- and more credibility with the
broadcasters themselves. Since his arrival at CPB in the
autumn of 1972, he and the board had been viewed in the
press and much of the public television community as the
surrogates of the White House in trying to take control
of the system and get rid of allegedly anti-
administration programs. Though he might often have

lacked a sense of diplomacy in his relations with the broadcasters, Loomis was, in fact, trying hard to mediate between them and the administration. As Herb Klein recalled, Loomis did not prove to be as pliable as some in the White House had hoped; but he appeared nonetheless to be carrying coals for Nixon and Whitehead. Loomis was aware that CPB's effort to take over PBS' decisionmaking authority to achieve greater decentralization was like "burning the village to save the village." But he hoped that if CPB got the power, "then the facts of life would show that we could be trusted and it would have been given back."[58] But the White House wanted control over public television and everyone involved knew it. Loomis was its hand-picked choice as CPB president and a majority of Nixon appointees controlled the Corporation board. Naturally, the rest of the system had interpreted the Corporation's actions as a White House plot and, to some extent, it was. "Oh, look," said CBS newsman Eric Severeid at a January conference on broadcasting and the First Amendment at the Center for the Study of Democratic Institutions, "John Macy was thrown out, and the President's own man, Henry Loomis, was put in there for the purpose of dismantling certain programming."[59]

"I will not buy the argument," said KCET's James Loper at the same meeting, "that the reorganized CPB and the administration are not synonomous."[60] CPB desperately needed to put some distance between itself and the Nixon administration. It could not hope to gain the allegiance of the panicky and poverty-stricken local stations unless it, too, lobbied for increased federal financing. But also, in cutting back drastically on public affairs programming, even Nixon's own appointees on the board felt they had done what had been called for in order to assure White House support for increased, long-term funding. They had taken a great deal of heat for their actions. It was time for them and for public television to reap some of the promised benefits.

Perhaps more importantly, by February of 1973 Henry Loomis had learned that the Corporation was not like any other government agency and should not be treated as one by any administration. He developed into an advocate of the advance funding concept and understood that the system could not make progress without more money that the White House was then offering. On February 1, Loomis and the Corporation counsel Tom Gherardi drafted a reply to OMB's Carlucci, which was sent under board chairman Curtis' signature. "Your letter to Mr. Loomis," it said, "may have followed a form which is used in your relations with Federal agencies. As you know, the Corporation is independent of any Federal control. The board of directors is composed of distinguished citizens nominated by the President and confirmed by the Senate. In my presentation to that independent board I will, of course, faithfully represent the President's views as you have expressed them. However, you must be aware that . . . your letter assumes a degree of compliance which is not consistent with the independence of the board of directors of the Corporation acting in pursuit of the aims and objectives of the Public Broadcasting Act of 1967."[61] Despite the powerful influence of administration supporters on the board, the White House was losing control of the Corporation. CPB officials and directors would go to Capitol Hill at the end of March to support a bill completely opposed to that of the administration -- two years, not one; $60 million and $80 million, not $45 million.

CPB's shifting position on funding and other matters can also be traced to the personal journey of its board chairman, Thomas E. Curtis. As a longtime Republican congressman from Missouri who had voted

against the Public Broadcasting Act of 1967, Curtis
seemed to be the most blatantly partisan of the
increasingly political appointments to the CPB board. He
began his tenure in basic agreement with Loomis and the
White House -- which had ordained his election through
its supporters on the board -- on CPB responsibility for
programming and the inappropriateness of public affairs.
But the growing enthusiasm with which he approached the
negotiations with Ralph Rogers opened a breach not only
with the White House, but with Loomis and his fellow
board members which had been long in the making. In the
weeks before Curtis' appointment in the summer of 1972,
Whitehead had warned Flanigan that Loomis and Curtis did
not complement each other well and might not make a very
good working team at CPB. Both men were strong-minded
"doers"; not "thinkers," like Whitehead's pet choice of
the chairmanship, Irving Kristol. Both were interested
in the day-to-day internal decisions. Only one of them,
however, could be the chief operating officer. Curtis
was the part-time chairman of the board. Yet in this
role, he involved himself to an unusual extent in the
daily affairs of the Corporation. He and Loomis clashed
over personnel and policy. Members of the CPB staff felt
that Curtis was arrogant, intolerant and rude in his
relations with them. Loomis recalled that women staff
members came to him in tears after dealing with Curtis,
"and men came in about ready to knock him flat."[62]

While Curtis entangled himself in the
Corporation's day-to-day activities, he seemed often not
to have a very firm grasp of the most important issue of
controversy, programming. The press had blasted him in
January for his admission that he had never even seen
many of the public affairs shows CPB had funded. A Los
Angeles Times editorial said that Curtis had
"demonstrated remarkable ignorance of some aspects of

public television programming."[63]   When he was asked at a
January 11 press conference to state his views about the
public affairs shows slated for cancellation by CPB,
Curtis admitted, "I do not know these programs." He was,
he said, "not exactly glued to the television set." The
off-handed reply drew also sharp criticism from John J.
O'Connor, who wrote a week later, "With all due respect,
Curtis might consider glueing himself to a TV set for a
while. If his decisions are not based on first-hand
knowledge, an innocent bystander might assume that they
are based on orders from higher powers."[64]

As board member Tom Moore recalled, Curtis and
Loomis "tangled almost from the very beginning," but by
early 1973 the two were at each other's throats.[65] The
effect of their personal battle was a debilitating
tension within CPB and a confusion of authority and
purpose in dealing with the outside. The Corporation
board, which under Frank Pace had operated in a collegial
atmosphere of friendly discussion and unanimous
resolutions, increasingly split along partisan lines.
Under Curtis, the very nature of board meetings
themselves changed. They became more formal as well as
more rancorous. Curtis could be harsh with his fellow
board members, scolding them if they arrived late to a
meeting and interrupted discussion. He treated the board
as if it were his own congressional committee.[66]

"Curtis began to become frustrated," one of his
few consistent supporters on the board, Jack Valenti,
remembered, "and lamented the way things were going,
because he was constantly being crossed by members of the
board. . . . Loomis wanted to go one way and Curtis
wanted to go another way and Loomis' views were being
upheld by a majority of the board members."[67]

Though Curtis proved to be a sometimes petulant
chairman, he was undoubtedly a man of high integrity.

The suggestions of impropriety infuriated him and he staunchly defended the independence of the CPB board -- and its chairman. His insistence on formality and proper procedures at board meetings grew out of a belief that the CPB directors should conduct their business with absolute propriety. Though he, like Loomis, agreed to meet with Whitehead and other administration officials, he did not want any of his board members to have such contact and was highly sensitive to any attempt by the White House to influence him, the thinking of the board, or the policies of the Corporation. Curtis even called his predecessor, John Macy, to tell him that he understood what Macy had gone through, that the White House was trying to control him [Curtis] also.[68] While Loomis found it perfectly acceptable for the President's advisors to air their views, Curtis saw little distinction between friendly suggestions and political tampering. The two of them attended one meeting in the White House with Whitehead, Flanigan, Frank Shakespeare, and Len Garment, who voiced their concerns about balance in programming. "It seemed to me that they were just saying what their views were," said Loomis, "just like we listen to a group of blacks and we listen to a bunch of educators say what their views are. I did not consider it a directive. . . . But it set off Curtis, who went through one of his temper tantrums and said that he would not be dictated to and he would not be interfered with and the Corporation was a private thing and he would resign . . . ." At first, Loomis thought that Curtis was overreacting, but the more he thought about it, the more he felt that the outburst about White House pressure was one of Curtis' better moves as CPB board chairman. "That experience began to make me think," Loomis recalled, "was I blind? Had I not recognized something going on there that I had not seen?"[69]

Yet Curtis did not have confidence in Loomis' freedom from White House influence and also began to question members of the board about their ties to the administration. In some cases, most notably those of Jack Wrather or Tom Moore, Curtis' doubts were entirely justified. They were working closely with the White House, trying to persuade the rest of the board to do what the administration wanted done. The board was sharply divided. But as Jack Valenti suggested, Curtis lost the support of some of the more neutral members -- "got their dander up" -- by implying that they were voting against him solely because of White House pressure. "Frankly," Valenti said, "I would have been a little ticked-off if I had been on the other side and somebody said to me, 'Well, the White House is pressuring you, I guess.'"[70] The growing conflict between Curtis and Loomis and the growing schism on the board would not surface until CPB's mid-April meeting, but as the Senate hearings on public television financing were about to begin, Curtis was taking a noticeably more conciliatory line towards Ralph Rogers and PBS. "This is," he said on March 26, "a time for mutual accommodation between CPB and the licensees, some of whom have distrusted CPB in recent months and believed the propaganda that a board with a Republican majority was out to create a 'Nixon network.'"[71]

The CPB chairman's new activism and support for increased funding and for CPB-PBS partnership were not well received within the White House. Whitehead felt his worst fears about Curtis' appointment had been realized. "Curtis liked the part about seizing control," Whitehead complained, "he didn't like the part about giving it away."[72] On March 27, the OTP wrote the following memorandum for the record:

> We were advised by the White House today
> that the President still sees serious
> dangers in the existence of a Federally-
> funded broadcasting network. He is
> strongly opposed to control of the
> interconnect and its scheduling anywhere
> other than with CPB. . . . The effort
> Mr. Curtis is making to seek more
> involvement by the boards of local
> public broadcast stations and a more
> active partnership with them in funding
> programs has much good in it. But the
> President would have to oppose that plan
> and Mr. Curtis personally, both strongly
> and openly, unless the principles of
> board responsibility and of safeguarding
> against excessive control by private
> organizations are clearly
> incorporated.[73]

By the time the March 28-30 Senate hearings began, every major leader and organization in the public broadcasting industry was in agreement on their support for the 1974-75 CPB funding bill, S. 1090. Representing the administration, Clay Whitehead alone opposed the two-year financing. Given the shocking veto of nine months earlier and his solitary stance on the proposed legislation, the OTP director might have expected another icy reception from the Communications Subcommittee. But whatever credibility he and the administration might have had was completely shattered less than two weeks before the hearings began by presidential special assistant Patrick J. Buchanan's appearance on a nationally televised talk show.

Pat Buchanan was an ideologue, an extremist seen by friends as a flamboyant Irish street fighter and by adversaries as a reactionary bully. He had been at the forefront of the Nixon administration's running battle with the news media since he drafted the first cannon shot of that battle for Spiro Agnew in November of 1969. He was the White House's watchdog over the press

and he kept his nose sensitive to even the slightest
scent of anti-administration bias in newspapers,
magazines, on television and radio. He doled out
scathing criticism on behalf of a President and a White
House that had believed themselves from the outset under
siege by the liberal press.

In the middle of the crucial month of
negotiations, meetings, and hearings regarding public
television, this cocky member of the Nixon "team"
committed -- to use his own metaphor -- a serious error
that would come back to haunt the White House in the
later innings of the game. Buchanan spoke at some length
about public television on ABC's Dick Cavett show in mid-
March. His performance, to public broadcasters, their
congressional supporters, the press, and his colleagues
in the administration, was a striking combination of
smugness and candor. Senate subcommittee chairman
Pastore was so amazed by Buchanan's unrestrained
description of the White House's hostility towards public
television that he felt obliged to open the hearings on
March 28 by reading it into the record. Buchanan had
said,

> . . . if you look at public television,
> you will find you've got Sander Vanocur
> and Robert MacNeil, the first of whom,
> Sander Vanocur, is a notorious Kennedy
> sycophant, in my judgment, and Robert
> MacNeil, who is anti-Administration.
> You have Elizabeth Drew . . . she
> personally is definitely not pro-
> Administration; I would say anti-
> Administration. 'Washington Week in
> Review' is unbalanced against
> us . . . you have 'Black Journal,' which
> is unbalanced against us . . . you have
> Bill Moyers, which is unbalanced against
> the Administration. And then for a fig
> leaf, they throw in William F. Buckley's
> program. So they sent down there a $165
> million package, voted 82-1 out of the
> Senate, thinking that Richard Nixon

would therefore -- he would have to sign
it, that he couldn't possibly have the
courage to veto something like that.
And Mr. Nixon, I'm delighted to say, hit
that ball about 450 feet down the right
field foul line right into the stands,
and got a whole new ballgame on
CPB . . . .[74]

When he heard about Buchanan's remarks, Clay
Whitehead "wanted to go hide somewhere." Though Buchanan
had faithfully expressed the prevailing view within the
White House, "he was not," said Whitehead, "the kind of
guy you would choose to articulate a policy position that
requires a lot of nuance."[75] Buchanan had stripped OTP's
policies of any philosophical importance. He
demonstrated beyond a shadow of a doubt that, from the
White House's perspective, the battle with public
television was simply a question of partisan politics.
"Buchanan's appearance was a disaster," said Henry
Goldberg, by then OTP general counsel. "Everyone was
tarred with the same brush. It was really a blunder."[76]
Buchanan had also made life much more difficult
for Henry Loomis and the CPB board, who had just canceled
Corporation funding for Moyers, MacNeil, and Drew only a
week earlier. "Anyone who boasts like that is foolish,"
Loomis said. "If in fact he did what he said he did, it
was stupid to say so; but he didn't do what he said he
did, which made it even worse."[77]
Understandably, the Senate committee had some
serious doubts about both White House and CPB intentions.
During the first morning of the hearings, both Loomis and
Curtis had to field numerous questions regarding the
Corporation's recent program decisions. They both
maintained that CPB was unalterably committed to public
affairs programming in principle and explained that the
cancellations of Firing Line, Washington Week in Review,

and <u>Bill Moyers' Journal</u> reflected purely fiscal, rather than political priorities. They and other CPB board members who testified expressed unequivocal support for the committee bill and disavowed Buchanan's statements. Board member Robert Benjamin declared that Buchanan's performance "was an outrage." "I thought he gave a wrong slant to the entire posture of the Corporation. And I don't think such statements influence the Board." "What influences the Board," he said, "is the priority question."[78]

Whitehead was the final witness of the first day of the hearings. In his opening statement he criticized what he called "the tendency toward centralized program decisionmaking by CPB and PBS," and said that reliance on federal monies to support public affairs programming was "inappropriate and potentially dangerous." He concluded, therefore, that multi-year funding must "await the resolution of the present uncertainties and deficiencies."

As soon as the OTP director finished his prepared remarks, Senators Pastore and Cook started to punch holes in his position. Their patience with his year-and-a-half of equivocation and double-talk had clearly worn thin.

> SENATOR PASTORE: Of course, you realize, Mr. Whitehead, you disagree with everything that was said here today.
> MR. WHITEHEAD: I hope not everything, Mr. Chairman.
> SENATOR PASTORE: You heard Mr. Benjamin. By whom was he nominated?
> MR. WHITEHEAD: As I recall, he was nominated by President Johnson.
> SENATOR PASTORE: Mr. Curtis by whom?
> MR. WHITEHEAD: Nixon.
> SENATOR PASTORE: Mr. Hughes by whom?
> MR. WHITEHEAD: By Johnson and Nixon.

SENATOR PASTORE: You heard them say they
need two years in order to get a program of
quality going. You disagree with that, don't
you?
MR. WHITEHEAD: Yes I do.
SENATOR PASTORE: You heard them say that
they need at least $55 million if they are to
do a respectable job delegated to them under
the law and by appointment to this particular
Corporation. You heard them say that?
MR. WHITEHEAD: I heard that.
SENATOR PASTORE: You disagree with that?
MR. WHITEHEAD: I think I do, Mr. Chairman,
it was always the case--
SENATOR PASTORE: You know, Mr. Whitehead, I
have a very, very firm conviction that, even
though you dress up your statement with sweet
words, you have an animosity toward this
Corporation and toward public broadcasting.
You praise it by one breath, and by the next
breath you suffocate it.

Now, when you come before this committee and
you tell us, in spite of the testimony that
has been developed here, not that you don't
have the money, but that $45 million is
enough to do a credible job and these
gentlemen say that they cannot do it.

When you come before this committee and say
one year is enough to put on a good program,
and the people who have the responsibility to
do it say it is impossible, it strikes me
that that is somewhat hostile; and then when
you take the things that Mr. Buchanan said on
the Dick Cavett show and you add everything
together, you begin to wonder whether you are
with us or against us.

I really think Mr. Whitehead, that you are
just against us.

Republican Senator Marlow Cook, whom Pastore
called, "the man who was master of ceremonies at the
inauguration of Richard Nixon," then launched into the
OTP director:

SENATOR COOK: Mr. Whitehead, I just want to say that there is one thing that kind of rankles me the wrong way. I honestly have to say this as a Republican. Maybe I'm not happy watching 'Washington Week in Review' and the 'Black Journal' and 'Bill Moyers' Journal' or Sander Vanocur, but I sure resent somebody saying they are unbalanced against us. . . . I resent the very lack of logic used in the accusatory labelling. . . . I didn't mind Mr. Buchanan speaking for himself, but when he goes on television and says 'they' are against us, he speaks for himself and he speaks for the responsibility and the position that he holds. In that instance, I am not quite sure he was up to the task.
SENATOR PASTORE: Not only that. Look at this fashion: New York or Washington, New York or Washington. Only this elitist New York and elitist Washington. It's always the same malarkey . . . this idea that every time you criticize someone, you have to knock them off the air, is beyond me. Beyond me.
MR. WHITEHEAD: Mr. Chairman, it is beyond me.
SENATOR PASTORE: Well, I don't know about that.[79]

On the second day of the hearings Ralph Rogers, Hartford Gunn, and NAEB chairman William Harley appeared before the committee. All three attacked Whitehead's testimony and said that the White House position on funding and decentralization was hypocritical and counterproductive. In Harley's words: "It is inconsistent for the administration to diminish or keep down the amounts of funds that are available to the stations if they say what they are really after is localism." Rogers, who described himself as being a Republican "before the OTP director was born," further explained the inherent absurdity of White House attitudes. Whitehead's proposal that all decisionmaking power be put in the hands of the Corporation on matters which concerned it at the national level was, Rogers

said, "in complete opposition to what everyone has been
advocating." "Frankly," Rogers continued, "if this
matter were not so serious, it would be amusing. Perhaps
we should ask him if he would also recommend that the
People of the United States abolish their legislatures
and leave it to the departments of the executive branch
to send out questionnaires for a plebiscite on every
matter which concerned them at the national level rather
than to elect persons of their own choice to represent
them."[80]

The committee was nearly unanimous in its
agreement with the public broadcasters, and its rejection
of the administration's position. Everyone supported the
idea of localism and nearly every witness reaffirmed that
the prime enemies of localism were one-year
appropriations and inadequate funds -- exactly what the
White House was advocating.

On March 30, PBS was reborn. By a 124 to 1
margin the public television licensees voted to be
represented by the new Public Broadcasting Service. The
new PBS was an aggregation of the original, station-
manager oriented organization, Rogers' chairman's
committee, and the Educational Television Stations
division of the NAEB. Two separate boards, a twenty-
five-member layman's group of station board members, and
a twenty-one-member professional's group of station
managers, would work together to govern the reconstituted
PBS. "Son of PBS," as Variety dubbed the new entity, was
more broadly representative of all the members of the
public television community -- particularly the non-
professional citizen board members, represented by the
Rogers group.[81] It could speak with a more respected and
authoritative voice than the old PBS, which CPB and the
White House felt represented only the interests of the

professional broadcasters. But the task of finding an accommodation with the Corporation was not yet complete.

By early April, the CPB board's ad-hoc negotiating committee reached a preliminary agreement with Rogers and the new PBS. On Wednesday, April 4, the committee, chaired by Tom Moore, met with Loomis and Curtis to discuss the proposal. The next day, the committee submitted its formal recommendations. The majority, consisting of Valenti and Killian, recommended to the CPB board a plan under which the Corporation would, in consultation with the Rogers group, decide all CPB-funded programs, through a CPB program department. Should the Rogers group -- that it, PBS -- dissent from any particular programming decision of the CPB programming staff, then it could appeal to the presidents of the two organizations. If these executives failed to agree, then the final appeal would go to the chairmen of the two organizations, whose decision would be final. Scheduling of the interconnection would be handled by PBS, in consultation with CPB. If CPB objected to any scheduling decision by PBS, then the same arrangement would hold. Killian and Valenti further recommended that all non-CPB funded programs should have access to the interconnection. If there were any conflicts of opinion as to the balance, fairness, and objectivity of any of these programs, a monitoring committee consisting of three CPB directors and three PBS directors would make a final judgment. It would take four votes of the monitoring committee to keep a program from national distribution via the interconnection.

Killian and Valenti submitted, along with the proposed agreement, a rationale for their affirmative recommendation. "The prime objective," they wrote, "is to extract the thorns of discontent, disaffection and

persistent controversy that have infected public and
private views of the current public broadcasting arena."

> By constructing a partnership with lay
> board chairmen, as the chosen instrument
> of local stations, we put to rest all
> the acrimony which has threatened to
> disfigure our public image, and rupture
> our congressional support.
>
> Nothing in these recommendations is set
> in concrete. If this arrangement proves
> unworkable, we can change it.
>
> But, let us give it a chance to work.
> We must understand that the Rogers group
> and the CPB board want the same thing,
> that is, a worthy, valuable public
> broadcasting medium providing a useful
> service to the people who view
> it . . . .
>
> We can trust each other because we are
> both working toward the same goal.[82]

The chairman of the negotiating committee, Tom
Moore, was not so enthusiastic about the partnership
agreement and filed a dissenting opinion. On April 9,
Moore delivered his minority recommendation to CPB over
the telephone. He, like Whitehead and the Nixon White
House, was not yet ready to trust the Public Broadcasting
Service with freedom from government oversight. He
opposed the agreement reached with Rogers and stated his
firm belief that the best interest of public broadcasting
could be "best served by CPB assuming, operating,
scheduling and trafficking the interconnections system."
"CPB," Moore said, "not only should operate the
interconnection; it is obliged to do so, and CPB cannot
delegate that authority and responsibility."[83]
Many members of the Corporation board and staff
believed that the agreement submitted by Killian and

Valenti was actually the product of personal discussions between Rogers and CPB chairman Curtis. Rogers, they felt, had carefully cultivated his alliance with Curtis in hopes of assuring passage of a partnership plan which would keep substantive control of the national program decisionmaking process and the interconnection in the hands of PBS. But Killian and Valenti had themselves long opposed any direct involvement of the CPB board in specific programming or scheduling decisions. They were hopeful that their proposal would be approved at the board's April 13 meeting and that the conflict between the Corporation and PBS would finally be resolved. Curtis and Rogers were full of confidence in the days prior to the CPB board's meeting. On April 10, after Curtis told him about the negotiating committee's recommendations, Rogers wrote the CPB chairman about the importance of establishing a working plan for the partnership. Rogers looked forward to a joint meeting of the two boards to formalize an interconnection contract and a national program process in late May or early June. He concluded, "The basic principles which will guide both of us in developing a plan of implementation for the partnership agreement are contained in the memorandum which you read to me. . . . The principles are entirely acceptable to our boards. We welcome the resolution of these principles and appreciate the fine spirit in which your board has worked with ours in creating these understandings."[84]

Rogers had assumed far too much; the passage of the partnership agreement would not prove to be so simple. Henry Loomis had serious qualms about the outcome of the negotiations with PBS. He and Corporation vice president Keith Fischer had themselves met with Ralph Rogers in Florida on March 15. Although they did not reach any sort of agreement at that time, Rogers had

promised to forward a specific plan to them at CPB in
Washington the following week. This plan, Loomis
reported to the CPB board, had not been forthcoming, but
Rogers had nonetheless gone ahead with his conversations
with Curtis. After his meeting with the PBS management
group, which presented him with their interconnection
cost analysis and national program selection process
outline, Loomis realized that the agreement reached by
Rogers and Curtis -- with Valenti and Killian -- was not
at all what he had expected. "We in the CPB management,"
he told the Corporation board, were "greatly concerned"
by what the PBS documents on programming and
interconnection represented. ". . . I feel that the PBS
proposals are very much opposed to the spirit of the
original discussions with Mr. Rogers, and, therefore, I
would ask the board to provide me with clear and specific
directions as to how to proceed with these
negotiations."[85]

Loomis and Curtis were on a collision course
over the partnership agreement. As it happened, Curtis
was on a collision course with much of the board and the
White House as well.

On April 11, Dick McCormack, a former CPB staff
member doing consulting work at the Corporation while
acting as an informal liaison to the White House, called
Whitehead to alert him about the power struggle that was
going on between Curtis and Loomis. McCormack, like the
current CPB staff, felt that Curtis had been "won over"
to the PBS cause during his discussions with Rogers, and
was conspiring with the PBS negotiator to initiate a
"campaign to discredit and ultimately remove Loomis as
President of CPB." "The conflict between Curtis and
Loomis simply must not be permitted to continue or
surface," McCormack said. "If this happens, and if there
is an open breach, Loomis' ability to influence the

outside will be sharply reduced; and we might as well pick up our marbles and go home."

Since the Rogers compromise had not yet been formally accepted by the CPB board, McCormack recommended that the White House "prevail upon Curtis to issue a statement of confidence in Loomis -- or that the board of directors as a whole give Loomis a vote of confidence" to squelch the whispering campaign. The White House, he said, should press the CPB board to support an "interim plan" confirming Corporation control over programming decisions, "while at the same time instructing CPB management to continue negotiations with PBS (and the Rogers group) and to report on recommendations in one year's time."

To defuse criticism of their last-minute deferral, McCormack suggested that the board should also "pass a resolution thanking Ralph Rogers for his selfless efforts thus far toward finding a common solution to the questions facing the public broadcasting industry." But the real need, he said, was for a "more effective buffer" between CPB management and the CPB chairman than the present secretary and general counsel, Tom Gherardi. McCormack concluded by warning Whitehead that administration objectives were in a precarious position because of the clash between Curtis and Gherardi and Loomis: "We have pretty much lost control of our board," he said, "and it's going to take a bigger man than Gherardi to get on top of the situation. In the ego conflict between Gherardi and Curtis, the only winner has been Ralph Rogers and Hartford Gunn. WE SIMPLY CANNOT AFFORD TO LET THIS SITUATION CONTINUE."[86]

On the next day, Whitehead met with Curtis and Moore in his office to explain the President's opposition to the compromise plan with PBS. Despite Moore's disenchantment with the interim agreement and White House

hostility, Curtis was apparently convinced that the
proposal worked out by the negotiating committee would be
acceptable to all parties and fully expected the entire
board to approve it on his recommendation at their April
13 meeting. But the Corporation board of directors
shocked its chairman by voting -- exactly as Moore
suggested to Whitehead -- ten to four to defer action on
the PBS proposal and to appoint a new committee to
conduct further meetings with representatives of the
Service. Three days after the surprising vote, Curtis
resigned from the CPB board claiming illicit White House
interference. In an April 16 letter to President Nixon,
he explained,

> A difference of opinion developed
> between myself and what Mr. Whitehead
> stated to me was your opinion in respect
> to the course of action the Corporation
> should be taking in working out its
> current relationship with PBS, the local
> stations and other organizations. . . .
> Mr. Whitehead suggested that if the
> board persisted in the course of action
> it seemed ready to pursue, a veto of the
> new authorization bill probably would be
> forthcoming. I responded by saying the
> board would proceed and if it did follow
> the course seemingly it was ready to
> follow, perhaps the results would be
> such that the board would be proven
> right and that a veto would not be
> advisable.

"Mr. Whitehead," Curtis wrote, "did not accept
this position." "[OTP's] approach," he charged, "was to
call individual members of the board without my knowledge
or the knowledge of the other members of the board and
presumably try to persuade them to the position that he
stated you had taken." According to Curtis, "this
resulted in the board deferring action on the resolution

and considerably altering the delicate negotiations in
progress with the new PBS organization and others
involved in public broadcasting."

Curtis concluded by saying, "the efforts of
Mr. Whitehead and others however well intentioned to save
the board from making what they deemed to be a serious
mistake had seriously undermined the independence and
integrity" of the board, "and placed me in a position of
not being able to defend the independence of the board
with the vigor required."[87]

On the same day, Curtis sent a four-page letter
to Killian, now acting chairman of the Corporation board,
forwarding copies to the other directors as well. Curtis
told his former colleagues that he had been deeply
disturbed during the preceding seven months over the
"constant and widespread attack in the news media on the
integrity of some of the board's major decisions."

> These attacks were primarily directed
> against the Nixon Administration; they
> alleged "a Nixon takeover" of the board.
> I have been disappointed to find the
> members of the board rather apathetic to
> these attacks; at least, in only rare
> instances did anyone other than myself
> speak out to rebut these attacks as
> being false and unfair. . . .
>
> . . . Frankly it shocked me to find that
> I was the only member who referred to
> the seriousness of what I think was
> rather apparent to all that there were
> indications that attempts had been made
> outside the board room to alter the
> judgment the board seemed about to reach
> in what up until then I thought was an
> orderly and considered manner. . . .

It was quite possible, Curtis wrote, that there
was an honest difference of opinion over what constituted
outside interference with the board's decisionmaking

THE WASHINGTON POST, April 19, 1973:

Violence On Television

©1973 HERBLOCK

---from Herblock On All Fronts (New American Library, 1980)

"I'll Decide What's Public and What Isn't"

process. He felt that the White House had clearly crossed that line and affected the outcome of the April 13 meeting. The board's acquiescence to this interference had proved what he had been denying for almost a year. He simply could not see how he "could be of any further value" to the board.[88]

For a week, Curtis refused to release the letters to the press or to comment publicly on his resignation or the board's April 13 decisions. During that time, speculation grew that the surprising vote was, as Curtis privately charged, the product of direct White House pressure. An April 19th New York Times editorial stated that "even minimal protection" of public television's basic freedom "appears to have been too much for the Administration's arbiters of public enlightenment." "Although Mr. Curtis had every reason by last week to believe that the compromise would be approved by the CPB board, the Administration's hardliners, again led by Mr. Whitehead, engaged in frantic last-minute lobbying to block it. The meeting that was to ratify the Curtis compromise turned into a rout of the moderates and a repudiation of Mr. Curtis."[89]

Curtis finally confirmed such reports on April 23, when he granted The New York Times an interview and made his first public comments since his resignation. He charged that members of the administration had tried to pressure the board, in express contradiction to assurances he had received. Curtis revealed that the White House talked constantly to members of the board, calling them privately and interfering with the process of deliberation. "When it became clear," he said, "that the White House was not respecting the integrity of the board, then I could not defend the integrity of the board the way I had." Curtis concluded, "When I felt I could no longer do that, I felt I better resign." He urged the

CPB board of directors to reassert its independence and integrity.[90]

OTP's Brian Lamb denied the allegations of a last minute telephone blitz by the White House staff. (Whitehead was in Mexico and not available for comment.) Board member Irving Kristol vigorously objected to the charges of White House influence. He spoke, he said, only because he was stung by Curtis' "going out of his way to cast aspersions on the integrity of all the members of the board." Kristol said he wanted to know, "What kind of pressure do you put on a board whose members are appointed for six years and who get no salary?"[91]

Yet calls had indeed been going back and forth between Whitehead, Flanigan, and certain board members throughout the partnership debate of the winter and early spring. The Republican directors were basically voting as a block, but usually against their chairman, whose attitudes and activities greatly annoyed both them and the White House. With the exception of Ralph Rogers, Curtis seemed to have annoyed just about everyone. The deferral of the proposed partnership agreement was not due solely to White House pressure. It was, at least in part, a very personal reaction by many of the board members against Curtis. The Corporation staff was hoping that the Chairman would resign over his defeat on April 13, and their reaction when he did was "Thank God!"[92]

"The concept that Curtis and Rogers would negotiate any agreement and come back and say, 'This is it,'" Loomis recalled, "had people in CPB up the walls, particularly the board [which felt] this was something that the board should do." Loomis himself had asked some legitimate questions about the details of the agreement, but he believed that the vote against the plan that Curtis had personally sponsored had less to do with the actual plan than with the way the chairman had handled it.[93] (Indeed, the partnership agreement submitted to and approved by the CPB board four weeks later was almost exactly the same.)

Curtis' resignation and the highly publicized charges of tampering -- as McCormack had predicted -- put the administration's year and a half effort in jeopardy. On April 20, OTP general counsel Henry Goldberg sent Whitehead a memo reviewing the administration's activities regarding public broadcasting and recommending a future course of action. Goldberg felt that the White House and the OTP director should make a tactical retreat while the surging opposition was still somewhat disorganized. "At this point," he said, "we are at or near the bottom of the 'slippery slope' we first set upon a year and a half ago." Goldberg felt, however, that the chaos within public broadcasting that had resulted from the administration's approach also "had its advantages." "The present disarray of our opponents," he said, "makes this an ideal time -- perhaps our last clear chance -- to restructure public broadcasting and to extricate ourselves . . . from continuous tinkering with [it]."

Goldberg felt that there were two approaches at hand. One was to find "competent, fair-minded and independent leadership for the Corporation both at the board and staff levels" and leave it to them to "rectify the deficiencies in the public broadcasting system" based on administration recommendations. Goldberg understood, however, that a competent, fair-minded, and independent group could not be expected to do what the White House wanted. Therefore, he recommended that the OTP itself should call together CPB, PBS, and other station interests to "work out a legislative restructuring of public broadcasting that we can all support."

Therefore, he said,

> I think that our own enlightened self-
> interest dictates that we use this
> opportunity to create something
> constructive and lasting by way of a
> public broadcasting policy. If not, the
> great expenditure in time and effort and
> personal sacrifice of your 'image' over
> the past two years will all be for
> naught. I would not like our record in
> public broadcasting to be one solely of
> creating, enhancing, and feeding upon
> chaos . . . .[94]

The events surrounding the April 13 CPB meeting
-- the tampering charges, Curtis' resignation -- gave
Whitehead a powerful jolt. He had increasingly
interjected himself into the CPB board's deliberations
because of Loomis', and particularly Curtis',
unwillingness to do what the administration thought
should be done. Now his entire effort was falling in on
him and it had become impossible to justify his
activities in terms of the purely structural objectives
he had claimed to seek. "It was clearer and clearer that
[the OTP] was just getting in the way of getting anything
productive or constructive out of public broadcasting,"
Goldberg felt. For the second time in a year and a half,
the OTP director had received a formal, internal
memorandum from his general counsel warning him about the
dangers of his doubled-edged public television policies.
In December 1971, as the White House's public television
offensive was gathering steam, Antonin Scalia (aided by
Goldberg) had told Whitehead that his association with
the White House's effort to control the system through
the CPB board would most likely prove a costly failure.
Its message, as Goldberg put it, was: "Don't do it.
It's not going to work, and it's just going to get you in

trouble." Now, in April of 1973, Goldberg was telling
Whitehead: "You did it. It didn't work. It's just
gotten you in trouble. Now stop it."[95]

But events moved too quickly for the frustrated
administration forces. The CPB board needed to prove its
independence after the Curtis embarrassment. It did so
by electing James Killian as its new chairman. Killian,
chairman of the Carnegie Commission, accepted the post on
the conditions that there would be no more White House
interference; that the negotiations with Rogers and PBS
be speedily completed; that long-range funding plans be
reconsidered in order to remove the Corporation's
activities from the political pressures of annual
appropriations; that local stations be strengthened with
autonomy and independence; and that public affairs
programming be reaffirmed as an essential responsibility
of public broadcasting.[96]

Killian's election as CPB's board chairman
changed the situation at the Corporation overnight. He
was universally respected and admired by his colleagues.
He was a man not only of great prestige, but of
unquestioned integrity and unstrained decency. Killian
was above the partisan battlefield and did not need to
raise his voice to be heard. Everyone listened. As past
chairman of the Carnegie Commission, Killian had more
knowledge about what public broadcasting was and what it
ought to be than anyone else. The board needed Killian's
credibility; it wanted his quiet leadership and was
willing to follow where he led. Loomis had a long and
warm association with Killian, both as his assistant at
MIT and as his staff director when Killian was
Eisenhower's advisor on science and technology. They
were a proven as well as a friendly team.

The board unequivocally supported Killian's
principles. Its May 9 statement quoted the original

Carnegie report, "'What we have sought to design is an
institution that will represent public television, that
in behalf of public television will receive and disburse
federal, state, and local government funds, as well as
private funds, and yet will be free of political
interference.' The Corporation is wholly devoted to this
requirement that it be independent and that government be
scrupulous in recognizing that it must be insulated from
political influence or the control of special interests."
The statement concluded,

> Just as an informed citizenry is
> essential to a functioning democracy, so
> public affairs programs are an essential
> ingredient of a healthy system of public
> broadcasting. Inadequate funds have
> forced CPB to cut back drastically on
> all our television program planning for
> the coming season and public affairs
> programs have suffered. If adequate
> funds become available we will move
> rapidly to fund more programs, including
> public affairs.[97]

At the same May 9 meeting, the CPB board
unanimously approved a four-point draft proposal for a
partnership agreement with PBS, as recommended by their
newest negotiating committee. It provided, first, that
CPB, in consultation with PBS, would decide all CPB
funded programs through the CPB program department.
Second, all non-CPB programs would have equal access to
the interconnection. Third, scheduling of the
interconnection would be done by a group of three
appointed by PBS and three appointed by CPB, with a
seventh participant chosen by the other six. The seventh
participant would have no connection with either
organization and would act as chairman. Finally, the
agreement with PBS would be mutually reviewed at the end
of a year of operation.[98]

Reaction from PBS was mixed at first. Rogers labelled the proposed joint committee a "seven-headed monster" and instead called for PBS scheduling of the interconnection with CPB approval. Although Rogers also wanted the agreement to last for five years instead of one, he agreed with the Corporation on the other substantive points. In something of a peace offering to Rogers and PBS, CPB announced on May 18 that it would continue to fund both Firing Line and Washington Week in Review through September. The new $300,000 grant was given "at the overwhelming request of the stations and because of a desire for partnership." It also represented a significant switch from earlier positions taken by Henry Loomis who, eight months earlier, had expressed doubt that any public affairs programs should be financed by CPB.[99]

On May 23 CPB and PBS negotiators agreed on a set of principles defining the relationship between the two organizations. The "Partnership Agreement" was formally approved by the boards of both organizations on May 31. In Boston, the Corporation board of directors and in Dallas, the PBS boards of directors unanimously resolved that:

> In order to effect a vigorous
> partnership in behalf of the
> independence and diversity of public
> television and to improve the excellence
> of its programs; to enhance the
> development, passage by Congress, and
> approval of the Executive branch of a
> long-range financing program that would
> remove public broadcasting from the
> political hazards of annual
> authorizations and appropriations; to
> further strengthen the autonomy and
> independence of local public television
> stations; and to reaffirm that public
> affairs are an essential responsibility
> of public broadcasting,

the two boards had jointly adopted a partnership agreement which incorporated the major points of the May 9 proposal. CPB in consultation with PBS would approve national program funding decisions. PBS would submit a schedule of those programs for national interconnection. Each organization could appeal a decision by the other for arbitration by the two chief executives, who would pass the problem along to the board chairmen if they could not reach an acceptable solution. Additionally, the agreement established a partnership review committee and called for CPB to pass an increasing percentage of its federal appropriations directly to the local stations as these appropriations increased: thirty percent at a $45 million level, forty percent at a $60 million level, forty-five percent at a $70 million level, and fifty percent when CPB's federal allocation reached $80 million.[100]

At the CPB board meeting, after several members expressed their support for the agreement, Killian read a letter from former chairman Frank Pace, affirming his support. He then "noted that Messrs. Cole, Wrather and Moore, who were necessarily absent, had each endorsed the adoption of the proposed agreements."[101] Killian declared after the meeting, "CPB and PBS have created a partnership to broaden the base, strengthen the independence, and quicken the promise of public television." "Of course," he added, "I stress independence. Public television must never become an instrument of propaganda or be politicized."[102]

During April and May, Congress quickly moved forward on the two-year funding legislation that would begin to make public television's independence a reality. Pastore's committee reported S. 1090 to the Senate with the declaration:

Government intrusion into the medium has
no more place than biased public affairs
programming. Whether it is the bludgeon
of patently inadequate funding or subtle
innuendoes of government officials, the
results are the same: a chilling effect
on the open and robust exchange of
ideas, and a diminution of the very
special service public broadcasting
brings to over forty million people.[103]

After accepting a proposal by Howard Baker on
May 7 to reduce the amount for 1975 by $10 million --
leaving the appropriation of $60 million for 1974 and $70
million for 1975, as well as $25 million in each year
from 1974 through 1977 for the HEW Educational Broadcast
Facilities program -- the Senate passed the two-year
funding legislation for CPB. When the House Commerce
Committee met to consider the legislation the Democratic
members favored the Senate bill, authorizing a total of
$230 million, while Republican members wanted a $175
million total package ($55 million in 1974 and $65
million in 1975 for the Corporation; $25 million in 1974
and $30 million in 1975 for facilities). To avoid the
possibility of another veto, the Democrats accepted the
Republican version. In July the House passed the measure
by a solid bipartisan vote of 363 to 14. The Senate
agreed to the House bill by a voice vote in less than a
week. On August 5, on Whitehead's somewhat wishful
recommendation that the recent developments in the public
broadcasting community had answered some of the
administration's criticisms and that the remaining issues
could be resolved within the framework of the new
legislation, President Nixon agreed to sign the two-year
authorization bill.[104]

CHAPTER SEVEN

GAVEL-TO-GAVEL

MacNEIL:	"In the Senate of the United States a resolution: to establish a select committee of the Senate to conduct an investigation and study of the extent, if any, to which illegal, improper, or unethical activities were engaged in by any persons, acting individually or in combination with others, in the presidential election of 1972 or any campaigning, canvass, or other activity related to it."
ANNOUNCER:	"From Washington, NPACT bring you gavel-to-gavel videotape coverage of today's hearings by the Senate Select Committee on Presidential Campaign Activities."

With those words, on the evening of May 17, 1973, public television began its historic coverage of the Watergate hearings. Watergate, a modern hotel-office-apartment complex on the edge of the Potomac River near the Kennedy Center of the Performing Arts in Northwest Washington, was the headquarters of the Democratic National Committee in 1972. On June 17 of that year, five men employed by the Committee to Re-Elect President Nixon broke into the DNC offices to plant electronic surveillance devices and gather potentially embarrassing information about prominent Democrats. At the time, there was little public comment about this unusual incident, but as the hearings would soon show, the Watergate break-in was both a product and a cause of the greatest political scandal in American history. Amid repeated denials of any wrongdoing on the part of those directly associated with the President, and a trial of the seven break-in conspirators that revealed little implicating anyone above them in the Committee to Re-Elect or the White House, Watergate made barely a ripple in the 1972 presidential election. Nixon won in a landslide. But by May of 1973, the President's two closest advisors, H.R. Haldeman and John Ehrlichman had resigned, along with Attorney General Richard Kleindienst and White House counsel John Dean, because of allegations that they had conspired to obstruct the investigation of the case. The President himself admitted that there had been an effort within the White House to conceal from him, and from the American people, the facts of the Watergate-related events. As one false White House statement after another was declared "inoperative" in light of new evidence and new allegations, it became clear by the spring of 1973 that there had been a massive cover-up involving not only the White House, but the Justice Department, the FBI, and the CIA. Watergate quickly became the umbrella term for a long list of abuses of executive power that included not only the break-in, but the payment of hush-money to the conspirators in exchange for guilty pleas and silence; the wire-tapping of reporters and officials; the break-in at the Los Angeles offices of the psychiatrist treating former Defense Department official Daniel Ellsberg; the use of millions of dollars in illegal cash contributions to the Nixon campaign; and the effort to conceal these and other illegal activities.

The Senate Watergate committee had been formed in early February of 1973, before any of the extraordinary revelations by the convicted burglars and before the resignations of Nixon's closest personal aides. Under the chairmanship of the seventy-six-year-

old North Carolina Democrat, Sam Ervin, the seven-member
committee finally began its long-awaited public hearings
in mid-May, as the Watergate scandal was enveloping the
Nixon White House. When the committee announced in
February that it would probably hold such hearings, NPACT
president Jim Karayn immediately went to PBS president
Hartford Gunn to discuss televising them. He was not
only interested in live, daytime transmission of the
events in the Senate Caucus Room, but in videotape
replays in the evening, prime-time hours, when most of
the country could watch them -- and, most likely, when
the commercial networks would show only their regular
entertainment schedules. "I went twelve weeks in a row,"
Karayn said, "every single day, five days a week, to see
Gunn . . . and try to get [him] to announce that public
broadcasting, if these hearings took place, would cover
them. He wouldn't do it. I kept saying, 'Hartford, this
is our issue. This is our real moment to make the whole
world realize that we are not the government network."[1]
Karayn argued that it did not matter whether the hearings
took place or not, but only that PBS made the declaration
of intent. It would mean that, for once, public
broadcasting would be out in front of commercial
television on vital special events coverage, instead of
merely following after it. In the winter and early
spring of 1973, while CPB and PBS battled over who would
control the future of public television NPACT fought for
the opportunity to broadcast the Watergate hearings.
Senior correspondent Robert MacNeil argued, as Karayn
did, that televising the Watergate hearings would put
public television on the map; it would "do for public
television what the Army-McCarthy hearings did for the
neophyte ABC network in the 1950's."[2] But with long-term
funding and the CPB-PBS dispute still unresolved, the
system was hesitant to cover the Watergate hearings.

There was still much to lose by antagonizing a White
House which had forced the system into near financial
collapse with the funding bill veto less than a year
earlier. Fear pervaded the thinking, said Karayn.
"Stations were at first afraid to run the Watergate
hearings for fear of annoying some of the prominent
Republicans on their boards or in fear that they might
lose some memberships or donations from conservatives."
Finally, in April, NPACT succeeded in convincing PBS to
conduct a poll of the 237 public television stations on
whether or not to broadcast the hearings. The outcome of
the vote was extremely close. By a slight 52 to 48
percent margin, the system elected to telecast complete,
gavel-to-gavel prime-time coverage of the Senate
hearings. There were those who told Karayn, "You've
finally had it; you've decided to commit professional
hari-kari!"[3]

On April 22, less than a week after Thomas
Curtis' resignation as chairman of the CPB board of
directors over the White House-influenced deferral by the
CPB board of the PBS partnership compromise, PBS
announced that NPACT's coverage of the Watergate hearings
would preempt their entire regular evening schedule.
While the three commercial networks remained undecided on
how they could handle the hearings, public television was
set for what Bill Greeley of Variety predicted to be its
"finest and most exciting public affairs spectacular
ever."[4] Ironically, one station that did not agree until
the very last minute to carry the event in prime time was
Washington's WETA, Channel 26. WETA was not only NPACT's
home base, but was, as Robert MacNeil pointed out,
"perhaps the most important outlet in the system" for the
Senate Watergate Committee coverage. The Capitol's
public station held out until two days before the
hearings were scheduled to begin, when, finally, WETA's

president Donald Taverner agreed to drop the showing of
previously advertised programs -- most of them repeats --
in favor of the NPACT coverage.[5]

The hearings, hosted by MacNeil and new NPACT
correspondent Jim Lehrer, former public affairs
coordinator for PBS, lived up to their advance billing.
They were a watershed, a turning point for both sides in
the struggle over the future of public television. In
May and June and throughout the entire summer of 1973 the
hearings became a phenomenon. Evening audience rating
figures for public television stations were often five
and six times above normal. On some evenings, New York's
Channel 13 outscored two of the three commercial networks
with the videotaped coverage.

Public television, wrote the Chicago Tribune's
Clarence Peterson, was receiving some complaints about
its nightly taped gavel-to-gavel coverage of the
hearings. Complaints like these: "Your coverage has
upset my life completely," crabbed a Seattle, Washington
physician. "I have watched more television in the past
week than in the past year."

"A woman from Atlanta, Georgia complained that
since the hearings began on public TV she had not 'sewn
on a button, taken a hem, or put the yogurt on to make.'"
"I do not know," said Peterson, "what 'putting the yogurt
on to make' means, but presumably it is something the
lady thinks she ought to be doing." The response, he
reported, "crossed all social, economic and geographical
lines. It has come from lifelong Republicans and from
Democrats who voted for President Nixon in the last
election."[6]

One New York woman, said NPACT's Karayn, sent
in $6,000 during the station fund drive saying that "she
had given three thousand dollars to the Committee to Re-
Elect the President and she felt the least she could do

"Just drinks, buffet, and then, at eight o'clock, we'll gavel-to-gavel."

Late Returns

---from Herblock Special Report (W.W. Norton & Co., 1974)

was to double it for the Watergate hearings."[7] The
hearings were having a tremendous impact on all America's
view of Richard Nixon. They provided the "Late Returns"
of the 1972 landslide. Public television had been the
first of the national news media to commit itself to
gavel-to-gavel coverage. It alone rebroadcast the
hearings in their entirety in prime time when most of the
country could actually watch them. Chances are that the
glum couple in Herblock's cartoon, seeing the reality of
the Nixon White House for the first time, was watching
its local PBS member station.

If the impact on the standing of the Nixon
administration was tremendous, the impact of the hearings
on public television itself was even greater. Viewer
support through membership contributions, which had been
increasing steadily throughout the first months of 1973,
took quantum leaps. WNET Channel 13 in New York averaged
about 1,200 new subscribers a week during the first
eighteen days of the Watergate hearings. Ten thousand
dollars was pledged in a single evening to Miami's public
station. Time magazine reported near the end of the
summer that the public television system had received
almost $1.5 million in donations since the time the
hearings began. WNET alone had collected over $250,000,
with the gifts still pouring in. The hearings gave
public television an incredible shot of support, both
monetary and popular. Karayn said that of the 75,000
letters NPACT had received by mid-August, two-thirds were
from people who said that they had never watched public
television before. "Nixon vetoed our bill," he told
Time, "cut our funding. Now he's given us our best
programming. It's sort of like being reborn."[8] As The
Washington Post reported in August, for public
television, the cloud of Watergate had a lining of
silver, gold -- and green.

> Beyond the members and staff of the
> Ervin committee, the big Watergate
> winner may well be the Public
> Broadcasting Service and the National
> Public Affairs Center for Television,
> which has been doing the highly popular
> nighttime reruns of the Watergate
> hearings.
>
> The success of the reruns has taken the
> heat off public television from the
> Nixon Administration that had threatened
> to gut it, and particularly NPACT.[9]

Karayn reported that NPACT coverage would continue, if
need be, until February of 1974 when the Ervin
committee's report was due. "For anyone to be talking of
NPACT in the terms of next February -- or even next month
-- would have been utterly bizarre last spring," said the
Los Angeles Times. "Nothing in public television was as
dead as NPACT. Clay T. Whitehead wrote its obituary when
he declared public TV shouldn't have public affairs."[10]
Public television had made its biggest splash in its
short history with the Watergate hearings. The NPACT
coverage was widely praised for its fairness and insight.
Its success confirmed not only the indispensability of
the non-commercial television system, but the importance
of public affairs programming to it. To illustrate how
much the atmosphere had changed, Karayn said in June,
"I've just received a letter from [Henry] Loomis praising
the Watergate coverage and saying this is precisely what
public television should do!"[11] It was, however, what
Nixon and Whitehead had been fighting all along. For a
time, NPACT and the rest of the public television
community could enjoy the irony that their greatest
success was at the expense of an administration that had
worked so hard to cripple and control them. "It's kind

of too bad," said one public broadcaster, "Clay Whitehead wasn't implicated in the Watergate scandal."[12]

The Watergate hearings did more than just improve ratings, membership drives and NPACT's image. They gave the entire system a renewed sense of vitality and excitement. They provided a context and a broadened viewing audience for the White House's sharpest critic on public television, Bill Moyers. Moyers and his program thrived on having the conflict with the Nixon administration out in the open. He had developed something of a personal battle with presidential special assistant Patrick Buchanan. Though Moyers believed that Clay Whitehead had legitimate concerns about publicly funded broadcast journalism, he also believed that men like Buchanan were using people like Whitehead to help silence opponents of the administration -- like Bill Moyers. "Because of that," Moyers said, "I had my appetite whetted. There's nothing more fun than beating a bully and Buchanan is a bully. He could be charming, as all Irish rogues can be charming and as Goebbels could at times, at dinner, be charming. But I think in his secret dreams, Buchanan saw a thousand year reich with Agnew as Fuhrer and himself as Goebbels. And I loved being in that kind of fight."[13]

In early 1973, Moyers -- whose program was slated for cancellation by the CPB board -- took his fight to Washington Post editor Ben Bradley. He asked Bradley if he could write a piece on what the White House was attempting to do to public television through CPB.

"What amused me," Moyers wrote, "are the gross contortions the CPB has assumed in order to announce the demise of public affairs with a straight face."

There is a denial of any White House influence on the decision [to cancel political programs]. Now, the littlest sports fan in Dallas knows that Coach Tom Landry is not sending Roger Staubach fond wishes when a messenger from the sidelines rushes to the huddle after each offensive play. Yet in Washington, where George Allen can hardly run a scrimmage without advice from the President, it is fervently avowed that the White House is not calling the plays. In an Administration whose lowest political operatives get their orders from the President's appointment secretary and their funds from the President's personal lawyer, we are asked to believe that a sparrow goes unnoticed. When the tiniest cheep of dissent can send Herb Klein to the telephone and Spiro Agnew to the thesaurus; when the President himself, in the slightly inelegant testimony of one who was there, 'dumped all over public television' in a private meeting with commercial broadcasters; when the White House enjoys an 8-7 majority on the CPB board; we are supposed to celebrate, without so much as a raised eyebrow, the emancipation of Henry Loomis.

Come, come, fellows -- the name of the game in this town is politics.

What was emerging, Moyers declared, was not public television, "but government television, shaped by politically conscious appointees whose desire to avoid controversy could turn CPB into the Corporation for Public Blandness."[14]

Moyers' words were prophetic. Two weeks after they appeared in newspapers around the country, Curtis tendered his resignation to the President, charging that the White House had tampered with the CPB board.

Buchanan's reactions to Moyers' piece are not reported, but a few months later, he made his feelings perfectly clear. As Clay Whitehead tried diplomatically to move the White House toward support for the long-promised increased, multi-year financing, a recalcitrant Buchanan stood firm in his strident hostility toward public television. He was not about to give up the fight. "My view," Buchanan wrote on October 14, "is that we should not quit."

> We should hold their feet to the fire;
> the President has the power to veto, and
> we should not hesitate to employ it on
> public broadcasting if that institution
> continues to provide cozy sinecures for
> our less competent journalistic
> adversaries. If they are going to have
> public broadcasting, and they are going
> to overload it against us, why should we
> approve any public funding at all. In
> that event, I would bite the bullet, and
> keep them at the present level of
> funding ad infinitum.[15]

Two weeks later, Moyers began the _Journal_'s 1973-74 season with what he considered to be one of the finest efforts of his broadcasting career, "An Essay on Watergate." The program pulled together some of the most revealing moments of that summer's Senate hearings, conversations between Moyers and longtime Washington journalists William S. White and Richard Strout, political scientists James David Barber and William Miller, historian Henry Steele Commager, and others in an attempt to gain some deeper understanding of the meaning of the Watergate affair. "An Essay on Watergate" was Moyers at his most passionate and eloquent.

Jeb Stuart Magruder was shown testifying that he and other members of the White House staff thought it was all right to break the law and violate the civil rights of anti-war activists because they thought [the administration] had a "legitimate cause." Moyers commented, "Government was supposed to protect society against lawlessness; now it became a lawbreaker, violating the Constitution, in effect, in order to save it and the lethal mutation occurred in the idea of national security. Anyone who disagreed with the view espoused by Jeb Magruder and his colleagues that the President was right became suspect. If his was the infallible last word on the national security and he the only one to save it, then re-electing the President was essential to the nation. The distinction between the President and the country paled, and critics of the official policy not only became a threat to the Republic but to his personal equilibrium."

John Dean spoke to the Ervin Committee of the proposed use of "thugs" to remove one solitary demonstrator from Lafayette Park outside the White House. Moyers remarked, "Life inside those iron gates takes on an existential quality. I think with the President's mind, therefore I am. To some extent this happens in every administration. But the men in and around the Nixon White House were measured by their zeal. Pity any grandmother who got in the way."

"Breaking the law is not out of bounds," Moyers said, "What the Constitution forbids, the President can permit."

From the hearings, Senator Herman Talmadge asked of John Enrlichman, "If the President could authorize a covert break-in, you don't know exactly where that power would be limited. You don't think it could include murder -- or other crimes beyond break-ins, do you?"

"I don't know where that line is, Senator,"
Nixon's former special assistant replied.

"There in brief is the Watergate morality
embedded in the Nixon White House," Moyers said.

> . . . a belief in the total rightness of
> the official view of reality and an
> arrogant disregard for the rule of law,
> the triumph of executive decree over due
> process. By arbitrarily and secretly
> invoking the national security, the
> President or his men can nullify the
> Bill of Rights and turn the Constitution
> into a license for illegitimate conduct.
>
> The President is set above ordinary
> standards of right or wrong. What's
> right is what works. And he alone
> decides what that is. One man, in
> effect, becomes the state.
>
> It was close. It almost worked. And it
> would have changed things for keeps:
> the public conscience smothered, the
> Congress intimidated, the press
> isolated, the political process rigged.
> The President would have been free to
> dictate the popular morality for his own
> ends. And we would have been at the
> mercy of unbridled, capricious, and
> arbitrary rules.
>
> It was close.
> It almost worked.
> But not quite.
> Something basic in our traditions held.

Moyers concluded his essay by asking why it
took "so great an affront to decency to make us realize
how hard won rights can be lost simply by taking them for
granted. So you come back, leaving behind the folk
stories and myths and wide-eyed innocence, believing that
what is best about this country doesn't need
exaggeration. It needs vigilance. I'm Bill Moyers.
Good night."[16]

Nixon and Buchanan clearly failed to silence their critics on federally supported public television. Their efforts had the opposite effect. Watergate had given public television in general and Bill Moyers in particular not only a cause, but an audience. "An Essay on Watergate" was an auspicious start to Moyers' third season on the air. The program had sent Buchanan "right up the wall" and made him "mad with rage," an administration source told Moyers. The public reaction to it and to a number of other controversial programs during the 1973-74 season was more encouraging. There were thousands of phone calls throughout the system, a tremendous surge in letters and requests for transcripts of the _Journal_. "That was the first time," Moyers recalled, ". . . that was when I realized, a hell of a lot more people watched public broadcasting across the spectrum of American life than I ever thought." There was, Moyers discovered, a silent but growing minority that was tuning in, and they were engaged by public affairs productions like the hearings and the _Journal_. "That was when I hit my stride," Moyers said. "And that was when I suddenly realized that I had found my audience . . . the 1973-74 season."[17] Because of Watergate, public television had made the kind of impact on the public that it had long sought. For a time it seemed to have emerged from its battle more vigorous and successful than it had gone in. The only loser in 1974 was Richard Nixon.

Clay Whitehead had hoped to leave government long before the autumn of 1973. He had been ready to leave after he set up the Office of Telecommunications Policy two years earlier. But he also had a great personal and professional investment in the policies he had created. He did not want to leave before he accomplished the objectives for which he had sacrificed

his non-partisan reputation. The period from the end of
1973 until the summer of 1974 was, Whitehead recalled, a
miserable one for him. "Things had degenerated [because
of Watergate]," he said. "It was pretty much an armed
camp within the White House." There were even some
people at the White House with whom the OTP director
refused to converse. But two goals he was determined to
achieve before he left the crumbling administration were
the completion of a long-range report on the future of
cable television and a long-term funding bill for public
television. "I felt I had a strong personal commitment
to do that," he said. "I had been the pointman in trying
to bring about this institutional change and had taken a
lot of heat, and things had come to the point where I
felt we had to stick by our commitments."[18]

The twelve-month period that began with Nixon's
signing of the two-year, $175 million funding package on
August 6, 1973 was one of near total retreat from
previously stated White House objectives in its battle
with public television. The day after the President
signed the Public Broadcasting Financing Act of 1973, a
White House spokesman told the press that the action
reflected the President's view that "public broadcasting
has much to offer the American people in the presentation
of educational and cultural programs of quality and
distinction."[19] The spokesman did not mention the
programs that had given public broadcasting its greatest
distinction to date, the Watergate hearings. But the
CPB-PBS partnership agreement had reaffirmed that public
affairs programming was an essential responsibility of
public television. NPACT's coverage of the hearings, the
growing popularity of Moyers and Buckley, made the
principle into a fact.

In October 1973, Whitehead drafted a memorandum
for the President in which he summarized the recent

developments in public broadcasting and urged swift
action to fill two new vacancies on the CPB board. He
wrote that the Ford Foundation intended to phase out its
support for public television over the next three to five
years. He called this "a hopeful sign of progress" in
diminishing the number of public affairs programs. But,
he admitted, CPB officials, PBS staff, and "many local
officials in the local stations still want a strong
complement of public affairs programming and the press
corps is highly supportive." The OTP director conceded,
"We have gone about as far as we can go with the old
strategy." Noting that the American Civil Liberties
Union had brought suit against him and Pat Buchanan,
alleging illegal interference in CPB actions, Whitehead
told the President that the administration was now
"keeping contacts with CPB to a minimum."

On funding, Whitehead painted an
extraordinarily rosy picture of White House successes in
decentralizing the structure of the public television
system and in getting Ford to phase out. "We have,
therefore, few grounds for opposing longer range
funding," he wrote.

> Long-range funding is supported not only
> in Congress, but by our friends on the
> Board who feel they have 'done a job'
> for us and want tangible evidence of
> support from the Administration. John
> Pastore is greatly upset by our attacks
> on CPB, and it has seriously
> deteriorated our relations with him on
> all communications issues. Our support
> for long-range funding would help this
> situation immensely.

With the President's approval, Whitehead
planned to develop a long-range funding plan as part of
the administration's program for 1974, "stressing

decentralization (to minimize the network character of the system), matching of non-Federal funds (to keep the Federal share down), and periodic review by Congress (to keep the use of Federal funds under scrutiny)."[20]

Though his comments about "hopeful signs of progress" were largely face-saving, the public television system was beginning to move towards greater decentralization. A year earlier, PBS president Hartford Gunn had developed the Station Program Cooperative plan for selecting national programs. Under the plan, CPB funds would be dispersed to the stations and the stations would then be free to purchase nationally-produced programs in a market system, or to utilize their basic grants for local programming.[21] The market plan, which was originally conceived in the fall of 1972 as a barrier to the political control of national programming by the White House-dominated CPB, was generally the kind of decentralization that Whitehead claimed to have been seeking from the start. The program cooperative illustrated that there was a mechanism by which the local stations could pool their resources to decide what they wanted in a national program service. Echoing some of the public broadcasters themselves, Whitehead called the SPC an "inherently more robust, stronger structure, much more capable of resisting government's improper attempts to manipulate programming, than having a small group of rather politically colored people sitting in Washington making those decisions unilaterally."[22]

Some within the White House, like Pat Buchanan, did not care a bit about structure or the SPC or past commitments to long-range funding. For them, the issue remained what it had always been, the programs themselves. "Why should we approve funding for the Administration's less-competent journalistic adversaries at all?" Buchanan asked. "As for the Ford Foundation

getting out [of public television], I'll believe that
when I see it," he replied to Whitehead. "My personal
view at this point is that we would be as well off with
not having the taxpayers contribute a single cent to
public television -- unless there is a clear, marked
disposition to provide balance on commentary . . . ."[23]
Evidently, Buchanan had an ally in the President.

By the end of 1973 Clay Whitehead had carried a
great deal of water for the White House. The debate over
structure and programming that he initiated had become
counterproductive in the process. For a time, his push
to decentralize funding and decisionmaking had fallen on
some very fertile ground within the public television
community. Many station leaders had long opposed
centralized control and resented the amount of money that
the national organizations bestowed on only a few of
their number. Until the summer of 1972, Whitehead was
able to manipulate this resentment. The administration's
support for the primacy of the local stations was
welcomed by many. The stations desperately needed the
money; and for some of them, sacrificing controversial
public affairs did not seen an unreasonable price to pay.

But after the June 1972 veto and the September
takeover of CPB, White House efforts had encountered
increasingly stiff and widespread resistance. The same
public broadcasters who had been bothered by centralized
control by NET were also wary of CPB domination.
Contrary to administration hopes, they were not
interested in trading one yoke for another. Until the
fall of 1972, administration posturings about localism
made sense and the White House had allies in its apparent
attempt to decentralize the system. But once CPB sought
to take all programming power away from the station-
orientated PBS, administration policies became a mass of
contradictions. It was centralization of power for the

sake of decentralization. As the gap between the image
and the substance of policy widened, increasing numbers
of public broadcasters and observers denounced the
hypocrisy.

The White House never seemed able to understand
or care that its position on funding and decentralization
was completely irrational. As Douglass Cater wrote in
January, 1973, "There is an irony in the Administration's
attitude toward public broadcasting. On the one hand,
the President's spokesmen have appealed for greater
diversity in programming and more allegiance to the
'bedrock of localism.' But they have failed to accept
the consequences that diversity and localism will cost
more, not less, for a system already showing fatal signs
of malnutrition."[24]

The contradictions in administration policy
reflected a sharp division within the executive branch.
One of the reasons that the debate over public television
became so counterproductive was that the different
elements of the Nixon administration were really trying
to accomplish very different objectives at the same time;
and each one was seeking to use the other to further its
own interests. The Office of Telecommunications Policy
had a consistent view favoring the decentralization and
the deregulation of the communications industry.
Anticipating the extraordinary development of new
technologies which would alter the structure of
broadcasting, OTP helped set a course in government
policy toward free market principles which remained
basically intact through subsequent administration. But
the lawyers, economists, and technocrats of the new
executive agency for communications matters did not
operate in a non-partisan political vacuum. The plain
fact was that Nixon hated the press. Many of his closest
advisors hated the press. They were willing to use

virtually any means available to them to stamp on or
stamp out their "enemies" in the media. The White
House's hostility created the context for all of the
administration's initiatives, even those that might have
been legitimately non-partisan. So it appeared as though
OTP was just providing the philosophical pretext for
breaking the "eastern liberal" control of the news media.

On the one hand, Clay Whitehead and his staff
tried very hard to differentiate the two different
strands of administration criticism of the media: the
political and the structural. He maintained that his
goals were purely long-range and philosophical in nature.
Privately, he complained that the White House's goals
reflected only short-term political gain and partisan
hostility. But to accomplish what he wanted to
accomplish, the OTP needed the White House's support and
influence. He therefore sold OTP's decentralization
policies to the President's men as a way of achieving
their political goal of diffusing liberal bias in
programming. His memos to the President and members of
the White House staff like H.R. Haldeman, John Ehrlichman
and Charles Colson told them what they wanted to hear
about ridding public television of New York liberal
control. Tapping into their hostility was a way of
developing a constituency for OTP within the White House,
for getting the President's attention, and for
accomplishing goals in other, less glamorous and less
politically charged areas of communications policy. But
this also raised White House expectations that OTP would,
in fact, take control of public television's programming,
dictating through CPB who should go on the air, and put
an end to the Ford Foundation's "propaganda network."
Hardly anyone at OTP was watching much public television,
or even cared about specific programs. They believed
that they could pursue their policies "for the right

reasons," said Henry Goldberg, doing what the White House wanted done "for all the wrong reasons." The key was to hold onto that White House power and support, to keep OTP where it could achieve as much as possible in developing government communications policy. Whitehead's success in keeping OTP in the thick of things by appealing to the partisan instincts within the White House justified, said Goldberg, going along on the issue of removing all public affairs programs from public television. The contradictions in OTP's public television policies were due, as much as anything else, to this bureaucratic imperative.[25]

Publicly, of course, neither Whitehead nor anyone else at OTP would denounce White House intentions. In his speeches to broadcasters and testimony before congressional committees, the OTP director could deny that single-year funding or the 1972 veto had anything to do with politics. Few believed him, and with good reason. Nixon and Colson and Buchanan clearly used Whitehead and OTP, also. If it was shrewd to try to use the White House's hostility to accomplish non-political goals, it was naive to think that the outside world would see the subtle differences of intent and accept them in good faith. The legitimate structural concerns about public television, and the simple desire to "control it or kill it" became so intermingled that it was impossible to separate them. Whitehead became involved in the workings of what was supposed to be a CPB board of directors independent of government control. Funding became a tool for political control and public television suffered immensely.

From the summer of 1972 until the spring of 1973, the rhetoric of localism rang increasingly hollow. After the Curtis resignation in April 1973, a New York Times editorial declared: "The Administration's record

of public broadcasting is a chronicle of double-talk.
When Mr. Nixon vetoed the public broadcasting
appropriations bill last year, he characterized the
Public Broadcasting Service as excessively centralized.
But with its latest coup, the Administration has, in
effect, let it be known that its goal is not a
decentralized PBS but one that is submissive to its will
-- and thus the disguised central control -- of the
Office of Telecommunications Policy."[26]

Clay Whitehead and his staff had nothing to do
with Watergate, but they were tainted along with the rest
of the Nixon White House. OTP counsel Henry Goldberg
told the director that his reputation had been sacrificed
in the battle over public television and that the
practical result of the administration's efforts to
influence the direction of the system had been chaos and
partisan division. Whitehead had done enough fighting
with the press and the public broadcasters. He was
intent on pushing through an administration-sponsored
long-term financing bill before he left OTP.

On April 2, 1974, he sent a memo to the
President outlining his proposal for a long-term funding
bill for public broadcasting. The legislation included:
long-range funding over a five-year period, without
annual appropriations but with annual oversight; a forty
percent matching formula with ceilings of $70 million in
fiscal 1976 gradually increasing to $100 million in 1980;
and a mandatory pass-through to the local stations of a
substantial portion of the federal matching grants. "The
bill," Whitehead told the President, "would not preclude
the use of Federal funds for news and public affairs
programs. While I share your view that such funds should
not be used for this purpose, it would not pass if we
attempted to deal with the problem legislatively. The
solution is best left to the Board of CPB."

Whitehead argued that the President's approval
of the bill offered the most likely way to reduce the
danger of control over public television, either by a
private foundation or by a future administration -- "one
that may not be as sympathetic to the role of the local
stations as we are." He also warned that Communications
Subcommittee chairman Pastore "in particular wants the
bill, and, if it is not submitted, could drag his feet on
our upcoming cable legislation and confirmation of our
nominees to CPB." The long-range bill would remove an
irritant in the administration's relationship with both
the Senate and House communications subcommittees and
therefore depoliticize the atmosphere surrounding the
hearings on the White House nominees to CPB. Finally, by
submitting the funding bill, Whitehead said, the White
House will have met its obligation and "if the Congress
does not support this bill, we are free to oppose any
other approach to long-range funding."[27]

President Nixon rejected Whitehead's
recommendation and refused to support the
administration's own funding bill. The OTP director was
angry and incredulous; but most of all, he was
frustrated. "When he rejected my proposal," Whitehead
recalled, "part of me said, 'He didn't understand; he
either didn't read my memo or somebody just ran it by him
and he really didn't understand what he was doing.' And
the other side of me said, 'He just didn't give a damn at
this point. He's being vindictive. He's saying, Let's
screw 'em,' Either way, I felt I had an obligation to go
back and appeal and make sure he understood what he was
doing."

"In the final analysis," Whitehead said, "he
was the President. And if he said, 'Screw 'em,' that was
his prerogative. He didn't <u>have</u> to support [the bill].
But I wanted to make sure that he understood that at

least, I felt that we had achieved some structural
change, and that it was important for him to try to
consolidate that and leave that behind."[28]

Whitehead appealed the President's decision.
On June 7, he sent a memo to White House chief of staff,
General Alexander Haig. "I have been informed," he
wrote, "that the President has disapproved the long-range
funding proposal for the Corporation for Public
Broadcasting, which I forwarded on April 2, 1974, and
wants to 'end' public broadcasting or submit a 'very
limited' budget proposal. I strongly disagree,"
Whitehead told Haig. "I cannot support such an action,
and request an appeal to the President."

> Rightly or wrongly, the commitment to
> Federal funding of public broadcasting
> has been made. For the President to
> attempt to back away from that
> commitment now is unwise, unworkable,
> and quixotic. An attempt to do so would
> isolate the President from public and
> Congressional opinion, and thus would
> deprive him of any effective
> participation in the constructive
> shaping of public broadcasting policy.

Whitehead also took issue with Nixon's personal
decision to appoint Nancy Chotiner, widow of one of
Nixon's oldest friends and supporters, Murray Chotiner,
to the CPB board. Whitehead called the nomination of
Mrs. Chotiner "most inappropriate." "While I do not know
Mrs. Chotiner personally," Whitehead told Haig, "and have
no adverse information about her, she appears to have no
particular qualifications for the Board, and her
appointment would be widely perceived as a purely
political appointment."[29] Nixon, it seemed, in the final
days of the administration was simply being vindictive
towards public television. With the denial of long-range

funding and the proposed appointment of Murray Chotiner's
widow, he was, it seemed, just trying to "screw 'em."

Nixon's longtime press aide, Herbert Klein,
wrote that within the many facets of the Nixon
personality, "there is a sadistic side, one which derives
satisfaction from thoughts of vengeance." By the spring
of 1974 those left in the administration had come to
realize that there was a "Jekyll and Hyde streak" in the
President. The conflict within the administration over
the real objective of its public television policies --
localism or censorship -- reflected a conflict within
Nixon himself. "There was a side of him that could argue
more passionately and more articulately than anyone I
have ever heard got for the need for the separation
between the government and the press," said Whitehead.
"The other side of him was the political infighter par
excellence who was not above using the resources of his
power to do the fighting."

> I could go to him and talk to him about
> these issues from a policy point of view
> and elicit one response, and you look at
> the transcripts of those tapes and you
> could see other people like Colson going
> to him, bringing out, almost the same
> day, an almost 180 degree opposite
> reaction. He was capable of having sort
> of a split mind, if you will. He would
> strongly support the separation of the
> government and the media, and a few days
> later he would meet with Colson to plan
> how they were going to use the FCC to
> have license renewal challenges filed
> against the Washington Post stations.
> On the one hand, he'd say we shouldn't
> have that kind of government control, we
> shouldn't have those kind of powers in
> the FCC, it's wrong. Two days later,
> he'd be saying, 'let's go get 'em.'
> There was a conflict within him that
> found its way into the conflicts within
> the Administration.[30]

Whitehead had a long meeting with Haig and felt that he had gotten a fair hearing out of it. But the President refused to budge. He rejected the long-term funding bill a second time.

"At that point," Whitehead recalled, "it was clear that I was not going to get the administration -- that I was not going to get the President -- to do what I wanted. I still wasn't convinced he knew what was going on." Nixon was under an intense amount of pressure in areas far more crucial to him than public television. For over a year he had been fighting the disclosure of his administration's and his own involvement in Watergate. But the scandal kept spreading. The President's personal role in a wide range of illegal and unethical activities was, by the late spring of 1974, widely acknowledged. Democrats and Republicans alike were calling for his resignation. Impeachment proceedings were begun against him in the House of Representatives. NPACT broadcast them over the public television system, in prime time, gavel-to-gavel.

"I didn't have any real confidence," said Whitehead, that the President had focused on the public television issue as much as he should have. "And so you make a judgment about what you think you ought to do," the OTP director explained. "One thing is to be a good soldier and say, 'okay.' But I was past that point. This was something I felt strongly about -- and felt I had the responsibility to carry on that debate. At that point, the only recourse I had was to take the debate between me and the White House public."[31]

Whitehead went to The New York Times with the story. The next day, June 10, there was a front page story. Attributing his information to "sources close to the CPB," Times television writer Les Brown reported that

President Nixon had "flatly rejected without discussion
or explanation" the OTP funding bill.

> The sources, who learned of the decision
> late last week, said that the President
> turned down the bill with a terse
> statement which suggested instead that
> Federal support for public television be
> scaled down.
>
> The proposed legislation was sent to the
> President in late April by Clay T.
> Whitehead. . . . Mr. Whitehead has been
> described as chagrined at the
> President's rejection of the bill.
> However, when contacted, Mr. Whitehead
> would not comment on the report of the
> President's action, but said that he was
> 'still pushing' to get a bill out for
> long-range funding of public television.

Brown reported that the funding bill, prepared
under Whitehead's supervision and approved by the CPB
board before it went to the White House, "had been
presumed certain" to receive presidential approval. "One
of the Corporation sources said he believed the President
had rejected the long-range funding bill because 'he has
never liked public television and probably never
will.'"[32]

The Times piece quickly generated editorials
critical of the President, not only from The Washington
Post, but from The Wall Street Journal, long a supporter
of the administration's public television policies. The
Journal pointed to public television's "excellent
performance in covering the Watergate hearings," in
improving the ideological balance of all its public
affairs programming, and in accepting the matching grant
approach to federal funding. It was unreasonable, The
Journal concluded, for the administration to abandon
public TV entirely, "especially in view of its recent
efforts to rectify its most glaring shortcomings."[33]

The next day, <u>The Washington Post</u> said,

> Ten months ago, it looked as if
> President Nixon might finally stop
> picking on public broadcasting. His
> sharp criticism of programs and policies
> had died down and he had reversed past
> form by signing a bill authorizing
> federal funds . . . over a two-year
> period.
>
> . . . but now comes the word that
> President Nixon doesn't want the [new,
> five-year] bill sent to Congress. . . .
> The taxpaying public -- listeners and
> viewers -- ought not be denied certain
> 'controversial' programs merely because
> the government doesn't like them, or
> because President Nixon doesn't happen
> to enjoy what he sees on the public
> channel.[32]

Whitehead's leak to <u>The Times</u> had the desired effect. "Ron Ziegler stood up and lied through his teeth and said the President had never made a decision," he said. "We ended up getting administration support for the long-range funding bill."[35]

On July 11, Whitehead received another terse memo from the White House: "Your April 2nd memorandum to the President on Public Broadcasting financing recommending a five-year advance funding program has been approved."[36]

At that point, Whitehead knew he had to resign. "I think that when you go public like that," he said, "you so poison the relationship between yourself and the White House that you really can't function. So I felt I had to resign." He stayed until he could get the administration publicly on record in support of the five-year funding by testifying before the Senate Communications Subcommittee. He pushed the bill through OMB, getting the necessary clearances and on August 6

went before Pastore's committee to support it on behalf
of the administration.

"It was four years ago," he said, "that I
appeared before you at the hearing regarding my
confirmation as director of the Office of
Telecommunications Policy. At that time, you reminded me
of this Administration's pledge to submit a long-range
funding plan for the Corporation for Public Broadcasting
and the local educational stations it is intended to
serve. I never realized then what an arduous journey it
would be before we could keep that promise."

After outlining the specifics of the bill and
the four-year history that finally led to its submission,
Whitehead concluded his prepared remarks:

> The financing of public broadcasting
> represents rare and unique circumstances
> in which the Executive and Legislative
> branches should give up some of the
> control they wield over federally funded
> programs by virtue of the annual
> authorization and appropriation process.
> This unusual funding mechanism is
> essential, if the public broadcasting
> system as conceived by the 1967 Act is
> to succeed. It's that simple. For that
> reason the Administration has put aside
> its own reservations and has proposed
> this bill. For the same reason Congress
> should loosen its control of public
> broadcasting's purse strings and pass
> this legislation.
>
> The past seven years have brought us all
> to a point at which we simply must trust
> the people who run the stations and the
> national public broadcast organiza-
> tions. . . . I am not asking Congress to
> have blind faith in public broadcasting;
> just as I did not ask that of the
> President in urging him to send this
> legislation to Congress. But we have
> created a system; it is a reality. We
> must now give it a chance to succeed

according to the original vision for a
truly independent and financially
insulated system of public broadcasting.
To do so, I have discovered, you must be
willing to respect both reality and
idealism. This bill is our best effort
to combine the two. I commend it to you
and your colleagues.[37]

On his way back from the Capitol, Whitehead
dropped off his formal letter of resignation in the White
House mail. Two days later, Richard Nixon himself
resigned.

CHAPTER EIGHT

A POETIC SYMMETRY

Public television survived Richard Nixon; but
not without paying a price. The battle with the
administration was a traumatic one, and it left its mark.
Though the Public Broadcasting Act of 1975 -- the end
result of the bill first offered to Congress by Clay
Whitehead before he resigned -- and the Public
Telecommunications Financing Act of 1978 finally gave
public television the kind of large, multi-year federal
appropriations that had been delayed by President Nixon,
they did not leave the picture for public television
entirely bright. With his signing of the 1975
legislation, President Ford declared that it would give
"more spine to the stations to produce daring and
controversial programs to match the tough problems of the
nation."[1] In the wake of Richard Nixon, however, public
television's record of support for daring and
controversial programs was mixed at best. Although the
Watergate hearings had proved to be an extraordinary
triumph for the entire system, the emphasis on
journalistic enterprises proved fleeting. The
decentralization long favored by Clay Whitehead had, to
some extent, been institutionalized in the Station
Program Cooperative method for selecting national program
offerings. While the market cooperative gave local
stations greater discretion over the shape of the
national schedule, it also seemed to result in fewer
programs that "matched the tough problems of the nation."

As NET's James Day had said when the station-oriented PBS replaced his organization as the system's national program authority, real diversity and daring in public television programming had to be planned from above by a strong, central authority. They would not occur democratically. Programming by committee, Day had said, led only to "bland decisions, blandly arrived at."[2] The years following the divisive struggle with Nixon and Whitehead seemed to prove Day's point.

With Nixon gone, the issue of how to balance local and national priorities, democracy and daring, remained. With greater reliance on a decentralized marketplace, the premium was put on the proven and popular, not the adventuresome and controversial. Thus, in the middle 1970's, journalism -- that most dangerous and delicate endeavor on public television -- became a scarce commodity. In 1973 Robert MacNeil departed from NPACT to return to the BBC, where publicly-supported broadcast journalism was a far more secure occupation. His exit followed by only eight months that of his controversial colleague, Sander Vanocur. Over the ensuing two years, the National Public Affairs Center itself withered away completely. What remained of its staff and its mandate to produce national public affairs programs from the nation's capital devolved upon Washington's station, WETA. WNET's Bill Moyers left public television for the much better endowed CBS News (he would later return only to depart again) because his critically acclaimed Journal could not seem to attract adequate support from the system. Public television gained a reputation for emphasizing programs that were, in the words of broadcast historian Erik Barnouw, "safely splendid:"[3] live opera, classical music, dance, British dramatizations of classic literature, and gala performances aimed at raising money for itself. By the

end of its first full decade, public television, said The
New York Times' John J. O'Connor, had become "a
repository for nicely reassuring, non-minority middle
class attitudes and values."[4] Public television seemed
to have become what many conservative critics charged it
would be when it was created in 1967, "a poverty program
for the well-to-do." There was no reason to disparage
the system's great successes in bringing cultural events
to an unprecedentedly wide and appreciative audience.
What disturbed some of public television's supporters was
not what was being broadcast on the Public Broadcasting
Service, but what was not. Risks were not being taken,
and experimentation did not seem to be nearly as welcome
as it once had been.

          In recognition of the fact that, even having
weathered the controversies and the political meddling of
1971 to 1973, all was not well in the nation's public
broadcasting system, a second Carnegie Commission was
formed in 1977. Its purpose was to examine what had
happened in the ten years since the first commission had
issued its report and, in light of that experience, to
make new recommendations for the future of public
broadcasting. "What public broadcasting tried to
invent," said Carnegie II, "was a truly radical idea: an
instrument of mass communication that simultaneously
respects the artistry of the individuals who create
programs, the needs of the public that form the audience,
and the forces of political power that supply the
resources. Sadly, we conclude that the invention did not
work, or at least not very well."[5] Carnegie II
acknowledged that journalism, in particular -- once
intended as public television's highest programming
priority -- had become its achilles heel. Under pressure
from the Nixon White House, many within the system had

been willing to amputate the troublesome limb in order to save the rest of the body.

Public affairs programing had been de-emphasized, and in the process, public television endured bitter internal struggles. "Herein lies the fundamental dilemma that has revealed itself over and over again in public broadcasting's brief history and led to the empanelment of this commission," said Carnegie II. "How can public broadcasting be organized so that sensitive judgments can be freely made and creative activity freely carried out without destructive quarreling over whether the system is subservient to a variety of powerful forces including the government?"[6] The second Carnegie Commission decided that the only way to keep the heat of institutional bickering from overshadowing the light generated by public television's programs was to have better insulation: A Public Telecommunications trust that would be more independent of government than the Corporation for Public Broadcasting, and within this new entity an even more sheltered Program Services Endowment. Since its creation, public television had been searching for a way to separate those who paid the piper from those who called the tune, sometimes, it seemed, with only limited success. CPB had proved unable to adequately safeguard the system from the political pressures -- inherent in government financing -- that were brought to bear by the Nixon administration. "Without attempting to judge the motives of the CPB board," said the Commission, "we observe that the board took action to downplay public affairs programming in order to avoid placing the entire federal appropriation in jeopardy."

> Rather than fight for the system's
> independence from political
> interference, CPB's decisions about
> NPACT, various public affairs series,

and the takeover of PBS functions seems
to us to have been an attempt to mollify
the administration in order to maintain
funding that was now life and death to
the system. . . . While one might argue
that CPB's decisions were arrived at
independently, they did, in fact,
coincide with the expressed objectives
of the administration and were widely
perceived as concessions.[7]

The Second Carnegie Commission concluded that the events
of 1971-73 "slowed the growth of public broadcasting and
left a psychological scar on the stations -- an enhanced
sensitivity to perceived threats to their independence --
which persists today."

But public television stations were highly
sensitive about controversy and perceived threats to
their independence before the Nixon White House began its
efforts to pressure them. The leaders of public
broadcasting had made a deliberate choice, with the
creation of the station-controlled Public Broadcasting
Service in 1970, to move the system away from the
creative and decisionmaking predominance of New York's
sometimes controversial network and national production
center, National Educational Television. This might have
been sound from an organizational point of view, but it
was a highly political decision as well. Congress, after
all, had approved a system based on grassroots localism;
and before Richard Nixon, Spiro Agnew and Patrick
Buchanan commenced their assault on the alleged "liberal-
left" bias of the New York-based commercial network news,
many local public broadcasters were themselves
complaining about the "left-wing" outlook and centralized
control of public television by NET. In March of 1969
the eight largest stations in the public system asked the
Corporation for Public Broadcasting and the Ford
Foundation to terminate funding for the politically
oriented Sunday evening Public Broadcast Laboratory

program. They wanted it replaced by a program that would put "stronger emphasis on cultural presentations and reduce the proportion of time accorded to news and public affairs."[8] The movement toward "establishment, up-scale" cultural programming in public broadcasting clearly began before the Nixon administration ever became involved in the development of the system; and the trend continued after Nixon left office. Indeed, such a shift was inevitable in a system that was trying to build a national audience and using millions of dollars of the government's money to do it.

New York Times Sunday editor Lester Markel wrote in January 1969 that public television had done too little in the area of public affairs programming, that it should take a more active role in shaping public opinion by providing a better, more useful flow of information to the American people.[9] Markel believed, like many others, that commercial network news was inadequate for the task. A great advocate of journalism on public television Markel did not, however, support continued production of the ideologically based "advocacy" documentaries for which NET had become noted. The leftist coloration of NET programming, he later wrote, "only served to hurt the cause of liberalism" and merely provided ammunition for those in government and the industry who wanted to end all public affairs programming on public television. The professional journalists who came to public television in its early years agreed with Markel's analysis. Bill Moyers, Robert MacNeil, Sander Vanocur and Jim Lehrer believed that polemical programs did not serve public television well. "I just felt," said MacNeil, "that you weren't going to build respect for journalism in this part publicly funded institution in the minds of all its opponents, within and without, unless you demonstrated professional, craftsmanlike, workmanlike, day-to-day

journalism, which meant fairness and objectivity."[10]
Vanocur described some of public television's public
affairs programs before 1971 as "gunslinging journalism."
And contrary to the popular impression, he did not join
NPACT to do his own gunslinging. He felt that NET's
reputation made it only more difficult to build the
credibility of the new public affairs center.[11]
Similarly, Lehrer said, "there were some programs that
NET did that were journalistically unsound." "They
were," he said, "poorly edited, sloppily done in terms of
reporting, and there's no question that they were done
from a point of view -- a liberal point of view."[12] There
were not many such programs, but it only took a few to
create a general impression. Lehrer accepted the post of
PBS public affairs coordinator in 1972 to help improve
the quality of journalistic programming around the
system. He, like NPACT founder and general manager Jim
Karayn, argued that public television should develop its
own "nightly public affairs presence."[13] Not superficial
news reports, not an echo of the commercial networks, but
television journalism that would, as Markel had
suggested, seek to educate viewers about the broader
implications of current issues and events. For a brand
new organization, NPACT was remarkably successful in 1972
and 1973 in doing this on a weekly basis.

"I consider myself a teaching journalist rather
than an advocating journalist," said Bill Moyers.[14] His
Journal, while it frequently offered strong political and
social critiques, was never predictably partisan or
actively polemical. It probed deeply, insightfully,
sometimes even passionately into controversial people and
issues that were rarely touched elsewhere in television.
There was nothing like it on commercial television.

These men felt that they could add something
unique to the public dialogue, while adding to the

prestige of the new television system only by not being "advocacy" journalists. They understood that public television could not hope to maintain support from the federal government if it continued to be perceived as a mouthpiece for the left. The shift away from works like "Banks and the Poor" and Paul Jacobs' FBI piece for <u>Great American Dream Machine</u>, was fueled in part by industry executives who were hesitant to create any pretext for threats to federal funding. But public television's expanding group of established journalists felt -- out of their own sense of professionalism -- that an increased emphasis on the journalistic values of balance and objectivity was needed. Both forces existed outside the context of the Nixon attack on public affairs programming and would have had their effect had that attack never occurred. And with or without Nixon, some producers and critics were bound to charge that public television had gone soft, bowing to political expediency and had become instead a government propaganda agency.

The public television system created in 1967 lacked financial and institutional independence from the federal government. Elected officials were so wary of establishing a national communications entity capable of capture by political opponents that they refused to confer the kind of freedom necessary for editorial creativity. The President chose members of the CPB board; Congress appropriated funds on an annual basis. This reality made it critical for public television, if it was to have journalism at all, to produce programs acceptable to a broad ideological spectrum. In any environment such evenhandedness would be a difficult task on television. Broadcast journalism has often been criticized simultaneously by conservatives for being too liberal, and by liberals for being too conservative. People seem instinctively to want to blame the messenger

for bringing messages that are disturbing to their own
beliefs. Public television's professional journalists
accepted the fact that their craft would be secure only
if those on both sides of the political equation felt
that their views were fairly represented. This indeed
had been NPACT's goal. But during an era of deep social
and political divisions in the nation and a presidential
administration deeply hostile to journalism that merely
gave attention to those who questioned official policy
such attempts at balance were to no avail.

The birth in 1975 and subsequent development of
the MacNeil-Lehrer Report into the MacNeil-Lehrer
Newshour is indicative of just how intractable the
situation had been for public television while Nixon was
still in office. Doing little fundamentally different
from NPACT's efforts, MacNeil-Lehrer, like the public
affairs center itself, would never have survived had it
gone on the air in 1971. MacNeil-Lehrer is now something
of a broadcasting institution, having won wide praise for
its in-depth, evenhanded treatment of important issues of
national concern. By giving equal time within each
night's program to proponents of various, conflicting
viewpoints from both in and outside of government,
MacNeil-Lehrer successfully defused charges of public
television's liberal editorial bias. The nightly report
represents a successful culmination of public
television's often painful search for a credible,
popular, probing, yet unoffensive national journalistic
presence. MacNeil-Lehrer was a direct descendent of
efforts begun and partnerships formed at NPACT, whose
demise was almost insured by the Nixon White House. The
antipathies of President Nixon even toward such balanced,
"journalism of record" were simply too great for public
television to have escaped.

In retrospect, it is difficult to understand
why the Nixon administration wasted as much time and
energy as it did in attempting to subdue an institution
as unthreatening as public television was in 1971.
Public television was then relatively unknown and its
viewership infinitesimal compared to that of commercial
television. An October 1971 survey of public television
viewing by Louis Harris and Associates demonstrated that
even public television watchers had only a dim awareness
that there was such a thing as a national non-commercial
broadcasting system. At the very time of Clay
Whitehead's speech to the National Association of
Educational Broadcasters in Miami criticizing the drift
toward centralization, sixty-one percent of public
television viewers believed that their local public
television station was independent of any network and
produced most of its own programs. The national system's
impact on the public awareness was clearly not very
significant. To onetime Carnegie Commission chairman
James Killian, the Nixon administration expressed a
degree of concern about centralization far out of line
with the actual case.[15] "They viewed us as much more
important a force on the American scene than we really
were," said CPB's first president John Macy. "They had
magnified a mouse into a lion. I can't help but be
amused at how exaggerated their estimate of what our
strength and influence really was. After all, there
weren't that many people watching."

    "I would have thought," Macy concluded, "that
an administration would have had other things to do that
would have been considerably more significant in building
their own record and serving the public interest."[16]
From within the administration itself, Office of
Telecommunications Policy counsel Henry Goldberg also
could not understand the White House's preoccupation. "I

still can't figure out why they all cared so much about
public broadcasting," he said. "It was amazing. It
occupied so much time which we could have better spent
worrying about AT&T, or something. It had an
insignificant number [of viewers]; why did they all
care?"[17] Of course, they cared for the same reasons they
cared about opposition from political foes, dissent in
the streets, and criticism in the news media. The Nixon
administration was conducting a war in Southeast Asia
which had become increasingly unpopular, particularly
among the very groups which had a prior history of
antagonism toward Richard Nixon himself: the "eastern
liberal establishment," and the national news media. The
opponents of the administration's policy of gradual
"Vietnamization" of the war -- many of them longtime
opponents of the President -- were, in the minds of many
at the White House, transformed into the enemies of
America's national security. "North Vietnam cannot
defeat or humiliate the United States," Nixon said in
November 1969. "Only Americans can do that." The many
twisted paths that led to the Watergate crisis four years
later were carved by a belief among the President and his
men that the television networks, The New York Times, The
Washington Post, the Democratic Party itself, were guilty
of giving aid and comfort to the enemy in Vietnam by
their opposition to the war. Nixon's pursuit of "Peace
with Honor," they felt, was undermined by a news media
that refused to tell the story their way. Their
analysis, too, was deeply colored by Richard Nixon's past
difficulties with the press and the "liberal
establishment" -- two institutions of which public
television seemed very much a part. Nixon saw himself as
an often helpless victim of a twenty-year conspiracy
against him by the news media, as someone who existed for
the press to "kick around." To him and many of his

aides, the nation's security and stability were inextricably tied to Richard Nixon's political security. Loyalty was placed above legality; if the President approved, then anything was permitted. Clearly, the intensity of such feelings gave the President and his staff a distorted sense of proportion in trying to muzzle a seemingly inconsequential, fledgling public television system.

Public television might have been weak. It might have been unnoticed by the vast majority of Americans. It might even have been actively seeking to de-politicize its journalistic programming; but public television in 1971 and 1972 was home to Sander Vanocur. Richard Nixon disliked the new media in general, but Sandy Vanocur was clearly one of those who stood out. He had been the first prominent broadcast journalist to predict disaster for American involvement in Vietnam and had continued to be one of the most outspoken on the issue. In 1960 he had earned then Vice President Nixon's enmity by his insistent interrogations during the presidential campaign. To Nixon, Vanocur was a Kennedy "sycophant," involved with other reporters sympathetic to the Democratic candidate in a "conspiracy" to undermine his own candidacy. Vanocur alone was remembered in Nixon's subsequent writings for his embarrassing question (about Eisenhower's sarcastic commentary on Nixon's vice presidential performance) during the first and most crucial nationally televised debate of the 1960 race.[18] Perhaps no one better personified the connection between past anti-Nixon and present anti-war attitudes than Sander Vanocur when he was named senior correspondent for NPACT. His hiring was like "waving a red flag" in front of the President's face, so many in the White House recall. For Nixon, it crystallized the public television issue as nothing else did. He reacted to it with a fury. He called for an immediate cut-off in federal funds to

the public system. He and others in the White House were
outraged at the notion that government money -- _their_
government's money -- would be used to underwrite an
adversary like Sander Vanocur.[19]

Vanocur himself comments, somewhat ruefully,
that because of the apparent lack of impact of his work
at NPACT he often "felt like a man who had walked across
a field of fresh snow, and looked back and there were no
marks at all."[20] But it is clear from their memorandums
and their private conversations that those within the
White House were deeply concerned about the effect that
Vanocur's ephemeral footprints might have. Like _The New
York Times_ or _The Washington Post_, Vanocur and public
television were perceived as enemies, and therefore as
threats to the administration. Although public
television presented a feeble threat, Robert MacNeil
said, the Nixon White House "wanted to cover every
mousehole." "There were some pretty tiny mice coming out
of it; but they wanted a cat by that mousehole."[21]
Indeed, every little mouse, from a lone anti-war
protester in Lafayette Park to a perceived imbalance on
the guest list of an _Advocates_ program dealing with the
issue of guaranteed minimum income, angered someone in
the White House. Every presidential administration seeks
favorable news coverage and complains about undue
criticism from the media, but the Nixon White House took
these tendencies to an unprecedented and illogical
extreme. To a President and an administration wholly
preoccupied, in the words of Jonathan Schell, with the
appearance of things rather than their substance, public
television was simply not permitted to expose any cracks
in the White House wall. It, like the rest of the news
media, threatened to tarnish the images of policy and
power that the Nixon White House sought so unceasingly to
create.[22]

The hostility of the Nixon White House might, at times, have been intimidating to the other media, but in the case of public television that hostility could be directly translated into government policy. Unlike The New York Times or CBS News, public television needed Richard Nixon's signature in order to pay its bills. Members of the Nixon administration were fond of saying that public television was dangerously vulnerable to political interference, from organizations like the Ford Foundation, or from the government itself. Yet the foundations and Congress had done admirably in keeping their hands off of program content. The only ones who actively interfered with the system's independence were those in the Nixon administration itself. It was they who demonstrated how much more public television was liable to political control than were the commercial media. As Clay Whitehead explained, "The separation we have, by and large, between the press and the government kept [the White House] from doing anything very meaningful with the rest of the media; but that separation blurred with public broadcasting and that gave them some levers, which they proceeded to utilize. You put a hammer in front of a little boy and he'll pick it up and pound something. That's what the funding of public television was to the Nixon political people."[23]

Jack Valenti, former aide to Lyndon Johnson and member of the CPB board of directors throughout the Nixon years, agreed that public television presented a tempting target. "If you're sitting in the White House," he said, "you can't do anything about Walter Cronkite and you can't do anything about David Brinkley, but you think, 'By God, I can sure do something about this.'"[24] Public television was vulnerable. It was open to political manipulation. It was hardly a threat to the Nixon White House, but if often made the President and his advisers

angry. When it did, they went for the hammer. The Nixon
administration's attempt to stunt the growth and
circumscribe the editorial freedom of public television
fit all too comfortably into the well-explored themes of
this scandalized presidency: the intimidation of the
news media; the attack on political "enemies"; the
internal pressure to follow orders and, if necessary, to
use extra-legal means to do so; the gaping division
between administration rhetoric about decentralization
and separation of powers, and its actions; the
aggrandizement of executive authority that brought about
the apex and the denouement of the "Imperial Presidency."
So, too, the fundamental issues surrounding government-
sponsored broadcasting were brought into sharper focus by
virtue of President Nixon's opposition to public
television. The natural tension that exists between
creative freedom and accountability to government was
greatly exacerbated by the Nixon White House. The built-
in conflict between local and national priorities in
programming was incalculably intensified because of
administration obstruction of adequate federal funding.
The intrinsic difficulties raised by journalism funded by
the government were immeasurably complicated because of
the administration's opposition to programs of this sort.

Public television's struggles during the Nixon
presidency nearly always boiled down to the not so simple
question of money: Where it came from and how it should
be used -- who paid the piper, who called the tune and
how to separate the two. Advocates of public
broadcasting knew that this was the single, crucial issue
when the system was being created in 1967. Broadcasters
and legislators agreed that long-term, politically
insulated federal financing would be the key to success
of the new venture. CBS President Frank Stanton,
testifying before the Senate Commerce Committee hearings

on the 1967 act, said that if public television was going
to experiment in programming it would "make mistakes
which could be costly in this narrow relationship between
money and operation."

"Of one thing we can be certain," Fred Friendly
told the senators with characteristic bluntness, "public
television will rock the boat." It would be essential,
he and Republican Hugh Scott agreed, to "insulate the
scratch," since someone in government was bound to
"scratch the insulation" when the boat did rock. Perhaps
more than the broadcasters, the politicians recognized
the threat they themselves presented to public
television. Senator Jacob Javits testifying before his
colleagues, said, "If I do nothing else but zero you in
on the fact that if you have a Presidential appointment,
advice and consent of the Senate, plus annual
appropriations techniques, you do raise the spectre, the
possibility of political influence." And yet, despite
widespread interest in keeping public television free
from governmental pressure, the legislation voted by
Congress and signed by President Johnson in 1967 lacked
any provision for insulated funding. Left without an
appropriations-free method of government financing, the
structures created in 1967 proved unable to meet the
challenge of what Senator Scott had called "the infinite
capacities of government to maneuver."[25]

Whatever structures should have been
established to separate politicians from programmers,
they are unlikely to have been effective in the face of
determined pressure from the Nixon White House. Perhaps
it is not very satisfying to say that the answer to
problems raised by government-sponsored broadcasting lies
in a personal determination on the part of those in
political power to simply stay out of the creative
process. But it is one we will likely have to live with.

There is no institutional or procedural substitute for good faith and integrity. The entire Watergate scandal illustrates that there will at times be those who will overstep whatever limits we impose on ourselves and our government.

The remarkable journalistic success of National Public Radio suggests that publicly financed broadcasting can be far more creative, controversial, and incisive than its commercial counterparts if only it is given the necessary breathing space. In the early 1970's, while public television was being pressured to drop its national affairs programming, NPR was able to establish and nurture its marvelous national news program, All Things Considered. The politicians were just not very interested in what was on the radio. Television was where the action -- and the battle -- was. Without the critical scrutiny given to the visual medium, NPR had the freedom to risk, to experiment, and to deal forthrightly with political issues without engendering the kind of controversy that inevitably surrounded such efforts on public television. (To be sure, NPR's nearly fatal financial crisis of the early 1980's reminds us that freedom from oversight can also be abused. If government does it part by appropriating the taxpayers' money without strings attached, then broadcasters must have a complimentary responsibility to spend it judiciously.)

Even in a less contentious political environment than that of the Nixon administration, public television has sometimes found it difficult to resolve the conflict between accountability to government and editorial freedom. In 1971 and 1972, documentaries like "Who Invited Us?", "Banks and the Poor" and Paul Jacobs' FBI piece caused a great deal of controversy. Newspaper editors like Lester Markel and A.M. Rosenthal of The New York Times thought such works shoddy journalism. They

provided justification for those in government and public
television itself who wanted to scuttle all public
affairs programming and get on to the more gratifying and
less troublesome business of bringing education, art, and
culture to the American people. In 1972 PBS decided that
it had to protect itself, its journalistic credibility
and the survival of its public affairs efforts by hiring
a good editor, a public affairs coordinator. Many
producers cried censorship.

In the spring of 1982, public television
broadcast three similarly controversial documentaries,
"Blood and Sand: War in the Sahara," "From the
Ashes . . . Nicaragua Today," and the "PBS Report on the
U.S. Role in Latin America." PBS' handling of these
highly political works brought sharp criticism from
President Reagan's chairman of the National Endowment for
the Humanities, which helps underwrite many public
television projects, and cries of censorship from their
independent producers. In July the executive producer,
Ned Schnurman, of public television's series on broadcast
journalism Inside Story charged that many of the
independent film journalists who complained about PBS
"censorship . . . have a hard time dealing with
straightforward factual presentations. They are
advocates, rather than journalists, clearly in need of a
tough, hard-nosed editor. Appointment of an editor-in-
chief at PBS with solid news background . . . working in
an environment familiar to traditional journalistic
endeavors, would blunt the complaints at the source and
leave free expression unimpaired."[26] The alternative,
voiced by the ranking Republican on the House
Telecommunications Subcommittee James Collins, is an
extreme one. It ominously echoes the view held by Clay
Whitehead and the intimidated CPB board of 1972-73.
"Documentaries," Collins said, "are a field [public

television] perhaps shouldn't be involved in,
particularly if they take a point of view."[27] History
might not be repeating itself, but the debate over the
propriety of independent journalism and the role of
federal funding certainly is. Ten years ago and today
(and probably in the future, as well) the consensus among
established journalists, programmers and legislators will
be that public television must be careful to play it
straight, to make its political programming balanced if
it expects to maintain credibility with viewers and
support among the politicians. We expect fairness from
all broadcast journalism. We tend to demand it from an
institution that benefits from our tax dollars. It will
never be easy to know where maintaining credibility ends
and guarding institutional survival begins. "Imagined
governmental censorship or displeasure is a convenient
and sometimes headline-making scapegoat from rejection
due to poor journalism" said PBS director of News and
Public Affairs Barry Chase.[28] The argument has an
undeniably familiar ring to it. In 1972 and 1973 many in
public television were actively trying to drop public
affairs programming completely because of official
displeasure. Such does not seem the case today. As long
as public television survives, it is clear that its
political programming will, too. A decade ago, the
survival of public affairs seemed much less sure. Those
who would have done away with public affairs were stopped
by those who remained steadfastly committed to journalism
on public television, and by an extraordinary stroke of
luck called the Watergate Hearings. For a few months of
what would have been uneventful, repeat-filled summer
evenings, the Senate Watergate hearings made public
affairs the most popular show in public television
history.

During the Watergate hearings it was frequently said that we have a government of laws, not a government of men, however much the history of the scandal and its discovery might suggest otherwise. Television programs, on the other hand, can only be made successfully by people, not statute. To some, this simple truth is an argument for the complete deregulation of broadcasting and an end to federal subsidy for public broadcasting. Since the need for public television, they say, is based on technological constraints that no longer exist, why depend on the judgment of a small group of broadcasters dangerously tied to the government when there is real editorial freedom in the private marketplace? Public television advocates had long reasoned that broadcasting, unlike book or magazine publishing, demanded government support. "Television channels," Carnegie Commission member Terry Sanford wrote in 1967, "are limited by natural laws and allocated by national laws." Television, said President Johnson's Secretary of Health, Education and Welfare John Gardner, was quite different from a bookstore or magazine stand, where the choice is so broad and varied.[29] But television today is looking more and more like a magazine rack with something to suit every taste. The scarcity of broadcast outlets has been overcome, but has the argument for a partially government subsidized alternative become obsolete because of it? Clearly not. There are indeed dozens of cable networks already in service. They provide not only entertainment programming to compete with the three broadcast networks, but "narrowcast" cultural, news and public affairs, consumer, and children's programming to the kinds of specialized audiences that public television was meant to serve. But proponents of an undiluted free market in the cable and satellite television services sometimes disregard fundamental problems of access at

both ends of the new endeavors. When viewers have to pay
for programs that have long been available over the air
for free there is clearly a danger of creating an
underclass of "information-poor." If we agree that
public schools and libraries and free concerts are
important enough to be freely available to all, why not
the increasingly vital electronic media as well? While
this is an admittedly political value judgment, equality
of access to our society's predominant form of
communication need not be a partisan issue. Republican
Senator Charles Percy wrote in 1982, "The most important
and far-reaching educational institution for millions of
our young is not our elementary schools, nor our high
schools, nor our colleges -- it is public broadcasting,
because everyone has access to it." Unless drastic
reductions proposed for the already modest support for
public broadcasting are reconsidered, said Percy, "we
shall indeed find ourselves being penny-wise and pound-
foolish." The cultural, educational and public policy
benefits of the Public Broadcasting System have come to
be enjoyed by seventy-three percent of all American
households, he argued. "So, we all must stand firm in
our resolve to insure that public broadcasting's high
quality educational and entertainment programming remains
with us in the future."[30] In an age of advanced
telecommunications, television, like public schools and
libraries, must be accessible to all.

One need not side with Percy on the political
and social value of high-quality television programming.
The pure economics on the supply-side of cable television
programming are already making clear that commercial
"narrowcasting" is not a viable alternative to a public
system. Making television programs costs a great deal of

money. Big audience or small, the production costs are
about the same. So cable television is really under the
same pressure as over-the-air broadcasting to maximize
its viewership. Perhaps there are now fifty or a hundred
possible channels available, but it seems unlikely that
we can afford to put programs on all of them. Many of
the organizations that provide the type of serious
programming once seen only on public television, are
losing millions of dollars because they cannot attract
enough advertising or subscription dollars. The most
acclaimed of them, CBS Cable, failed to sustain itself
economically. Others are finding it equally difficult to
develop expensive, high-quality schedules on the strength
of a small audience. So what good are the new
technologies of program delivery if only a very few
organizations can actually prosper by utilizing them?
Clearly, we still need a non-commercial alternative, and
it is deserving, as Percy says, of our government's
support.

Deciding that some "elitism" in television
programming is a good thing -- that is, having a service
that need not conform to the lowest common denominator
theory of audience maximization -- returns us to a
painful question: Whose elitism, yours or mine? Who
should decide what voices shall be heard in a system that
has a mandate to fulfill many needs and reflect many
views: the local station, the national programmer, the
government-appointed public trustee, or the government
itself? The only thing we seem to agree on is that we
don't want the government telling us what we can see and
hear. And yet, as the Nixon years vividly show, the
politician's hand can come dangerously close to the
editorial and creative process. "Who should decide?"
will always be a particularly difficult question in the
area of journalism. In striving to answer it, we are

sure to have conflicts and controversies. Specific
programs will always be criticized and the freedom to
produce them will sometimes be challenged. Public
television's first great journalistic coup -- coverage of
the Watergate hearings -- proved that fighting off the
challenges from within and without is usually
accomplished by individuals rather than the institutions
that house them. As Arthur Schlesinger said of the
Watergate crisis as a whole, "If the independent
judiciary, the free press, Congress and the executive
agencies could not really claim too much credit as
institutions for work performed within them by brave
individuals, nonetheless they all drew new confidence as
institutions from the exercise of power they had
forgotten they possessed."[31]

Though many within the system never acquiesced
to the Corporation for Public Broadcasting's
administration-inspired attempt at centralization for the
sake of localism, making public television safe for
public affairs programming, even the "journalism of
record" variety, would have been impossible without the
work performed by a few brave individuals and without
Watergate. If NPACT had not gotten the opportunity to
flex public television's muscles by covering the Senate
Watergate hearings, the system might well have traded in
news and public affairs for a guarantee of federal
funding from the Nixon White House. Had Watergate never
come to light, the Nixon White House would likely have
succeeded in muzzling public television as it might have
succeeded in muzzling all its opponents.

Before 1973, as NPACT executive Al Vecchione
put it, public television was just a "young fowl" trying
to stand up on its legs for the first time.[32] It was
barely standing up under the weight of its internal
conflicts when Richard Nixon came into office. And yet,

it managed to survive blatant and determined efforts by
his administration to control it. It is not unreasonable
to suggest that the institutional changes of the spring
of 1973 alone might not have saved journalism on public
television. The hearings were the turning point, for
news and public affairs programming, for the entire
system, and for Richard Nixon himself. Without them, any
subsequent effort for major coverage of important
political issues and events by public television might
never have been undertaken. WETA's refusal to carry the
Watergate hearings in the nation's capital until two days
before they were to commence starkly illustrated the
weakness of the commitment to news and public affairs at
many stations. The unprecedented popular success of the
Watergate coverage and the contributions that it brought
forced the nervous doubters throughout the system to see
that national public affairs programming could not be
ignored. The hearings had brought them the recognition
and popularity they had been searching for. They caused
a tremendous outpouring of financial support from viewers
and praise from former critics. They were, in short, a
watershed for public broadcasting. Even in intervening
years when public affairs seemed much less a priority,
the Watergate hearings remained a legacy which public
broadcasting could never entirely forget. They had
demonstrated the indispensability of news and public
affairs within the public system and the efficacy of the
system as part of the national media.

        The story of public television from 1969 to
1974 serves as a revealing metaphor for what the Nixon
administration attempted to do to our system of
government and to our free press. Viewed in context of
the larger themes of the Nixon presidency, public
television's plight was far from extraordinary; rather,
it was highly symbolic of those larger themes. Nixon's

battle with public television, his attack on the press
and his administration's various attempts to circumvent
the Constitution and create a "super-presidency" came
close to succeeding. That they did not was, perhaps,
just luck. As Fred Friendly put it, "if it hadn't been
for the tape on the door, if it hadn't been for Woodward
and Bernstein, Richard Nixon might still be President of
the United States, and I might be in jail, or even more
of a eunuch than I am."[33] But Nixon demonstrated a
remarkable talent for self-destruction and there was, in
Friendly's words, a "poetic symmetry" for public
television in his downfall. As Herblock's May 1973
Washington Post cartoon illustrated, public television's
Watergate hearings proved to be the "Late Returns" from
President Nixon's landslide re-election of only a few
months before.[34] A year later, as White House Office of
Telecommunication's policy director Clay Whitehead
testified before a Senate committee in support of a long-
term funding bill for public television, the House
Judiciary Committee's hearings on Richard Nixon's
impeachment were being broadcast, gavel-to-gavel on PBS
by NPACT. There was great irony to the notion that the
one news media organization which the White House had a
genuine ability to crush, was the organization that gave
the country the opportunity to see Watergate -- and the
Nixon presidency -- unravel on its television screens.
Public television owed its first great flush of success -
-and public affairs programming its survival -- to
Watergate and Richard Nixon. Richard Nixon's inability
to survive Watergate can, at least in part, be attributed
to public television, an institution his administration
very nearly succeeded in destroying. Therein lies a
truly "poetic symmetry."

NOTES

INTRODUCTION

1. Anthony Smith, The Shadow in the Cave (Urbana, Illinois: University of Illinois Press, 1973), p. 140.
2. Public Law 73-416, The Communications Act of 1934.
3. Smith, The Shadow in the Cave, p. 55.
4. W.L. O'Neill, Coming Apart, An Informal History of America in the 1960's (Chicago: Quadrangle, 1971).
5. Lyndon Johnson, The Vantage Point (New York: Holt, Rinehart and Winston, 1971).
6. Patrick Buchanan, The New Majority (Girard Bank of Philadelphia, 1973), p. 11.
7. The New York Times, November 4, 1969, p. 1.
8. Entire speech reprinted in Marvin Barrett, ed., The Alfred I. DuPont-Columbia University Survey of Broadcast Journalism 1968-1969 (New York: Grosset & Dunlap, 1969).
9. Buchanan, The New Majority, p. 11.
10. Herbert Klein, Making It Perfectly Clear (Garden City, N.Y.: 1980), p. 69.
11. See Harry Ashmore, Fear in the Air (New York: Norton, 1973).
12. Public Law 90-129, The Public Broadcasting Act of 1967.
13. The Carnegie Commission on the Future of Public Television, Public Television: A Program for Action (New York: Bantam Books, 1967).
14. Quoted in The New York Times, July 21, 1972, p. 31.
15. CBS News, Sixty Minutes, March 26, 1973.

CHAPTER ONE

1. The New York Times, January 25, 1969, p. 28.
2. Among the best descriptions I found of public television's institutional history is the series of articles by Robert Pepper and Robert Avery, "The Interconnection-Connection: The Formation of PBS," and "Interconnection-Disconnection: The Evolution of the CPB-PBS Relationship 1970-1973," Public Telecommunications Review, IV (January/February, 1976) and IV (September/October, 1976); and George Gibson, Public Broadcasting, The Role of the Federal Government 1912-1976 (New York: Praeger, 1977).

3. See Erik Barnouw, A Tower in Babel (New York: Oxford University Press, 1966) and The Golden Web (New York: Oxford University Press, 1968).
4. Public Law 73-416, The Communications Act of 1934.
5. Barnouw, The Golden Web, p. 39.
6. Ibid., pp. 24-25.
7. Ibid., p. 293.
8. Ford Foundation Ativities in Noncommercial Broadcasting 1951-1976 (New York: The Ford Foundation, 1977), p. 4.
9. Barnouw, The Golden Web, p. 294.
10. The New York Times, May 17, 1970, Section II, p. 15.
11. Wilbur Schramm and Lyle Nelson, The Financing of Public Television (Aspen, Colorado: Communications and Society, 1972), pp. 1-4.
12. Ford Foundation, pp. 7-10.
13. Fred Powledge, Public Television: A Question of Survival, An ACLU Report (Washington, D.C.: Public Affairs Press, 1972), p. 3.
14. Public Television: A Program for Action (New York: Bantam Books, 1967).
15. Ibid., pp. 4-9.
16. As quoted in Powledge, ACLU Report, p. 6.
17. Schramm and Nelson, Public Television Financing, pp. 2, 22.
18. James Burke, "The Public Broadcasting Act of 1967," Educational Broadcasting Review, VI (June 1972), p. 185.
19. Ibid.
20. Burke, "The Public Broadcasting Act of 1967," p. 261.
21. Ibid.
22. Public Law 90-129, The Public Broadcasting Act of 1967, November 7, 1967.
23. The Network Project, The Fourth Network (New York: The Network Project, 1972), p. 18.
24. Interview with John Macy, January 29, 1981, Washington, D.C.
25. Ibid.
26. The New York Times, January 13, 1969, p. 95.
27. Pepper and Avery, "Interconnection-Connection," p. 9.
28. Interview with James Day, November 24, 1980, New York City.
29. Macy interview.
30. Anthony Smith, The Shadow in the Cave (Urbana, Ill.: University of Illinois Press, 1973), p. 210.
31. Ford Foundation Activities, p. 13; Network Project, The Fourth Network, p. 12; duPont-Columbia Survey, p. 64.
32. The New York Times, March 9, 1969, p. 1.
33. Ibid., April 9, 1969, p.
34. October 1, 1969, Appendix document contained in PBS Staff Paper, "National Program Decision Making Within Public Television," October 17, 1972, hereafter cited as PBS Staff Paper.

35. <u>Ibid</u>., pp. 3-4.
36. <u>Ibid</u>., Appendix document, October 1, 1969.
37. <u>The New York Times</u>, February 26, 1970, p. 79.
38. Macy interview.
39. After it was reported that the station manager at Washington station WETA had phoned Friendly about the firing of "Newsroom" editor William Woesstendick because of his wife's new job as press secretary to Martha Mitchell, Friendly was called before the House Subcommittee on Communications to explain the Ford Foundation's role in public television programming decisions. Before the committee, Friendly said, "Speculation in the press that I was in some way involved in the decision regarding Mr. Woesstendick had been particularly painful to me, not only because it is false, but because I have spent my entire professional career at CBS and later at the Ford Foundation fighting for the independence of broadcast journalism."
40. <u>The New York Times</u>, February 26, 1970, p. 79.
41. <u>Ibid</u>., April 22, 1969, p. 95.
42. <u>Ibid</u>., April 29, 1969, p. 34.
43. <u>Variety</u>, March 4, 1970.
44. <u>Ibid</u>., April 29 and July 8, 1970.
45. <u>Ibid</u>., March 18, 1970.
46. NET Information Services, January 10, 1970, from the files of the Public Broadcasting Services, Washington, D.C., cited hereafter as PBS.
47. Interview with James Lehrer, February 15, 1980, Arlington, Virginia.
48. <u>Variety</u>, March 4, 1970.
49. <u>The New York Times</u>, June 16, 1971, p. 91.
50. <u>Variety</u>, November 18, 1970.
51. Pepper, "Interconnection-Disconnection," p. 11.
52. "The Banks and the Poor," NET transcript, November 9, 1970, PBS.
53. <u>The New York Times</u>, November 25, 1970, p.
54. Text of Gunn remarks to PBS membership meeting, November 10, 1970, from the files of the Corporation for Public Broadcasting, Washington, D.C., hereafter cited as CPB.
55. CPB Board Minutes, November 20, 1970, CPB.
56. <u>Ibid</u>.
57. CPB Board Minutes, January 14-15, 1971, CPB.
58. <u>The New York Times</u>, June 16, 1971, p. 91.
59. Macy interview.
60. <u>Ibid</u>.
61. James Day to Hartford Gunn, April 12, 1971, in appendix of PBS Staff Paper, October 17, 1971, PBS.
62. "Aspen Document," June 18, 1971, in appendix of PBS Staff Paper.
63. PBS Staff Paper, pp. 12-13.
64. <u>The New York Times</u>, July 5, 1971, p. 39; <u>Variety</u>, July 7, 1971.

CHAPTER TWO

1. Richard Nixon, Six Crises (Garden City, N.Y.:
    Doubleday, 1962), p. 69.
2. Herbert G. Klein, Making It Perfectly Clear (Garden
    City, N.Y.: Doubleday, 1980), p. 78.
3. Earl Mazo and Stephen Hess, Nixon, A Political Portrait
    (New York: Harper and Row, 1968), pp. 4, 6; Ralph
    DeToledano, One Man Alone, Richard Nixon (New York:
    Funk & Wagnalls, 1969), p. 216.
4. Herbert Block, Herblock Special Report (New York:
    Norton, 1974), p. 40.
5. Klein, Making It Perfectly Clear, p. 385.
6. Block, Herblock Special Report, p. 40.
7. Nixon, Six Crises, p. 358.
8. Theodore H. White, The Making of the President, 1960
    (New York: Atheneum, 1961), as quoted in Richard Nixon,
    RN, The Memoirs of Richard Nixon (New York: Grosset &
    Dunlap, 1978), p. 225.
9. Klein, Making It Perfectly Clear, pp. 89-91.
10. Melvyn Bloom, Public Relations and Presidential
    Campaigns (New York: Thomas Y. Crowell Co., 1973),
    p. 99.
11. Klein, Making It Perfectly Clear, p. 86.
12. White, The Making of the President, 1960, p. 377.
13. Nixon, Six Crises, p. 360.
14. Nixon, Memoirs, p. 242.
15. Ibid.
16. Ibid.
17. Tim Crouse, The Boys on the Bus (New York: Random
    House, 1972), p. 183.
18. Ibid.
19. Nixon, Memoirs, p. 330.
20. Edith Efron, The News Twisters (Los Angeles: Nash,
    1971), as quoted in Nixon, Memoirs, p. 330.
21. George Reedy, The Twilight of the Presidency (New York:
    World Publications, 1970), pp. 112 and 114.
22. Anthony Smith, The Shadow in the Cave (Urbana, Ill.:
    University of Illinois Press, 1973), p. 102. Smith's
    book is a brilliant discussion both of the ideology of
    broadcast journalism and of the troubling issues
    inherent in broadcasting and politics.
23. The New York Times, November 4, 1969, p. 1.
24. Interview with Tom Moore, May 26, 1982, New York City.
25. Moore interview.
26. Who's Who in American Politics, 1979-1980, Jaques
    Cattell Press, ed. (New York: R.R. Bauker, 1979);
    Herbert Klein, Making It Perfectly Clear (Garden City,
    N.Y.: Doubleday, 1980), p. 5.

27. Personal interview with Clay T. Whitehead, February 20, 1981, Arlington, Virginia.
28. The New York Times, March 12, 1969, p. 95.
29. This is the first reference to the Nixon Administration Documents dealing with public broadcasting, released under the Freedom of Information Act by the Commerce Department at the request of the second Carnegie commission on Public Broadcasting, February 22, 1979. Hereafter, each document will be listed by its author, its recipient(s) and its date, along with the general reference, FOIA. This first memo is thus noted as Whitehead to Chapin; May 6, 1969, FOIA.
30. Whitehead to Nathan; July 20, 1969, FOIA.
31. Whitehead to Flanigan; October 30, 1969, FOIA.
32. Flanigan, "Memorandum for the President's File;" October 27, 1969, FOIA.
33. Flanigan to Mayo; October 24, 1969, FOIA.
34. Quoted in Richard Armstrong, "Mac Bundy Confronts the Reachers," The New York Times Magazine, April 20, 1969, p. 27.
35. "McGeorge Bundy and the New Foundation Style," Fortune, LXXVI (April, 1968), p. 104.
36. The New York Times, February 13, 1969, p. 32.
37. Jeffrey Hart, "The New Class War," National Review, September 9, 1969, p. 896.
38. The New York Times, Februeary 21, 1969, p. 1.
39. Hart, "The New Class War," p. 900.
40. Whitehead to Flanigan; October 30, 1969, FOIA.
41. Ibid.
42. Flanigan to Whitehead; November 3, 1969, FOIA.
43. Whitehead to Flanigan; November 4, 1969; FOIA.
44. Duke to Flanigan; November 4, 1969, FOIA.
45. Interview with Henry Goldberg, January 28, 1981, Washington, D.C.
46. Interview with John Macy, January 29, 1981, Washington, D.C.
47. Moore interview.
48. Whitehead interview.
49. Whitehead to Flanigan, Garment, Hanks, Shakespeare, and McWhorter; February 6, 1970, FOIA.
50. Whitehead to Harlow, Haldeman, and Ehrlichman; April 3, 1970, FOIA.
51. U.S. Congress, Hearings before the Subcommittee on Communications and Power of the Committee on Interstate and Foreign Commerce, House of Representatives; April 14, 15, 27, and May 1, 1970, p. 1.
52. Flanigan to Cole; November 9, 1970, FOIA.
53. Cole to Flanigan; November 21, 1970, FOIA.
54. Moynihan to Macy; December 1, 1970, FOIA.
55. Moynihan to Haldeman; December 1, 1970, FOIA.
56. Fred Esplin, "Long-Range Funding: The Forgotten Chapter," Public Telecommunications Review, III (July/August 1975), p. 30.

57. Goldberg interview.
58. Whitehead interview.
59. Goldberg interview.
60. Ibid.
61. Esplin, "Long-Range Funding," p. 32.
62 Macy interview.
63. Whitehead interview.
64. Scalia to Whitehead; June 4, 1971, FOIA.
65. Wrather to Flanigan; June 22, 1971, FOIA.
66. CPB Board Minutes, July 15-16,1971; from the files of the Corporation for Public Broadcasting, Washington, D.C.
67. Goldberg interview.
68. Whitehead, "Action Memorandum for the President," July 9, 1971, FOIA.

CHAPTER THREE

1. The New York Times, August 25, 1971, p. 75.
2. NPACT Press booklet, from the personal files of James Karayn, Philadelphia, Pennsylvania.
3. Interview with James Karayn, December 10, 1980, Philadelphia, Pennsylvania.
4. Interview with James Day, November 24, 1980, New York City.
5. NPACT resume; from the personal files of James Lehrer, Arlington, Virginia; Karayn interview.
6. Karayan interview.
7. The New York Times, August 25, 1971, p. 75.
8. NPACT resume, Lehrer files.
9. Karayn interview.
10. NPACT resume, Lehrer files.
11. CPB Board Minutes, September 17, 1971, from the files of the Corporation for Public Broadcasting, Washington, D.C., hereafter cited as CPB.
12. NPACT Press Release, September 22, 1971, Nixon era documents dealing with public broadcasting released by the Commerce Department under the Freedom of Information Act, at the request of the Carnegie Commission on Public Broadcasting, February 22, 1979, hereafter cited as FOIA.
13. Huntsman to Haldeman, Flanigan, and Butterfield, September 23, 1971, FOIA.
14. Interview with Clay Whitehead, February 20, 1981, Arlington, Virginia; interview with Tom Moore, May 26, 1982, New York City; interview with Brian Lamb, June 21, 1982, Washington, D.C.

15. Richard Nixon, <u>Six Crises</u> (Garden City, N.Y.: Doubleday, 1962), p. 339.
16. Interview with Sander Vanocur, November 28, 1979, Washington, D.C.
17. Whitehead Draft, September 23, 1971, FOIA.
18. Interview with Brian Lamb, Washington, D.C.
19. Interview with Henry Goldberg, January 28, 1981, Washington, D.C.
20. Whitehead, "Draft Memorandum for the President"; October 4, 1971, FOIA.
21. Colson to Flanigan and Whitehead; October 12, 1971, FOIA.
22. Klein to Whitehead; October 7, 1971, FOIA.
23. OTP Office log; October 12, 1971, FOIA.
24. Rose to Higby; October 15, 1971, FOIA.
25. All quotations from the FBI film are taken from the full transcript <u>Behind the Lines</u>, October 8, 1971, from the files of the Public Broadcasting Service, Washington, D.C., hereafter cited as PBS.
26. Day interview.
27. <u>Behind the Lines</u>, transcript, October 8, 1971, PBS.
28. <u>Ibid</u>.
29. <u>Chicago Sun-Times</u>, October 9, 1971.
30. <u>Long Island Newsday</u>, October 12, 1971.
31. <u>Indianpolis News</u>, October 14, 1971.
32. <u>Behind the Lines</u>, transcript, October 8, 1971, PBS.
33. Interview with James Lehrer, February 15, 1980, Arlington, Virginia.
34. Interview with John Macy, January 29, 1981, Washington, D.C.
35. Whitehead to the President; November 15, 1971, FOIA.
36. Whitehead, text of speech to NAEB convention; October 20, 1971, FOIA.
37. <u>Variety</u>, October 27, 1971.
38. Macy interview.
39. Witherspoon, memo to public television stations managers, November 5, 1971, Lehrer files.
40. <u>National Journal</u>, IV (April 29, 1972), p. 736.
41. Lamb interview.
42. Wilson to Whitehead; October 26, 1971, Lehrer files.
43. Karayn to Whitehead; November 4, 1971, FOIA.
44. NAEB, ETS Managers Council to Whitehead; November 21, 1971, PBS.
45. <u>The New York Times</u>, October 20, 1971, p. 46.
46. <u>Variety</u>, October 27, 1971.
47. <u>Broadcasting</u>, November 8, 1971, p. 30.
48. Karayn interview.
49. Snyder to Flanigan; November 22, 1971, FOIA.
50. Whitehead to Haldeman; November 24, 1971, FOIA.
51. CPB Board Minutes, November 19, 1971, CPB.
52. NPACT Board Minutes, November, 1971, from the personal files of Frank W. Lloyd, Washington, D.C., hereafter cited as FWL.

53. The New York Times, December 3, 1971, p. 83.
54. Lamb interview.
55. Karayn interview.
56. Vanocur interview.
57. Interview with Bill Moyers, February 13, 1981, New York City.
58. Karayn interview.
59. Moyers interview.
60. Interview with Robert MacNeil, December 10, 1979, New York City.
61. Whitehead to Flanigan; December 1, 1971, FOIA.
62. The New York Times, January 8, 1972, p. 52.
63. The Christian Science Monitor, December 10, 1971.
64. The Los Angeles Times, December 20, 1971.
65. The New York Times, December 23, 1971, p. 52.
66. Whitehead to Flanigan; December 2, 1971, FOIA.
67. Flanigan to Haldeman; December 1, 1971, FOIA.
68. Flanigan to Whitehead; December 7, 1971, FOIA.
69. Flanigan to Whitehead; December 22, 1971, FOIA.
70. Scalia to Whitehead; December 23, 1971, FOIA.
71. Goldberg interview.
72. Whitehead interview.
73. Goldberg interview.
74. Lamb interview.
75. National Journal, IV (April 29, 1972), p. 736; Goldberg interview.
76. Whitehead interview.
77. Goldberg interview.

CHAPTER FOUR

1. Whitehead to Flanigan, January 14, 1972, Nixon era documents dealing with public broadcasting released by the Commerce Department under the Freedom of Information Act at the request of the Carnegie Commission on Public Broadcasting, February 22, 1979, hereafter cited as FOIA.
2. Whitehead to the President, January 24, 1972, FOIA.
3. CPB Board Minutes, January 21-22, 1972, from the files of the Corporation for Public Broadcasting, Washington, D.C., hereafter cited as CPB.
4. Karayn to Macy, January 18, 1972, from the personal files of Frank W. Lloyd, Washington, D.C., hereafter cited as FWL.
5. Interview with James Karayn, December 10, 1980, Phialdelphia, Pennsylvania.
6. The New York Times, January 24, 1972, p. 79.

7. George Gibson, Public Broadcasting (New York: Praeger, 1977), p. 177.
8. The New York Times, February 2, 1972, p. 79.
9. Ibid., February 7, 1972, p. 63.
10. The New York Times, February 7, 1972, p. 63.
11. Gibson, Public Broadcasting, p. 180.
12. The New York Times, February 7, 1972, p. 63.
13. Interview with Brian Lamb, June 21, 1982, Washington, D.C.
14. The New York Times, February 7, 1972, p. 63.
15. The New York Times, February 14, 1972, p. 28.
16. Cleveland Plain-Dealer, January 9, 1972, FWL.
17. Christian Science Monitor, March 7, 1972, editorial pages.
18. Indianapolis News, February 2, 1972, FWL.
19. St. Louis Post-Dispatch, February 18, 1972, FWL.
20. Chicago Tribune, January 31, 1972, FWL.
21. New Yorker, February 5, 1972.
22. Fred Powledge, Public Television: A Question of Survival (Washington, D.C.: Public Affairs Press, 1972), pp. 48, 50.
23. Variety, February 23, 1972.
24. Commerce Department Summary, p. 59.
25. Los Angeles Times, March 28, 1972, sec. II, p. 6.
26. Washington Post, March 2, 1972, p. B1.
27. Variety, March 15, 1972.
28. The New York Times, February 23, 1972, p. 82.
29. Ibid.
30. Hartford Gunn, Report to the PBS Board of Directors, March 6, 1972, from the files of the Public Broadcasting Service, Washington, D.C., hereafter cited as PBS.
31. Private screening of videotape, part of interview with James Day, November 24, 1980, New York City.
32. The New York Times, February 15, 1972, p. 67.
33. Ibid.
34. The New York Times, February 23, 1972, p. 82.
35. Ibid., March 8, 1972, p. 87.
36. Interview with James Lehrer, February 15, 1980, Arlington, Virginia.
37. Day interview.
38. The New York Times, February 7, 1972, p. 63.
39. PBS Fall Season 1972 Program Evaluation, p. 60, reprinted in Hearings before the Subcommittee on Communications of the Committee on Commerce, U.S. Senate, March 28-30, 1973, No. 93-10, p. 294.
40. Variety, February 16, 1972.
41. Vanocur interview.
42. MacNeil interview.
43. Whitehead to the President, April 27, 1972, FOIA.
44. Robert MacNeil, The People Machine (New York: Harper & Row, 1968).

45. All descriptions of NPACT programming come from two sources, official NPACT transcripts of Election '72: A Public Affair from the files of PBS and FWL, and from private screenings of selected programs at PBS in Washington, courtesy of Allan Lewis, PBS archivist.
46. Washington Post, February 3, 1972, FWL.
47. NPACT background book, compiled by Frank W. Lloyd, October 9, 1972, FWL.
48. Lloyd to Karayn, October 24, 1972; Lloyd to Maj. Charles A. May, USAFA, August 29, 1972.
49. Seattle Post-Intelligencer, February 9, 1972, FWL.
50. Broadcasting (April 17, 1972), p. 68.
51. Vanocur interview.
52. MacNeil interview.
53. Karayn interview.
54. CPB Board Minutes, April 13, 1972, CPB.
55. Karayan to James, April 28, 1972, FOIA.
56. Moore to Whitehead, May 11, 1972, FOIA.
57. Whitehead to the President, April 27, 1972, FOIA.
58. CPB Board Minutes, April 17, 1972, CPB.
59. Interview with James R. Killian, July 14, 1982, Cambridge, Massachusetts.
60. Whitehead to the President, April 25, 1972, FOIA.
61. Rep. Robert Michel to Brian Lamb, May 11, 1972, FOIA.
62. Ibid.
63. Statements prepared for congressmen by OTP, May 1972, FOIA.
64. Gibson, Public Broadcasting, p. 183.
65. Statements prepared for congressmen by OPT, June, 1972, FOIA.
66. Gibson, Public Broadcasting, p. 175.
67. Fred Friendly, "Politicizing TV," Columbia Journalism Review, March/April 1973, p. 13.
68. Interview with Clay Whitehead, February 20, 1981, Arlington, Virginia.
69. Whitehead, Memorandum for the Record, June 21, 1972, FOIA.
70. Variety, July 12, 1972, entitled "Nixon's Hot Romance with TV/Election Year, Remember?" reported that there was already speculation about the connection between the June 22 meeting with commercial broadcasters and the CPB funding bill veto. Nixon, it said, "crunched public TV just as it was about to make significant inroads into commerical broadcasting."
71. Whitehead to the President, June 26, 1972, FOIA.
72. President's veto message, June 30, 1972, FOIA.
73. Interview with Henry Goldberg, January 28, 1981, Washington, D.C.

CHAPTER FIVE

1. George Gibson, Public Broadcasting (New York: Praeger, 1977), p. 185.
2. Variety, July 5, 1972.
3. Washington Star, July 5, 1972, from the personal files of Frank W. Lloyd, Washington, D.C., hereafter cited as FWL.
4. Variety, July 5, 1972.
5. Ibid., July 12, 1972.
6. Memphis Press-Scimitar, July 3, 1972, from the files of the Public Broadcasting Service, Washington, D.C., hereafter cited as PBS.
7. Chicago Tribune, August 20, 1972, sec. 1A, p. 54.
8. Los Angeles Times, July 5, 1972, sec. II, p. 6.
9. Louisville Times, July 5, 1972, PBS.
10. Christian Science Monitor, July 8, 1972, PBS.
11. Transcript of White House briefing, June 30, 1972, PBS.
12. The New York Times, July 21, 1972, p. 31.
13. The New York Times, July 21, 1972, p. 31.
14. Charlotte Obesrver, July 198, 1972, PBS.
15. Commerce Department Summary of Nixon era documents dealing with public broadcasting, Washington, D.C., February 22, 1972, p. 87.
16. Public Law 92-411; Gibson, Public Broadcasting, p. 187. As a final indignity and incovenience to the public broadcasters, the $45 million CPB appropriation was included in an HEW-Labor Department bill which the President also vetoed in his running battle with Congress over government expenditures. All agencies covered in the bill were continued by resolution at the same budgetary levels as the 1972 fiscal year. Under the continuing resolution CPB received only $35 million of the $45 million mandated for fiscal 1973.
17. Whitehead to the President, June 30, 1972, Nixon era documents dealing with public broadcasting released by the Commerce Department under the Freedom of Information Act at the request of the Carnegie Commission on Public Broadcasting, February 22, 1979, hereafter cited as FOIA.
18. Robert Pepper, "Interconnection-Disconnection," Public Telecommunications Review, September/October, 1976, p. 28.
19. CPB Board Mintues, March 17-18, 1972, from the files of the Corporation for Public Broadcasting, Washington, D.C., hereafter cited as CPB.
20. The New York Times, August 11, 1972, p. 59.
21. Interview with Sander Vanocur, November 28, 1979, Washington, D.C.

22. Macy to Whitehead, July 24, 1972; Whitehead to Macy, August 18, 1972, FOIA.
23. The New York Times, August 11, 1972, p. 59.
24. Macy interview.
25. Interview with Jack Valenti, January 29, 1981, Washington, D.C.
26. Interview with John Macy, January 29, 1981, Washington, D.C.
27. The Washington Post, August 17, 1972, p. C-12.
28. Variety, August 23, 1972.
29. Moore to Flanigan, August 1, 1972, FOIA.
30. Whitehead to Flanigan, July 5, 1972, FOIA.
31. Moore to Flanigan, August 1, 1972, FOIA.
32. Interview with Frank W. Lloyd, January 27, 1981, Washington, D.C.
33. Variety, August 9, 1972.
34. Interview with Robert MacNeil, December 10, 1979, New York City.
35. Variety, August 16, 1972.
36. Interview with Bill Moyers, February 13, 1981, New York City.
37. Christian Science Monitor, August 28, 1972, FWL.
38. Newsweek, September 4, 1972, FWL.
39. U.S. Senate, Hearings before the Committee on Commerce, September 8, 1972, FWL.
40. Valenti interview.
41. Interview with Henry Loomis, January 26, 1981, Middleburg, Virginia.
42. Loomis interview.
43. Broadcasting, October 30, 1972, from the personal files of James Lehrer, Arlington, Virginia, hereafter cited as JL.
44. Interview with James Karayan, December 10, 1980, Philadelphia, Pennsylvania.
45. Loomis interview.
46. OTP Office log, August 1, 1972, FOIA.
47. Interview with Clay T. Whitehead, February 25, 1981, New York City.
48. Interview with Henry Goldberg, January 28, 1981, Washington, D.C.
49. Interview with Brian Lamb, June 21, 1982, Washington, D.C.
50. Colson to Snyder, September 16, 1972, FOIA.
51. Variety, November 22, 1972; John J. O'Connor wrote in a New York Times November 5, 1972 piece entitled "Above All, Let's Not Be Rude to the White House," "Among the more ingenious Administration tactics was a demand that more power and authority be given to the local stations instead of a central agency smelling of eastern Establishment biases.

"But Henry Loomis, the new president of CPB, indicates that the Corporation will be directly involved in the form and content of all programming which brings everything back to the point of maximum pressure."

52. Transcript of Loomis meeting with stations, September 20, 1972, PBS.
53. Variety, October 4, 1972.
54. Loomis transcript, September 20, 1972, PBS.
55. Interview with Robert MacNeil, December 10, 1979, New York City.
56. Whitehead to Flanigan, October 6, 1972, FOIA.
57. Loomis to Whitehead, November 7, 1972, FOIA.
58. Loomis interview.
59. Interview with Michael Hobbs, November 5, 1980, Washington, D.C.
60. National Program Decision Making within Public Television, a PBS Staff Paper, October 15, 1972, PBS.
61. NPACT Briefing Book for Henry Loomis, October 9, 1972, FWL.
62. Moyers interview.
63. Loomis interview.
64. Fauci to Gunn, October 17, 1972, PBS.
65. Gunn to Fauci, October 24, 1972, PBS.
66. Loomis interview.
67. Los Angeles Times, September 30, 1972, PBS.
68. Gunn Report to PBS Board, September 20, 1972, PBS.
69. Variety, September 27, 1972.
70. Harry Ashmore, Fear in the Air (New York: W.W. Norton, 1973), p. 101. Minow made the comment at a January 1973 symposium at the Center for the Study of Democratic Institutions in Santa Barbara, California. Ashmore's book is a report on the symposium which dealt with broadcasting, the Nixon Administration and the First Amendment.
71. Wilbur Schramm and Lyle Nelson, The Financing of Public Television (Aspen Program on Communications and Society, October, 1972), p. 21.
72. Ibid., p. 28.
73. Ibid., p. 25.
74. Interview with Al Vecchione, December 20, 1979, New York City.
75. Lloyd interview.
76. MacNeil interview.
77. Vanocur interview.
78. MacNeil interview.
79 TV Guide, November 5, 1972, PBS.
80. Variety, November 22, 1972.
81. Loomis interview.
82. Loomis message to stations, November 9, 1972, FWL.
83. The Washington Post, November 10, 1972, p. B-1.
84. The New York Times, November 11, 1972, p. 67.

85. _Variety_, November 15, 1972.
86. _Ibid._, November 29, 1972.
87. Loomis interview.
88. All remarks taken from transcripts of _All About TV_,
    November (undated), 1972, PBS.
89. Slater and Sinel to PBS Board, December 14, 1972, PBS.
90. CPB Draft Statement on CPB-PBS Relationship, Decmeber
    15, 1972, CPB.
91. PBS Draft Statement of CPB-PBS Relationship, December
    15, 1972, PBS.
92. Transcript of PBS Executive Committee meeting, December
    15, 1972, PBS.
93. Interview with Norman Sinel, November 5, 1980,
    Washington, D.C.
94. Interview with Thomas Gherardi, November 11, 1980,
    Washington, D.C.
95. Loomis interview.
96. PBS meeting, December 15, 1972, PBS.

CHAPTER 6

1. CPB board of directors meeting, January 10, 1973, from
   the files of the Corporation for Public Broadcasting,
   Washington, D.C., hereafter cited as CPB.
2. _The Los Angeles Times_, January 15, 1973, Sec. IV,
   p. 12.
3. OTP logs, January 4, January 26, and February 5, 1973;
   Fischer to Lamb, January 31, 1973, Nixon era documents
   dealing with public broadcasting released by the
   Commerce Department under the Freedom of Information
   Act at the Request of the Carnegie commission on Public
   Broadcasting, February 22, 1979, hereafter cited as
   FOIA.
4. _Variety_, January 17, 1973.
5. See Robert Pepper, "Interconnection-Disconnection, The
   Evolution of the CPB-PBS Relationship 1970-1973,"
   Public Telecommunications Review, IV
   (September/October, 1976).
6. Interview with Jack Valenti, January 29, 1981,
   Washington, D.C.
7. As quoted in speech by Robert MacNeil to the Consumer
   Federation of America, January 26, 1973, from the
   personal files of Robert MacNeil, New York City.
8. Herert Klein, _Making It Perfectly Clear_ (Garden City,
   N.Y.: Doubleday, 1980), p. 223.
9. Interview with Henry Loomis, January 26, 1981,
   Middleburg, Virginia.

10. *Variety*, January 10, 1973.
11. See Whitehead to Flanigan, October 11, 1972, FOIA.
12. *The New York Times*, January 6, 1973, p. 66.
13. *Chicago Tribune*, January 5, 1973, sec. 2, p. 13.
14. *Variety*, December 27, 1972.
15. *The New York Times*, January 6, 1973, p. 24.
16. *Variety,*, January 17, 1973.
17. NAEB *Newsletter*, XXXVIII (January 22, 1973).
18. *Los Angeles Times*, January 17, 1973, sec. IV, p. 14.
19. *Ibid.*
20. Charles Northrip to Thomas Curtis, January 12, 1973, PBS.
21. Fedderson Cable to Schenkkan, Janaury 15, 1973, PBS.
22. Gordon Tuell to Thomas Curtis, January 19, 1973, PBS.
23. Tuell to Senator Warren Magnuson, January 19, 1973, PBS.
24. *Variety*, January 3, 1973.
25. *Ibid.*, January 17, 1973.
26. *The New York Times*, January 24, 1973, p. 82.
27. *Ibid.*
28. *Ibid.*, January 21, 1973, sec. II, p. 17.
29. *Chicago Tribune*, January 19, 1973, p. 12.
30. *Ibid.*, January 31, 1973, p. 83; Harry Ashmore, *Fear in the Air* (New York: W.W. Norton, 1973), p. 95.
31. *Variety*, January 17, 1973.
32. *The New York Times*, February 21, 1973, p. 87.
33. *Variety*, February 21, 1973.
34. MacNeil speech, January 26, 1973, MacNeil files.
35. Herbert Klein, *Making It Perfectly Clear* (Garden City, N.Y.: Doubleday, 1980), p. 388.
36. Quoted in Harry Ashmore, *Fear in the Air* (New York: W.W. Norton, 1973), p. 113.
37. Arthur Schlesinsger, *The Imperial Presidency* (Boston: Houghton Mifflin, 1973), pp. 230-1.
38. Quoted in Ashmore, *Fear in the Air*, p. 17.
39. Interview with John Macy, January 29, 1981, Washington, D.C.
40. Interview with Bill Moyers, February 13, 1981, New York City.
41. Richard Nathan, *The Plot That Failed; Nixon and the Administrative Presidency* (New York: Wiley, 1975), p. 81.
42. MacNeil speech, January 26, 1973, MacNeil files.
43. *Variety*, March 7, 1973.
44. Loomis interview.
45. CPB Press Release, February 8, 1973, CPB.
46. Rogers' statement to CPB Board, February 6, 1973, CPB.
47. NAEB *Newsletter*, XXXVIII (February 14, 1973).
48. *Boston Globe*, February 22, 1973, PBS.
49. Whitehead, Memorandum for the Record, February 12, 1973, FOIA.

50. The New York Times, December 19, 1972, p. 1.
51. Interview with Clay T. Whitehead, February 25, 1981, New York City.
52. Interview with Brian Lamb, June 21, 1982, Washington, D.C.
53. U.S. Senate, Committee on Commerce, Subcommittee on Communications, Hearings on OTP Overview, February 20, 1973, PBS.
54. Variety. March 14, 1973.
55. The New York Times, March 8, 1973, p. 79.
56. CPB Press Release, March 7, 1973, CPB.
57. Carlucci to Loomis, January (undated) 1973, CPB.
58. Loomis interview.
59. Ashmore, Fear in the Air, p. 99.
60. Ibid., p. 100.
61. Curtis (draft) letter to Carlucci, February 1, 1973, CPB.
62. Loomis interview.
63. Los Angeles Times, January 15, 1973, sec. II, p. 6.
64. The New York Times, January 21, 1973, sec. II, p. 17.
65. Interview with Tom Moore, May 26, 1982, New York City.
66. Interview with Thomas Gherardi, November 11, 1973, Washington, D.C.; interview with Michael Hobbs, November 5, 1973, Washington, D.C.; Loomis interview.
67. Valenti interview.
68. Interview with John Macy, January 29, 1981, Washington, D.C.
69. Loomis interview.
70. Valenti interview.
71. The New York Times, March 27, 1973, p. 94.
72. Whitehead interview.
73. Whitehead, Memorandum for the Record, March 27, 1973, FOIA.
74. Hearings before the Subcommittee on Communications of the Committee on Commerce, United States Senate, March 28-30, 1973, No. 93-10, p. 8.
75. Whitehead interview.
76. Interview with Henry Goldberg, January 28, 1981, Washington, D.C.
77. Loomis interview.
78. Senate hearings, March 28-30, 1973, p. 46.
79. Ibid., pp. 88-92.
80. Ibid., p. 129.
81. Variety, March 31, 1973.
82. Report of the Ad-Hoc Committee commissioned to negotiate with the Rogers Group, April 5, 1973, CPB.
83. Moore to CPB Board, April 9, 1973, CPB.
84. Rogers to Curtis, April 10, 1973, CPB.
85. Loomis Report to the CPB Board, April 13, 1973, CPB.
86. McCormack to Whitehead, April 12, 1973, FOIA.
87. Curtis to the President, April 16, 1973, FOIA.
88. Curtis to Killian, April 16, 1973, CPB.

89. The New York Times, April 19, 1973, p. 42.
90. Ibid., April 24, 1973, p. 81
91. Ibid., April 26, 1973, p. 87.
92. Gherardi interview.
93. Loomis interview.
94. Goldberg to Whitehead, April 20, 1973, FOIA.
95. Goldberg interview.
96. CPB Board Minutes, May 9, 1973, CPB.
97. CPB Board Minutes, May 9, 1973, CPB.
98. The New York Times, May 10, 1973, p. 91.
99. Ibid., May 19, 1973, p. 75.
100. CPB Board Minutes, May 31, 1973, CPB.
101. Ibid.
102. The New York Times, June 1, 1973, p. 1.
103. George Gibson, Public Broadcasting (New York: Praeger, 1977), p. 194.
104. Ibid., p. 202; Whitehead to the President, July 27, 1973, FOIA.

CHAPTER SEVEN

1. Interview with James Karayn, December 10, 1980, Philadelphia, Pennsylvania.
2. Interview with Robert MacNeil, December 10, 1979, New York City.
3. Los Angeles Times, June 20, 1973, p. IV, 1.
4. Variety, April 25, 1973.
5. Robert MacNeil, "Is Anybody Watching?" Washingtonian, IX (October, 1973), p. 61.
6. Chicago Tribune, July 12, 1973, p. II, 9.
7. Los Angeles Times, June 20, 1973, p. IV, 1.
8. Karayn interview.
9. The Washington Post, August 25, 1973, p. A2.
10. Los Angeles Times, June 2, 1973, p. IV, 1.
11. Ibid.
12. Chicago Tribune, March 16, 1973, p. III, 11.
13. Interview with Bill Moyers, February 13, 1981, New York City.
14. The Washington Post, April 1, 1973, p. B-1.
15. Buchanan to Paulson, October 14, 1973, Nixon era documents dealing with public broadcasting released under the Freedom of Information Act by the Commerce Department at the request of the Carnegie Commission on Public Broadcasting, February 22, 1979, hereafter FOIA.
16. Transcript of "An Essay on Watergate," Bill Moyers' Journal, October 31, 1973, courtesy of Mr. Bill Moyers.

17. Moyers interview.
18. Interview with Clay T. Whitehead, February 25, 1981, New York City.
19. White House Press Conference, August 7, 1973, FOIA.
20. Whitehead to the President, October 3, 1973, FOIA.
21. Hartford Gunn, "Public Television Program Financing," Educational Broadcasting Review, VI (October, 1972).
22. Whitehead interview.
23. Buchanan to Paulson, October 14, 1973, FOIA.
24. Variety, January 3, 1973.
25. Interview with Henry Goldberg, January 28, 1981, Washington, D.C.
26. The New York Times, April 19, 1973, p. 42.
27. Whitehead to the President, April 2, 1974, FOIA.
28. Whitehead interview.
29. Whitehead to Haig, June 7, 1974, FOIA.
30. Whitehead interview.
31. Ibid.
32. The New York Times, June 10, 1974, p. 1.
33. The Wall Street Journal, June 11, 1974, FOIA.
34. The Washington Post, June 12, 1974, p. A-22.
35. Whitehead interview.
36. Cole to Whitehead, July 11, 1974, FOIA.
37. Whitehead statement before the Senate Communications Subcommittee, August 6, 1974, FOIA.

CHAPTER EIGHT

1. George Gibson, Public Broadcasting (New York: Praeger, 1977), p. 218.
2. Interview with James Day, November 24, 1980, New York City.
3. The Village Voice, February 25, 1980, p. 33.
4. The New York Times, March 23, 1980, Sec. IV, p. 35.
5. The Carnegie Commission on the Future of Public Broadcasting, A Public Trust (New York: Bantam Books, 1979), p. 11.
6. Ibid., p. 10.
7. Ibid., p. 49.
8. The New York Times, March 9, 1969, p. 1.
9. The New York Times, January 25, 1969.
10. Interview with Robert MacNeil, December 10, 1979, New York City.
11. Interview with Sander Vanocur, November 28, 1970, Washington, D.C.
12. Interview with James Lehrer, February 15, 1980, Arlington, Va.

13. Interview with James Karayn, December 10, 1980, Philadelphia, Pa.
14. Interview with Bill Moyers, February 13, 1981, New York City.
15. Interview with James Killian, July , 1982, Cambridge, Ma.
16. Interview with John Macy, January 29, 1981, Washington, D.C.
17. Interview with Henry Goldberg, January 28, 1981, Washington, D.C.
18. Richard M. Nixon, <u>Six Crises</u> (Garden City, N.Y.: Doubleday, 1962); <u>RN, The Memoirs of Richard Nixon</u> (New York: Grosset & Dunlap, 1978).
19. Interview with Clay T. Whitehead, February 25, 1981, New York City; Goldberg interview.
20. Vanocur interview.
21. MacNeil interview.
22. See generally Jonathan Schell, <u>The Time of Illusion</u> (New York: Knopf, 1976).
23. Whitehead interview.
24. Interview with Jack Valenti, January 29, 1981, Washington, D.C.
25. Senate, Committee on Commerce, Subcommittee on Communications, <u>Public Television Act of 1976, Hearings on S1160</u>, 90 Cong., 1 Sess.
26. <u>The New York Times</u>, August 1, 1982, Sec. II, p. 21.
27. <u>The New York Times</u>, April 26, 1982, p. C11.
28. <u>The New York Times</u>, August 1, 1982, Sec. II, p. 21.
29. Senate, Subcommittee on Communications, <u>Hearings on S1160</u>.
30. <u>The New York Times</u>, September 11, 1982.
31. Arthur Schlesinger, <u>The Imperial Presidency</u> (Boston: Houghton Mifflin, 1973), p. 277.
32. Interview with A. Vecchione, December 20, 1979, New York City.
33. Interview with Fred Friendly, December 5, 1979, New York City.
34. Herbert Block, <u>Herblock Special Report</u> (New York: W.W. Norton, 1974), p. 145.

INDEX